GISELA VON BUSSE · HORST ERNESTUS

Libraries in the
Federal Republic of Germany

REVISED AND ENLARGED ENGLISH EDITION

DISTRIBUTED IN THE UNITED STATES

BY THE AMERICAN LIBRARY ASSOCIATION, CHICAGO

1972

OTTO HARRASSOWITZ · WIESBADEN

A revised and enlarged version of the original German edition, Das Bibliothekswesen der Bundesrepublik Deutschland (Harrassowitz 1968), translated by John S. Andrews and Gregory Walker.

Distributed in the United States by
The American Library Association
50 East Huron
Chicago, Illinois 60611
ISBN: 0-8389-0135-2   (1972)

© Otto Harrassowitz, Wiesbaden 1972
This book may not be reproduced in whole or in part by any means without the publisher's permission
Production: MZ-Verlagsdruckerei GmbH, Memmingen
Printed in Germany
ISBN   3 447 013 79 6

Contents

Contents

4 Some Aspects of Library Administration and Services 179

Contents

Preface

The librarian visiting another country to study its libraries wants to understand something familiar to him in its special local form: he would like to gain an overall picture and an acquaintance with individual library structures and problems; he would like to know what libraries in the country visited look like, how they are administered and how the library profession is organised; also it may well interest him to learn what links there are with other countries and where he might find starting points and areas of contact for possible co-operation. Above all however the visitor wishes to construct for himself out of the cross-section that he sees a picture of what we term the "librarianship" of a country. He will want to record what is similar to the practice of his own country and to understand what diverges from it because of differing historical, political, social, economic and academic structures and developments.

The desire to supply this reader with a vade mecum showing general and specific aspects of the contemporary state of librarianship in the Federal Republic of Germany is the intention of this book and its raison d'être.

We have however also had the general reader in mind. If by chance one or more library users should light on this book and in so doing gain some insight into the world of libraries and discover something of the inner movement and kaleidoscopic nature of these institutions (which to him may often seem ponderous and monotonous), then we shall be especially pleased.

For the first time we attempt a conspectus of all types of libraries, in particular the two large groups, academic and public libraries, which are normally treated separately. This provides a panorama of librarianship in the Federal Republic.

This was the most difficult part of our task. To pave the way for understanding we had to explain the historical development of this division, so hard for the visitor from abroad to understand. Our description was intended to provide an overall picture. Frequently however we had for practical reasons to treat the particular professional problems of each of the two types separately within the same context. We were uneasy about this because we ourselves believe that librarianship does need libraries serving different purposes, but that the twofold division into academic and public libraries is misleading especially with an eye to the future.

11

We are also conscious that the concepts "Bibliothek" on the one hand and "Bücherei" on the other can often no longer be used without ambiguity[1]. However, we were unable to eliminate those inconsistencies and overlappings that actually exist or to achieve in the discussion a degree of integration that has not been achieved in reality.

Faced with the superabundance of facts and problems inherent in the subject matter we could only attempt to reveal main outlines, to suggest a few themes and to provide an initial practical approach to further contact with librarianship in the Federal Republic. Limitations occasionally arose from the lack of sufficient data for particular areas of the field. The selection of many detailed aspects treated in the work is explained by questions with which the authors were confronted time and again in many professional conversations with colleagues from abroad.

Conscious of touching on controversial topics in professional matters and in library policy, we have endeavoured to present the situation and the possible trends objectively and without polemics. In such matters changes are occurring nowadays so rapidly that even while this book is in the press fresh developments must be allowed for. For example, in 1971 the journal "Bücherei und Bildung" became "Buch und Bibliothek".

The Bibliothekarische Auslandsstelle ("International Relations Office for Libraries") first suggested this book, the Deutsche Forschungsgemeinschaft ("German Research Association") commissioned it. We have ventured upon this responsible and far from easy task. We were able to use our own experiences as a basis, but could not have completed the work without the assistance of others. We owe a debt to all those who have made contributions in professional literature on the topics under discussion. We ask those colleagues who have co-operated with unwearying advice in the composition of the manuscript to accept here our thanks without our naming them individually. It only remains for us to mention that Appendix III, "Halts on a Library Study Tour", was executed in Berlin by the Arbeitsstelle für das Büchereiwesen ("Study Centre for Public Libraries"), although conceived jointly with the authors and completed in close collaboration with them.

In the interests of a clear layout and of easy reading we have done without a system of notes and references to sources. Similarly we have not supplied a bibliography; instead, we have referred at the end of each

---

[1] *Translators' note:* Traditionally "Bibliothek" has been reserved for academic libraries, "Bücherei" for non-academic ones.

chapter to some titles felt to be particularly significant; the brief selection, to which we have limited ourselves, cannot be always satisfactory.

We thank the Deutsche Forschungsgemeinschaft for making the publication of this book possible and hope that it will be useful to our friends from abroad. We realise that this first attempt at an introduction to the whole library service in the Federal Republic requires in many respects supplementing, improving or correcting. Suggestions to that end will be gratefully received.

GISELA VON BUSSE   HORST ERNESTUS

Translators' Note

The problem whether or not to translate names and titles in a foreign language admits of no ideal solution. Since the present book will be used for reference purposes, we consider that unambiguity is essential. Where a name or title is distinctive, especially where it has no precise equivalent in English, we prefer to retain the original form. Otherwise the reader will not always be sure, for example, which library association is intended by the "Association of German Librarians". For clarity's sake we add, where necessary, an English paraphrase in parenthesis; such additions have been normally confined to the first use in the book of the German name or title. It is assumed that those readers who wish to follow up the suggestions for "further reading" will have sufficient command of the language not to need the translators' assistance.

We are grateful to the authors for their many detailed suggestions and to the publishers for their ready co-operation. Finally, we should like to thank Mrs. Penelope Andrews for her help in various ways and Miss Dianne Bell for her careful typing of our manuscript.

JSA   GPMW
Lancaster   Oxford

Plates

1. Frankfurt: Deutsche Bibliothek, book tower.
   (Photograph: Wolf & v. Schweinitz, Wiesbaden)

   between pp. 56 and 57

2. Berlin: Staatsbibliothek Preußischer Kulturbesitz, model of the new building, design by Hans Scharoun.
   (Photograph: Reinhard Friedrich, Berlin)

   between pp. 56 and 57

3. Marburg: Universitätsbibliothek Marburg.
   (Photograph: Klingelhöfer, Marburg)

   between pp. 56 and 57

4. Berlin: Amerika-Gedenkbibliothek / Berlin Central Library.
   (Photograph: Gnilka, Berlin)

   between pp. 56 and 57

5. Hamburg: Hamburger Öffentliche Bücherhallen, Public Library at Hamburg-Eppendorf.
   (Photograph: Scheel, Hamburg)

   between pp. 104 and 105

6. Hamm (pop. 72,000): Stadtbücherei, Central Library.
   (Photograph: Jucho, Hamm)

   between pp. 104 and 105

7. Munich: Bayerische Staatsbibliothek, reading area in the wing.
   (Photograph: Bayerische Staatsbibliothek)

   between pp. 104 and 105

8. Hanover: Technische Informationsbibliothek / Bibliothek der Technischen Universität, public catalogue room.
   (Photograph: Günther Fischer, Hanover)

   between pp. 104 and 105

9. Hanover: Stadtbüchereien Hannover, Branch library at Hanover-Ricklingen.
   (Photograph: Friedrich, Wülferode/Hanover)

   between pp. 152 and 153

10. Bremen: Volksbüchereien der Freien Hansestadt Bremen, Youth and School Library in Graubündener Straße.
    (Photograph: Landesbildstelle Bremen)

    between pp. 152 and 153

11. Bad Friedrichshall (pop. 9,800, Kreis Heilbronn): Stadtbücherei (responsibility of the Staatliche Büchereistelle Stuttgart).
    (Photograph: Landesbildstelle Baden-Württemberg)

    between pp. 152 and 153

12. Wolfenbüttel: Herzog-August-Bibliothek, converted modern exhibition room.
    (Photograph: Heinrich Heidersberger, Wolfsburg)

    between pp. 152 and 153

13. Stuttgart: Stadtbücherei Stuttgart, Central Library in the Wilhelmspalais.
    (Photograph: Planck, Stuttgart)

    between pp. 216 and 217

14. Bamberg: Staatsbibliothek in the Neue Residenz, modern converted interior.
    (Photograph: Staatsbibliothek, Bamberg)

    between pp. 216 and 217

15. Rendsburg: Büchereizentrale Rendsburg, Überlandbücherei 3 000 (a special mobile library holding 3,000 vols.).
    (Photograph: Bursinsky, Büdelsdorf)

    between pp. 216 and 217

16. Bochum: Universitätsbibliothek der Ruhr-Universität Bochum, automated charging procedure.
    (Photograph: Packmohr, Essen)

    between pp. 216 and 217

Abbreviations

BTH Bibliothek der Technischen Hochschule (cf. 1.222)
DB Deutsche Bibliothek (cf. 2.11)
DBV Deutscher Büchereiverband (cf. 3.21)
DGD Deutsche Gesellschaft für Dokumentation (cf. 6.223)
EKZ Einkaufszentrale für Öffentliche Büchereien (cf. 3.25)
FU Freie Universität Berlin
FUB Freie Universität — Bibliothek
IFLA International Federation of Library Associations
KGSt Kommunale Gemeinschaftsstelle für Verwaltungsvereinfachung (cf. 1.56, 4.14)
LB Landesbibliothek (cf. 2.2)
LHB Landes- und Hochschulbibliothek (cf. 2.31)
SB Staatsbibliothek (cf. 2.2)
StB Stadtbibliothek (cf. 2.51)
StUB Stadt- und Universitätsbibliothek (cf. 2.31, 2.51)
SUB Staats- und Universitätsbibliothek (cf. 2.2, 2.31)
THB Technische Hochschulbibliothek (cf. 2.31)
TIB Technische Informationsbibliothek (cf. 2.41)
TU Technische Universität (cf. 1.222)
TUB Technische Universitätsbibliothek (cf. 2.31)
UB Universitätsbibliothek (cf. 2.3)
UStB Universitäts- und Stadtbibliothek (cf. 2.31, 2.51)
VDB Verein Deutscher Bibliothekare (cf. 3.21)
VdDB Verein der Diplom-Bibliothekare an wissenschaftlichen Bibliotheken (cf. 3.21)
ZfBB Zeitschrift für Bibliothekswesen und Bibliographie (cf. 8.11)

1   The General Background

1.1   Government and Administration

The institutions of cultural and academic life in the German Federal Republic are multifarious and bewildering to the foreign observer. Their structure, comprehensible only against the background of the constitution and government regulations, is based on the federal, decentralised pattern laid down in the constitution by the Basic Law of 23 May 1949.

The federal and municipal administration is organised from the bottom upwards: from the Gemeinden ("local authorities") to the Länder ("states" or "provinces") and the Bund ("State" or "Federation"), the main administrative burden falling on the Länder. The Bund, Länder and Gemeinden are independent regional corporations with their own sovereign rights and their own incomes from rates or taxes.

The Federal Republic consists of eleven Länder: the states of Baden-Württemberg, Bavaria, Hesse, Lower Saxony, North Rhine-Westphalia, Rhineland Palatinate, Saarland, Schleswig-Holstein, together with the city states of Bremen, Hamburg and West Berlin. Berlin has a special status owing to the restrictions placed upon it by the Allies and by the constitutional laws of the Länder. Since 1945 the latter have been reorganised, partly in accordance with historical tradition partly as new creations. Divergence from tradition became especially necessary with the dissolution of the largest of the former German territories, the state of Prussia.

Legislative and administrative powers are divided between the Bund and the Länder; in principle authority rests with the Länder, unless expressly reserved for the Bund under the Basic Law. Public responsibility for cultural affairs and for the whole sphere of education is vested almost exclusively in the Länder. Only as recently as the autumn of 1969 a Bundesministerium für Bildung und Wissenschaft ("Federal Ministry for Education and Research"), with the two new departments for Bildungsplanung (educational planning) and Forschungsplanung (research planning), has been formed out of the Bundesministerium für wissenschaftliche Forschung ("Federal Ministry for Scientific Research"), which had been primarily responsible for promoting and co-ordinating major research in natural science and technology. Besides there are existing cultural

19

departments in the Bundesministerium des Innern ("Federal Ministry of the Interior") and the Auswärtiges Amt ("Foreign Office").

Wide legislative and administrative decentralisation in cultural matters and the differing financial resources of the individual Länder necessitate co-ordination and co-operation and even common financial support in certain activities. Institutions are established and agreements reached on a voluntary basis.

The legislative bodies of the *Länder* are their parliaments; at the head of the administration of each Land is its government, in which the Kultusminister ("Minister of Culture and Education") is responsible for library matters. In most Länder there are *Regierungsbezirke* ("administrative areas"), which perform some of the duties of the Länder, including the general control of the Gemeinden. In the Länder Staatliche Büchereistellen ("State Public Library Offices") exercise their influence predominantly within the administrative framework of the Regierungsbezirke. Finally, in a number of Länder *Landkreise* ("rural districts") and *Stadtkreise* or kreisfreie Städte ("urban districts") assume the functions of minor administrative authorities.

The organs of municipal government (local autonomy is firmly laid down by the Basic Law) are the *Gemeinden,* the overall term for towns and smaller local authorities. Towns (mostly those with over 20,000 inhabitants) that enjoy the same legal and independent status as the Landkreise are designated kreisfreie Städte (Stadtkreise). In contrast, the kreisangehörige Städte ("towns within the jurisdiction of a Landkreis") are subject to local control through the Landkreise.

Functions of local government and responsibilities delegated by the Länder for which the resources of individual Gemeinden are inadequate are taken over by *Gemeindeverbände* ("associations of Gemeinden"). Ämter ("districts"), which comprise several small Gemeinden, enjoy the legal status of regional corporations. Occasionally they act as library authorities. Landkreise include Ämter and Gemeinden that are independent of Ämter. Among their duties is the support of local libraries. In some Länder *Landschaftsverbände* ("regional associations") as the largest associations of Gemeinden assume responsibilities which the kreisfreie Städte and Landkreise cannot undertake on their own. *Ad hoc associations*, formed by Gemeinden for specific purposes, could be significant for the development of efficient library units.

Local government in the Gemeinden is controlled by byelaws, which differ from one Land to the next. Basically the Gemeinden are responsible for all public work in their district unless the law decrees otherwise. Among the local government responsibilities of the Gemeinden a distinction should be made between those that are mandatory, e. g. social welfare, and those that are voluntary, which include the support of secondary schools, museums and libraries.

Regulations concerning the Gemeinden differ because of their differing constitutions. One element common to all is that discussions and resolutions on affairs of a Gemeinde are entrusted to *the popularly elected representatives*. For particular tasks special *committees* may be appointed, say an education committee, which will in larger towns often form sub-committees, e. g. for adult education. Special library committees are rarely found.

The resolutions of the Gemeinde representatives are carried out by the *Gemeinde administration*. Its head is the chief officer, who is freely elected just as the Stadträte ("town councillors") are elected for particular duties. The head of the public library service is responsible to this administration.

The *financial needs* of the Bund, Länder and Gemeinden are met by rates and taxes, the allocation of which is settled by the Basic Law. Between the Bund and the Länder some limited financial flexibility is permitted in case the ratio between income and expenditure changes as their respective responsibilities are discharged. Similarly, the Gemeinden receive part of the revenue of the Länder apart from earmarked grants for specific purposes. The responsibilities of the Landkreise are financed by the annual Kreis assessment, to which the Ämter and the kreisfreie Städte contribute. Grants for specific purposes, e. g. libraries, are covered out of the general income not out of specific funds. The level of income and expenditure is accounted for in detail in the estimates. If the taxpayer wants information, he, too, must examine these, since on the tax demands no figures are given about the purpose for which the money is required.

1.2   The Public Educational System

1.21   General and Vocational Education

1.211 General Education

The legal foundations for education in schools are laid down by the individual Länder. Although this leads to differences between one Land and another, a certain essential uniformity has been achieved so far.

Schools in the public sector are supported jointly by the Länder, Gemeinden and the Gemeindeverbände. With non-state schools the cost of staffing is usually borne by the Land, that of materials by the Gemeinden. Compulsory schooling lasts from the end of the 6th to the end of the 18th year of age. Besides the compulsory full-time schooling usually lasting 9 years there is an obligation upon everyone not pursuing higher education to attend a vocational course.

The foundation of general education and the lowest stage common to all pupils is the *Grundschule* or *Volksschule* ("primary school"), consisting of 4 or in certain Länder 6 classes. Whereas in some Länder the Grundschule offers instruction free of denominational or ideological emphasis, in other Länder there are also Roman Catholic and Protestant schools maintained by the state and a few ideological ones.

On the basis of the Grundschule are built the secondary schools: these are termed Hauptschule, Realschule and Gymnasium and in certain Länder there are even other designations. The aim of the *Hauptschule* is to impart fundamental knowledge and skills so as to enable pupils to enter upon a career. The aim of the *Realschule*, which ends with the 10th class, is the preparation for those duties in practical life that entail increased technical, economic and social responsibilities. The leaving certificate opens the way to commercial and technical institutions and engineering schools. The traditional basic types of the *Gymnasium* are the classical schools, the modern language ones, and those specialising in mathematics and natural science. Of recent years further differences have arisen. The Gymnasium is intended to provide the essential preparation for a university or college course. The leaving certificate is the Reifeprüfung (Abitur), which is taken after the 13th year, by which time the candidate is usually 19 years old. Possession of the Reifeprüfung entitles one to admission to universities and institutions of comparable status, including library schools.

In general efforts are being made today to facilitate transfers from one type of school to another. Moreover, adults can prepare for the Reifeprüfung by evening study or (under certain conditions) by lectures in the Kolleg, a new type of full-time school.

1.212 Vocational Schools

To meet the requirements of the various trades and professions there are very many types of vocational schools. These schools demand differing standards of previous education (e. g. the leaving certificate of a Hauptschule or a Realschule, or the completion of an apprenticeship or a period of practical training), and they lead to differing levels in professional life. Among such schools are those linked with an apprenticeship or a job (to the end of the 18th year of age), the Berufsfachschulen (such as commercial schools and colleges, domestic science schools, and schools for technical assistants of various kinds), Berufsaufbauschulen ("intermediate vocational schools"), Fachschulen (e. g. trade, industrial, and technical schools) and höhere Fachschulen or Akademien, as they are usually called nowadays (e. g. commercial and engineering colleges). The trend is towards planning vocational education in such a way that standards are achieved equivalent to those in general education. The school-leavers are then expected to reach higher grades and can thereby have a belated chance of taking the university entrance examination.

1.22 Universities and Colleges

1.221 Specialist Institutions of Higher Education

In the Federal Republic there are many — about 100 — professional colleges, mostly called Hochschulen, though some have the more traditional name of Akademien. They are principally colleges of education, colleges or academies of art, colleges or academies of music, and colleges of physical education. The entrance requirement is the Reifeprüfung or a special examination which restricts the student to the study of a subject field related to his profession. Courses and duration of studies are specified, and the training is completed by an examination. These colleges produce primary school teachers and teachers of art, music and physical education, as well as members of other professions. The equivalence of the semesters spent at these state or state-recognised institutions to courses at universities varies. In some Länder the colleges of education are affiliated to universities.

1.222 Universities and Colleges of University Status

Hitherto the state universities and equivalent institutions have fallen into three groups: universities; colleges of advanced technology; and colleges with a restricted range of teaching and research subjects such as those for medicine, agriculture, veterinary medicine, and economic affairs. Recent developments have made this tripartite structure out of date. An active reform movement, still in progress, is about to re-draw the traditional boundaries.

Alongside the old-style universities, which offer universality of knowledge (admittedly mostly without agriculture and engineering), there have sprung up new reformed universities, which lack certain faculties (e. g. medicine or theology). In the colleges of advanced technology the arts faculties have been reinforced; accordingly some have been redesignated technical universities and others simply universities. Colleges with a restricted range of teaching and research subjects add new faculties and thereby also become universities. Soon therefore there will be a distinction only between full universities and partial universities, and the boundary between the two will remain fluid. In all there are 39 institutions of university status situated in the following towns (U — University, TU — Technical University, TH — Technische Hochschule ("College of Advanced Technology"), H — Hochschule (other College of university status)):

Aachen TH, Berlin U and TU, Bielefeld U (under construction), Bochum U, Bonn U, Brunswick TU, Bremen U (at the planning stage), Clausthal TU (the former Mining Academy), Cologne U, Darmstadt TH, Dortmund U (under construction), Düsseldorf U (the former Medical Academy), Erlangen-Nuremberg U, Frankfurt U, Freiburg U, Giessen U, Göttingen U, Hamburg U, Hanover TU (also Medical H and Veterinary H), Heidelberg U, Karlsruhe U (the former TH), Kiel U, Konstanz U (under construction), Mainz U, Mannheim U (the former Commercial H), Marburg U, Munich U and TH, Münster U, Regensburg U (under construction), Saarbrücken U, Stuttgart U (the former TH), Stuttgart-Hohenheim U (the former Agricultural H), Tübingen U, Ulm U for Medicine and Natural Science (under construction), Würzburg U.

For the training of theologians besides the university theological faculties (which do not exist in all universities) there are a number of either state- or church-maintained Philosophisch-Theologische (Roman Catholic) and Kirchliche (Protestant) Hochschulen, which form a group on their own. The courses are completed by state-recognised examinations; some of the colleges have also the right to confer doctorates.

Protestant colleges are to be found in: Berlin, Bethel, Neuendettelsau, Oberursel/Taunus, and Wuppertal. There are Roman Catholic ones in: Augsburg, Bamberg, Dillingen, Eichstätt, Frankfurt (Sankt Georgen), Fulda, Königstein/Taunus, Paderborn, Passau and Trier. The former Philosophisch-Theologische Hochschulen at Freising and Regensburg have recently been closed.

Apart from the denominational ones all colleges of university status are state institutions; the estimates appear in the education budgets of the Länder. The Federal Republic has neither a federal nor a private university. Administratively the universities are autonomous corporations; they each elect their own Rektor ("vice-chancellor") and decide in the Senat ("university court or council") on all matters affecting the institution. Participation of junior teaching staff and students in the administration, a privilege hitherto restricted to full professors, is one of the demands for reform currently being made and already partly granted.

The whole university is divided into faculties: with the chairs go institutes, seminars or laboratories of which the professor is director. Reorganisation of this structure forms an important part of the reforms. The existing "monocratic rule by professors" has been attacked in the light of the Anglo-American departmental system, which is better fitted especially to research in the natural sciences. A start at reorganisation has been made in some of the existing universities. It is however predominantly the new foundations that have drawn up new plans: either there are to be no institutes of the old style at all (this is the intention at Konstanz and Regensburg) or, alternatively, several or all the chairs in a given field are to be brought together in one large institute (as at Bielefeld, Bochum, Bremen and Dortmund).

Study is based on the principle of the freedom of teaching and learning for teachers and taught. This means for the student that he can freely organise his course of study with lectures and participation in advanced classes and can himself decide when he takes the examinations.

Behind this is the concept of the university as an establishment for research and teaching, a concept upon which Humboldt set his seal at the beginning of the 19th century, a concept that was again asserted to be normative in West Germany during the reconstruction after the 1945 collapse, a concept that is also today emphasised by the universities and the Wissenschaftsrat ("Science Council", covering also the humanities and social sciences), and yet a concept that is being disputed in public discussion. The mass competition for university places, the growing need for academically educated people in teaching, industry, commerce and local government causes the vocational aspect of education, that is teaching, to come to the fore. On the other hand, however, the swift development of research in every modern industrial state calls for constant progress and for the attraction of qualified recruits, a call that the universities must obey if they are not to lose their importance.

Plans for reform, under discussion as long ago as 1948, have been presented from about 1960 onwards with increasing force from various sides: from the universities themselves, first from some of the senior teaching staff, recently also from students and the junior staff; from scholars and administrators jointly represented on the Wissenschaftsrat; from local government through the Länder, as a result of which certain laws were passed affecting universities; from the Bund; and not least from the public through the media of the press and radio. Among the plans are tightening the university curricula and shortening the length of courses; freeing university teachers from too much administration and making their personal research easier by sabbatical semesters; removing the narrow limitations of separate subject fields and strengthening inter-disciplinary research; establishing a firmer administrative organisation by making the office of Rektor a permanency; and finally granting greater independence to junior teaching staff.

In addition there is a plan developed by the Wissenschaftsrat to lay down special research fields for the individual universities; such fields are to be supported by providing all the necessary finance for staff and equipment, whereas in other fields retrenchment will have to take place. A carefully worked-out, graded system is to be set up linking universities and special research institutes.

The new universities will in their own ways put such reforming ideas into effect; but even the existing universities are undergoing a similar transformation. Of course the whole movement for reform has considerable impact upon university libraries.

1.23 Adult Education

A characteristic of adult education in the Federal Republic is the multiplicity of institutions differing from one another in structure and presuppositions. With regard to their aims there is substantial agreement inasmuch as there is today a reaction against merely imparting facts. The knowledge that each person gains is expected to assist him in his personal life or in his career and to help him find his bearings in and become a full member of the democratic society. The most important role in adult education is played by the Abendvolkshochschule ("evening institute") — called Volkshochschule for short — which has grown greatly since the twenties. Akin to the "university extension" concept in purpose and manner of working, it is distinguished by the fact that the individual Volkshochschulen are independent and local bodies. The Volkshochschule recognises no restrictions whatever in its syllabuses or audiences.

Other adult educational institutions include: the co-operative venture of the trade-unions and the Volkshochschulen, Arbeit und Leben ("Work and Life"); the Heimvolkshochschulen ("adult education institutes providing full-time short courses"); the Protestant academies; the political academies; Roman Catholic social and theological seminaries; the mothercraft classes and many small educational associations.

Just as varied as the adult educational institutions are the authorities responsible for them. Statistics here are incomplete. In general it may be said that Gemeinden, Landkreise, churches, trade-unions, professional associations, charitable and private organisations all appear as authorities; of these the Gemeinden come first as the main sponsors of the numerically largest group of institutions, namely the Abendvolkshochschulen. In 1969 there were in the Federal Republic 1194 Volkshochschulen, of which 588 were directly supported by the Gemeinden. 209 Volkshochschulen had a full-time head, 985 only a part-time one.

The State is not responsible for adult education except under the special conditions of the city states. The other Länder make grants by virtue of differing, partly statutory regulations. German adult education has however always insisted upon its independence of state control.

There is no head organisation at federal level representing adult education as a whole, although there are associations representing establishments of a similar type. Among them the Deutscher Volkshochschulverband plays a leading part. In 1957 it set up a central educational study centre in Frankfurt am Main.

Co-operation between public libraries and adult educational institutions leaves on the whole much to be desired. In certain Gemeinden however there are successful ventures; sometimes the Volkshochschule and the public library come under the same head and even share the same accommodation.

1.3   The Book Trade

The book trade, which is heir to a long tradition in Germany, enjoys considerable cultural prestige.

According to international statistics book production in the Federal Republic ranks fourth after that in the USSR, USA and Great Britain. In 1968 about 32,000 titles were published, of which 84 per cent were first editions, with 1,548 titles appearing as paperbacks. Out of about 5,000 fiction titles about 28 per cent were translations from other languages.

In the "Adreßbuch des deutschsprachigen Buchhandels 1967/68" ("Directory of the German Book Trade, 1967/68") there are for the Federal Republic and West Berlin about 10,000 enterprises concerned with the trade, among them about 2,600 firms concerned with manufacture and about 7,300 concerned with distributing the publishers' products. These include book, periodical and music publishers and publishers' agents, retail booksellers and middlemen, circulating libraries and other outlets, railway-station bookstalls, mail-order firms, wholesalers and book clubs. The leading position held by Leipzig as the publishing centre of Germany until the Second World War is today shared by several cities, including Munich, West Berlin, Stuttgart, Hamburg and Frankfurt. In each of 30 towns there are now more than 20 firms of the distributive book trade.

Book clubs, of which the first ones, e. g. the Büchergilde Gutenberg, arose from ideas about popular education, developed into a special and important form of sales promotion. Their number has sharply increased since the end of the Second World War. The lists of book titles, from which subscribers can select and order on favourable terms, is usually very comprehensive. The number of members reaches several millions.

As a basis for bookselling practice the standard has long been the "Sale and Trading Regulations" of the Börsenverein des Deutschen Buchhandels ("Organisation of the German Book Trade"). Certain rules had to be altered by virtue of the 1958 law against restrictive practices. As before, direct supply to libraries from publishers is forbidden, and there is still retail price maintenance. Instead of library discounts being settled horizontally by the "Sale and Trading Regulations" they are negotiated vertically by the individual publisher. By far the majority of publishers however have fixed this discount in accordance with the old rule of 5 per cent (for academic libraries) and 10 per cent (for public libraries) of the shop price; other publishers allow a uniform 5 per cent, while some have refused to allow any discount at all. A basis for average book prices, on which public libraries rely, is offered by the annual returns of the Arbeitsstelle für das Büchereiwesen ("Study Centre for Public Libraries") (cf. 3.24).

As the central organisation the Börsenverein des Deutschen Buchhandels in Frankfurt am Main unites the manufacturing and the distributive trades in the Federal Republic. The annual International Frankfurt Book Fair is due to its initiative. The Börsenverein also makes its influence felt in the education of booksellers. Besides the three-year apprenticeship combined with attendance at a vocational school an opportunity is offered the young bookseller of attending the course at the German Book Trade School in Frankfurt. The organ of the Börsenverein is the twice-weekly "Börsenblatt des Deutschen Buchhandels — Frankfurter Ausgabe". Apart from numerous publishers' advertisements and notices it contains current news and contributions from the book-world.

Attempts by using questionnaires to investigate the reading interests and habits of people in the Republic have led to widely differing results and at the moment scarcely justify any generalisation. However, it is to be expected that economic and sociological research, as it is now being pursued by the Hamburg Institut für Buchmarktforschung ("Institute for Market Research on the Book Trade"), will be intensified in the years ahead.

1.4 Bund (Federal Government), Länder (States) and Gemeinden (Local Authorities) as Bodies Responsible for the Library Service

As far as state responsibilities go, libraries come according to the Basic Law under the sole jurisdiction of the Länder. The *Bund* however sponsors its own libraries, e. g. that of the Federal Parliament, those of the Federal authorities and of a number of Federal research establishments. It is also responsible for German libraries abroad. The problem of financing libraries whose function and significance extend wholly or largely outside their own area has been solved in several ways. Funds are received either from the Bund (as from 1969 onwards in the case of the Deutsche Bibliothek in Frankfurt am Main), in other cases collectively from the Länder — on the basis of an agreement drawn up at Königstein in 1949 — (this applies, e. g. to the Technische Informationsbibliothek in Hanover and to the Library of the Institut für Weltwirtschaft in Kiel). An administrative agreement between *Bund* and *Länder* dating from 1964 on "joint financial support outside the terms of the Königstein agreement" opened up the possibility of such joint support; examples of such support are the libraries of the Max Planck Institutes. The State Library of the Preußischer Kulturbesitz ("Prussian Cultural Foundation") and the Bibliothek des Iberoamerikanischen Instituts ("Library of the Latin-American Institute") in West Berlin are both sponsored by the Stiftung Preußischer Kulturbesitz, which was established by the Bund, West Berlin and three Länder. As a collective operation outside the terms of the Königstein agreement the Bund and the Länder maintain the central professional Arbeitsstelle für das Büchereiwesen of the Deutscher Büchereiverband in Berlin. It should finally be mentioned that the foreign activities of the library associations are supported by the Bund.

The *Länder* maintain numerous libraries within their territories. They finance Landes- and Staatsbibliotheken as well as the libraries of by far the majority of universities and comparable institutions. The library schools, apart from the denominational ones in Bonn and Göttingen, are maintained wholly or partially by the Länder. Other regional enterprises such as union catalogues, co-operative acquisitions programmes, extension courses, conferences of library associations and the publication of professional journals are made possible by grants of varying amounts from the Länder. The municipal libraries and in certain Länder even the denominational libraries receive differing degrees of support from the Länder. Almost all the Länder make grants to individual libraries, some for buildings as well. The appropriate allocation of the funds earmarked for municipal public librarianship devolves upon the Staatliche Büchereistellen, which are maintained for this purpose by the Länder. Their significance for the overall development of librarianship in the Länder will be discussed in detail in the following chapter (2.53).

Among the library authorities the *Gemeinden* play a major role. The privilege of maintaining public libraries, which in the interests of local autonomy is granted to even the smallest Gemeinde, is still being exercised (according to the 1968 figures) by some 8,800 out of 23,629 Gemeinden in order to retain an independent service of permanent libraries. Moreover, some of the larger towns still maintain independent academic libraries. Through the co-operation of their libraries in the Deutscher Büchereiverband and the Arbeitsstelle für das Büchereiwesen the towns made a decisive contribution to the growth of public librarianship.

The *Landkreise* at present vary a great deal as regards their participation in librarianship. Most of them make grants to particular Gemeinde libraries. A number maintain central Kreis libraries, often jointly with the library belonging to the chief town of the Kreis, with full lending facilities including interloans. Recently certain Kreise have begun sponsoring mobile libraries. Nowhere however is there already in existence a Kreis library, which (like the American or British county library) is responsible for a central library system with a sizeable number of permanent branches in the Gemeinden.

In the Federal Republic neither the expenditure of the state nor that of the Gemeinden and Gemeindeverbände is laid down by law. The Bund is not empowered to introduce such legislation. The support of youth libraries within the framework of the Federal Youth Plan had to be withdrawn after a few years for constitutional reasons; and the balancing of accounts between the Bund and the Länder encourages both sides to insist upon their respective rights. So for the time being it seems impracticable to introduce even a law offering federal support, such as has materialised in the equally strongly federalist USA with its Library Services and Construction Act. However, an amendment to the Basic Law of the Federal Republic passed in 1970 makes joint efforts of the Bund and the Länder possible in educational planning. This may offer new prospects.

Laws affecting libraries in individual Länder come up against other difficulties. Some Länder, such as Schleswig-Holstein, consider their present solutions adequate for the development and protection of library interests. The Länder are reluctant to commit themselves to long-term grants to municipal or denominational libraries, especially as the grants for library purposes in the Länder and the Gemeinden have to some extent to compete with very much higher financial responsibilities for other cultural institutions. In addition the Gemeinden fear lest the sphere of their voluntary tasks and scope for self-government should be restricted. On the other hand the overall significance of a network of efficient public libraries has hitherto not been sufficiently recognised.

However the increasing attention that the Bund, the Länder and Gemeinden have recently paid to public librarianship in the context of educational planning as a whole has strongly revived the discussion about library legislation. And indeed in some Länder (e.g. Lower Saxony, Hesse, North Rhine-Westphalia) public library legislation is under serious discussion now. The two associations of public libraries and public librarians therefore felt the need to set up a joint committee, which in 1970 presented a document entitled Grundsätze und Normen für die Büchereigesetzgebung in den Ländern der Bundesrepublik Deutschland ("Principles and standards for public library legislation in the Länder of the Federal Republic of Germany"). The suggestions made by the committee are based on the assumption that public library laws in the Länder would not make public library service mandatory for local authorities, but would rather aim to create an incentive to meet and even surpass certain standards und to accept responsibilities within the frame-work of regional library co-operation by offering conditions to be laid down in such legislation. State aid should also be guaranteed for various region-wide activities. The general standards for public library service in this document are based on those already contained in other publications (cf. 3.14 and 4.14).

1.5 Supra-Regional Bodies of Importance for Librarianship

In the following pages only some of the corporate bodies and institutions of significance to librarianship are described. Permanent contact however exists also with other bodies, such as the cultural departments of the Bundesministerium für Bildung und Wissenschaft, the Bundesministerium des Innern and the Auswärtiges Amt (cf. 1.1). On the German Unesco Committee there is one representative for academic libraries and another for public ones so that the library projects of Unesco are dealt with in close collaboration with the professional library associations of the Federal Republic.

1.51 Wissenschaftsrat

As far as academic libraries are concerned the Wissenschaftsrat ("Science Council") established in 1957, is today an institution whose authority is recognised and in whose Empfehlungen ("Recommendations") great confidence is placed. Ever since its foundation the Wissenschaftsrat has pursued step by step the investigations laid down in its terms of reference: "to evolve an overall plan for the advancement of the arts and sciences and thereby to co-ordinate the plans of the Bund and the Länder". The two further related tasks, that of "determining emphases and priorities" and that of "making recommendations for the expenditure of those funds that are available in the budgets of the Bund and the Länder for the advancement of the arts and sciences", have in part already been accomplished. Detailed recommendations have been published for universities and colleges (1960 and 1967), for academic libraries (1964), for research establishments outside universities, and for academies of science, museums and academic special collections (1965). It is hoped to produce the master plan in the near future.

The Wissenschaftsrat was created by an administrative agreement between the governments of the Bund and of the Länder in September 1957. Of its 39 members 17 are representatives of the Bund (6) and of the Länder (1 each — they are the ministers of culture or finance), and 22 are scholars or public men of acknowledged standing. The academic members are appointed by the President of the Bund: 16 on the joint recommendation of the Deutsche Forschungsgemeinschaft, the Max Planck Association and the Westdeutsche Rektorenkonferenz ("Conference of West German Vice-Chancellors"), 6 on the joint recommendation of the Bund and of the Länder. The work is carried out by two committees, an academic and an administrative one, which can for their researches set up expert sub-committees. Resolutions and the publication of statements require the approval of the full Council.

For academic libraries, whose interests are here for the first time considered in close relationship with those of academic institutions in general, the 1964 Empfehlungen are an important document. In the present book reference is frequently made to them. Besides practical special recommendations for 82 libraries and model estimates for university libraries (cf. 4.11) the volume contains fundamental observations on the structure of academic libraries together with suggestions and recommendations for improvements in general and in detail.

The Wissenschaftsrat does not content itself with recommendations. It follows up the results and reports again if improvements, which it had recognised as essential, remain unachieved. It also publishes new statements as soon as developments make them necessary.

1.52 Deutsche Forschungsgemeinschaft

Like the Wissenschaftsrat the Deutsche Forschungsgemeinschaft ("German Research Association") is supported by the Bund and the Länder. Its funds come from grants from the Bund and the Länder in equal proportions; in addition there are contributions from industry through the Stifterverband für die deutsche Wissenschaft ("Donors' Association for German Arts and Sciences") and the Fritz Thyssen Foundation. On the main committee of the Forschungsgemeinschaft, consisting of 29 members, there are representatives of the arts and sciences (15), the Bund and the Länder (6 each) and also of commerce and industry (through 2 members of the Stifterverband). The terms of reference of the Wissenschaftsrat and the Forschungsgemeinschaft are however completely different.

Alongside the planning organisation for institutions is the organisation for promoting research and the interests of those engaged in it. The functions of the Forschungsgemeinschaft are as follows: the financial support of research projects, promoting co-operation between research workers, advising parliaments and governments on academic matters, keeping in touch with research work abroad, and a concern for encouraging and training the rising generation of research workers. Unlike the Wissenschaftsrat, which is a new creation and which had first to evolve its modus operandi, the Forschungsgemeinschaft has links with a tradition forged by the Notgemeinschaft der deutschen Wissenschaft ("Emergency Association for German Arts and Sciences"), which had existed in Berlin from 1921 to 1945. In its organisation and structure it follows for the most part the pattern laid down by its predecessor. It is an autonomous organisation of the German arts and sciences, which formulates its own rules and freely elects the academic members of its bodies. It is neither a state authority nor a public corporation. The members of the Forschungsgemeinschaft are all the universities together with the large learned academies, the Max Planck Association and some learned societies and institutions. A major role in planning research and establishing emphasis is played by the senate, which is composed exclusively of academics. Decisions on the use of funds are made by the main committee. The latter relies in such matters on the judgement of 338 honorary consultants, who are elected every four years by a total of 10,000 research workers from every special field.

The Forschungsgemeinschaft has included in its programme the advancement of academic librarianship as an indirect means of furthering research and is in this respect advised by its libraries committee (cf. 3.23). Aid to libraries is subject to restrictions arising from the position and function of the Forschungsgemeinschaft as a central organisation for the advancement of research financed by the Bund and the Länder. Since the Länder are responsible for the upkeep and the current endowment of academic libraries, the Forschungsgemeinschaft cannot support individual libraries in fulfilling their own normal duties or in compensating for inadequate budgets. It limits itself rather to supporting co-operative library ventures and central institutions, as well as to making initial grants for new developments. The first category includes obtaining foreign literature through the co-operative acquisitions scheme, compiling union catalogues, union lists of periodicals, catalogues of manuscripts and indexes of literature; the second category includes help for central specialist libraries; the third category includes a number of projects and models designed to rationalise library procedure. The measures in general and their effect upon the organisation of academic librarianship in the Republic are discussed later in their appropriate context.

1.53 Deutscher Bildungsrat

In 1965, as a counterpart to the Wissenschaftsrat, the Deutscher Bildungsrat ("German Education Council") was established by a further agreement between the Bund and the Länder. The Bildungsrat is to draft plans for the requirements and developments of the German educational system, make proposals for the structure of the system, draw up financial estimates, as well as to make long-term recommendations for the various stages of the system.

In composition and functions the Bildungsrat resembles the Wissenschaftsrat. There is an administrative committee consisting of one representative from each Land, 4 representatives of the Bund and 4 representatives put forward by the associations of local authorities. Then there is the education committee, comprising 18 members appointed by the President of the Republic on the nomination of the Ministerpräsidentenkonferenz ("Conference of Prime Ministers") of the Länder, the Bund and the associations of local authorities. For co-operation with the Wissenschaftsrat in matters of fundamental importance the constitution of the Bildungsrat provides for a co-ordinating committee.

The Bildungsrat has so far set up several committees, such as a structural committee, the sub-committees of which deal with detailed questions relating to the means and methods of education, e. g. pre-school education, educational opportunity, education of the gifted child, length of schooling, and the training of teachers.

The sub-committee for adult education deals with, inter alia, the possibilities of vocational training and all aspects of "life-long learning". It is to be expected also that public librarianship will be included in future deliberations of the Bildungsrat.

1.54 Ständige Konferenz der Kultusminister der Länder

The decentralised structure of the Federal Republic makes it difficult to initiate co-operative and uniform plans in any cultural sphere. The Wissenschaftsrat, the Forschungsgemeinschaft and the Bildungsrat put forward many suggestions and recommendations on this problem. Even in 1948, before the Federal Republic was established, the Kultusminister ("Ministers of Culture and Education") of the West German Länder recognised the need for a continuous dialogue with each other and set up the Standing Conference, which has since become a permanent institution. The Conference lays down in its main committee, to which the Kultusminister belong, the direction and priorities of its work and passes resolutions which, if they are to be binding on all the Länder, have to be unanimous. Specialist work is delegated to four large committees: the schools committee, the universities and colleges committee, the committee for the arts and adult education (formerly simply the committee for the arts), and the committee for education abroad; subcommittees are appointed where necessary. Attached to the secretariat is an international department and a documentation centre. After the first years, devoted to reconstruction, the emphasis was until 1957 (when the Wissenschaftsrat was founded) placed especially upon the advancement of research; since then the reform movements in education have come to the fore. Specialist questions of academic librarianship, such as professional training, the 1966 loan regulations, and the Institut für Bibliothekstechnik ("Institute for Library Technology"), all these have been the concern of the universities and colleges committee either alone or jointly with the committee for the arts. Appropriate recommendations have been made by the Conference. Occasionally the universities and colleges committee has conferred with the libraries committee of the Forschungsgemeinschaft on its measures to promote library services.

With regard to public librarianship, which is treated together with adult education, the Conference has made fundamental recommendations for the extension of library services and has taken the initiative in the regional planning of libraries; this is something in which it is at present actively engaged. Outline agreements for library education have pointed the way to unified developments in this sphere. As a result of a Conference resolution, moreover, the Länder agreed to participate in the current financing of the Arbeitsstelle für das Büchereiwesen of the Deutscher Büchereiverband.

1.55 Associations of Local Authorities

Gemeinden and Kreise in the Federal Republic have joined forces to form associations of local authorities, whose functions are to represent the interests of the Gemeinden and the Gemeindeverbände to parliaments, governments and other bodies, to keep the public informed about achievements and requirements and to facilitate the exchange of ideas on all subjects between members. Among the specialist committees the education ones are responsible for public library affairs. In the larger Länder regional associations have been set up and entrusted with functions of regional scope.

Virtually all the kreisfreie Städte and many kreisangehörige Städte from South Germany belong to the Deutscher Städtetag. Other kreisangehörige Städte have joined the Deutscher Städtebund. Smaller Landgemeinden and Ämter have founded the Deutscher Gemeindetag, and the Landkreise the Deutscher Landkreistag. All four bodies co-operate in the Bundesvereinigung der kommunalen Spitzenverbände ("Federal Union of Local Authority Associations"), the formal direction of which is vested in the Städtetag. (On the terms used in this paragraph see also 1.1.)

On basic and specialist library problems these four associations have produced opinions, reports and recommendations. Delegates of the four co-operate in the bodies for the regional planning of libraries. The Städtetag publishes every two years statistics of local authority public libraries in its Statistisches Jahrbuch Deutscher Gemeinden ("Statistical Yearbook of German Gemeinden"). Moreover, the foundation of the Deutscher Büchereiverband, the Verband der Bibliotheken des Landes Nordrhein-Westfalen and the Arbeitsstelle für das Büchereiwesen is partly due to the initiative of the Städtetag. Between these bodies and associations of local authorities there is close contact.

1.56 Kommunale Gemeinschaftsstelle für Verwaltungsvereinfachung

As a central institution technically independent even of the associations of local authorities there is the Kommunale Gemeinschaftsstelle für Verwaltungsvereinfachung ("Municipal Centre for Administrative Simplification"), which is financed by over 300 regional corporations. Its function is to investigate the organisation and the cost effectiveness of municipal administration and by means of information, recommendations and reports, principally intended for members, to contribute to rationalisation and to an increase in productivity.

The Gemeinschaftsstelle employs a small staff of principal consultants, supported by the experience and co-operation of the municipal administrations themselves and of individual specialists. In this way the findings are based upon practice and are therefore treated with due respect. In the sphere of local cultural activity the Gemeinschaftsstelle has carried out the first detailed investigation into the organisation and cost effectiveness of municipal public libraries (cf. especially 4.14).

Recently the Gemeinschaftsstelle has also concerned itself in a similar way with academic libraries.

1.57 Trusts and Foundations

Private foundations, which promoted science and research without restricting beneficiaries to specific tasks and interests, did not exist in the Federal Republic until the establishment of the Fritz Thyssen Foundation in July 1959. Shortly afterwards, in May 1961, when the Volkswagen works were transferred to private ownership the Volkswagen

Foundation was set up. We must mention as the largest German private foundation the Gemeinnützige Vermögensverwaltung Robert Bosch GmbH, which however is not devoted exclusively to the advancement of science and research; it supports also other work of value to the community. We limit ourselves here to a few facts about the first two foundations, since they both support academic librarianship.

On the important matter of where to draw the line between their functions and those of the State, both follow the principle of granting aid where the State cannot, or at all events cannot do so speedily. They keep in close touch with each other and with the Forschungsgemeinschaft in order to avoid overlapping and in order to agree on basic matters and individual projects. Each of the foundations is governed by a board of trustees, on which sit personalities from science and industry and, in the case of the Volkswagen Foundation (which owes its existence to an agreement between the Bund and the Land of Lower Saxony), also from public administration; the board decides about individual projects and lays down the guidelines for future grants. Moreover each of the foundations gave its own distinctive character to its activities during the early years.

Since neither body wished, as a stopgap measure, to assume functions for which the State is responsible (even if the latter does not adequately perform them), both bodies have restricted the assistance that they will give to libraries. Of the library undertakings that have been supported we have here singled out only a few, especially those for which initial ad hoc grants were made.

The Volkswagen Foundation has given individual libraries considerable sums for book purchases; but this assistance has been restricted to cases of special need. Influence upon future development has been exercised by their initial grants for the setting up and extension of text-book collections in university libraries (cf. 2.31). Similarly, it is hoped that the preparation of a model stock for an "educational library" and the placing of such model libraries in four universities, made possible by the Thyssen Foundation, will stimulate the establishment of students' libraries (cf. 2.31). The Thyssen Foundation also supports the Arbeitsgemeinschaft der Kunstbibliotheken ("Study Group of Art Libraries") in its various projects.

1.6 Development of German Librarianship from the Beginning to the Middle of the Century

This book provides an introduction to present-day librarianship in the Federal Republic. It contains no library history. Only briefly can we look back and outline the historical development in the first half of the twentieth century in so far as it is necessary for an understanding of contemporary circumstances. In 1900 there existed side by side wissenschaftliche Bibliotheken ("academic libraries") and — as they were then termed — Volksbüchereien ("people's libraries"). The long period of independent development of the two types is a peculiarity of German library history, which distinguishes it from other countries, especially Anglo-Saxon ones. This will become clearer to the reader from the following historical sections. Whereas academic libraries have merely had to adapt their time-honoured functions to the demands of modern times, the still young Öffentliche Büchereien ("public libraries") have managed to clarify their role in public life only after severe clashes of opinion.

From about 1950 onwards and increasingly of recent years both sides have striven to build bridge-heads, to see the library profession as a whole with easier possibilities of transfer and to reorganise their systems accordingly.

The normal development of both kinds of library was interrupted in this century by the First World War (1914–1918), National Socialism (1933–May 1945) and the Second World War (1939–May 1945). The first years after the collapse were for all libraries a phase of wearisome reconstruction, in which there was only the inkling of new forward-looking ideas. We close our historical retrospect with the end of this phase, about 1945–1950.

In this period falls the most significant crisis in German post-War development, the division into a western and an eastern zone, the Federal Republic and the centralised German Democratic Republic. The divergent forms of government, the distinctive development of political, economic and social as well as intellectual and cultural life, have also torn librarianship asunder into two systems with different structures.

The founding of the Federal Republic in 1949 and the process of economic reconstruction paved the way for a new period, which began then and still continues today. The description of the present situation in the later chapters of this book covers the years since 1950.

1.61 Academic Libraries

The development of academic librarianship in this period is determined by two major conflicting, yet closely interrelated, trends. The first, corresponding to the development of research itself, is the increased emphasis upon specialisation and therefore upon isolation; the second is the striving for co-ordination and co-operation. The first third of the 20th century is moreover taken up with the consolidation of the general academic library and with that of the library profession. Connected with this are the attempts to create a national German Library and to maintain contacts with foreign librarianship.

The first trend, specialisation, is seen in the formation of libraries for a single subject field, *special libraries* (cf. 2.42), a large number being in the realm of commerce and industry and in pure and applied science. The same trend is evident in the emergence of learned institutions attached to universities, of newly established research institutes, museums and archives, governments, parliaments and law-courts, and therefore also in the social sciences and the humanities. This development, foreshadowed in the 17th and 18th centuries, began properly in the late 19th century, but came to full fruition in the 20th. In many instances such libraries consisted at first merely of basic reference material with a few books and periodicals but not subject to professional supervision.

At a rate unusual by earlier library standards there grew out of many of them in a few years extensive and heavily used collections. Yet, since they were attached to their institutions and had primarily to serve them, they were frequently inaccessible except to a restricted circle of readers. It was only gradually that they became open to a wider public and were incorporated in the general library service.

The second trend, that of consolidation, began with *general libraries*, partly as a result of government measures, partly as a result of co-operative ventures initiated by librarians. The underlying cause was the peculiar situation in Germany, on the one hand with an abundance of separate libraries, whose holdings (in some cases centuries old), diverged sharply from one another, and on the other hand with the lack of a central national library. A step which proved to be decisive for the future was taken by the Prussian Kultusministerium in 1910 when it grouped together six university libraries by allotting each of them a "special subject field". This was because there were insufficient funds for an all-round increase in stocks; it was therefore a kind of rational economy drive. In

1921 the plan was converted into an activity supported by the Notgemein-schaft der deutschen Wissenschaft for the acquisition of foreign literature, and it was extended to cover eight university libraries. For inter-library co-operation certain truly professional joint undertakings were launched: the Preußischer (later: Deutscher) Gesamtkatalog ("Prussian — German — Union Catalogue", cf. 3.121), the inter-library lending scheme (cf. 3.13), and the Auskunftsbüro der deutschen Bibliotheken ("Information Office for German Libraries", cf. 4.61). Although they were begun in the last decade of the 19th century, these ventures, much altered and extended to cover the whole Reich, are library achievements of the 20th century; as a result the scholar in Germany was offered good study facilities, and the German library service earned respect abroad.

The stages of the librarian's career were governed by regulations concerning admission, training, examination, and promotion (cf. chap. 7). The activity of the Verein Deutscher Bibliothekare ("Association of German Librarians") (cf. 3.21) founded in 1900, helped to form a kind of professional consciousness and esprit de corps.

Many matters would have been easier if a national German library had existed as a focus for all endeavours. There was however no such library even after the founding of the Reich.

The realisation that a library that would collect German literature comprehensively and exploit it bibliographically was indispensable led the German book trade in 1913 to establish the Deutsche Bücherei ("German Library") in Leipzig (cf. 2.11). As a deposit library for all literature in the German language and as compiler of the Deutsche Nationalbibliographie ("German National Bibliography") it exercised some of the functions of a national library. In 1940 it was declared a public corporation.

Between the World Wars the Preußische Staatsbibliothek ("Prussian State Library") (cf. 2.12), the largest academic library open to the public in the largest of the Länder and situated in Berlin, the Reich capital, consciously aimed at becoming the national library. It too collected German literature comprehensively, including official publications; it acquired on a large scale new learned publications from abroad in all subject fields and published lists of new foreign accessions; it was the headquarters of the Deutscher Gesamtkatalog, the Auskunftsbüro der deutschen Bibliotheken, the Gesamtkatalog der Wiegendrucke ("Union Catalogue of Incunabula"), and the training institute for educating new entrants to librarianship; it saw to the representation of German libraries abroad.

Alongside it however, with similar significance for South Germany although without such a concentration of central functions, was the *Bayerische Staatsbibliothek* ("Bavarian State Library") (cf. 2.13) in Munich with its wealth of manuscripts, incunabula and older literature, with valuable special collections of orientalia, maps and music, and also with a school of librarianship.

Further large and famous Landesbibliotheken such as Dresden and Stuttgart followed suit.

The elevation of a single library to be the central national library has never taken place. The collapse of May 1945 and the resultant end of the German Reich and the Prussian State marked the end of a chapter. The national library question had to be considered all over again.

In spite of all the disorders and losses of two World Wars the other academic libraries have been able to maintain continuity with their past; but even for them it was not easy. Twice in twenty years German libraries were prevented for four or five years from acquiring foreign works and any information about recent publications and library activity abroad. Twice, after 1918 and 1945, great endeavours had to be made at the end of a war to regain contact with foreign material, to fill gaps in periodicals, to catch up on the purchase of monographs, and to gain information about current developments. On both occasions the Notgemeinschaft der deutschen Wissenschaft — established in 1920, re-established in 1949 (cf. 1.52) — came to the rescue. On both occasions the assistance was supplementary to whatever the libraries had available from their own funds. The difficulties were great, the financial resources limited, and budgets were scarcely adequate for current requirements; on top of this came a strict national regulation of foreign exchange and, especially marked after 1920, devaluation.

In 1945 the recommencement was much harder than in 1919 for two reasons. Bombs had destroyed the substance of the libraries themselves; book losses of as many as 25 million volumes (about a third of the holdings of academic libraries alone), completely or partially destroyed library buildings, loss of catalogues — all this had turned the former order into chaos. The era of National Socialism hit the public libraries more severely than the academic ones. Nevertheless it lies in the nature of a dictatorial doctrinaire one-party regime to keep all cultural institutions under its control. Academic libraries were, it is true, able to continue functioning after a fashion, book acquisitions were left to them, but the distinction between "desirable" and "undesirable" books was also made. Everything that was not politically congenial had to be concealed, and restrictions placed on its issue. Foreign literature could no longer be acquired as formerly; shortage of foreign currency was the reason given. The removal of "non-Aryan" and politically suspect colleagues, the constant political supervision burdened and impeded the once free co-operation between colleagues. Notwithstanding, even in those years scholarly works were obtained by the libraries, where they were put to scholarly use.

The years 1945–1949 cannot be counted as a period of positive progress. For that the damage was too great, the distress too acute. Each library on its own had to cope with immediate problems, to tidy up, to obtain material for urgent repairs to the fabric, to erect work-rooms for the library staff, and, as soon as the building could be reopened for readers, to retrieve books from the places to which they had been dispersed and as far as possible to restore order in the library and in its catalogues. Slowly the procedures for acquiring books and periodicals were set in motion again, though hampered until 1951 by restrictions on foreign currency. Thoughts and plans about professional organisation and co-operation were not lacking even in those early days, but whatever was possible was still at first limited by the boundaries of the occupation zones; certain relief was obtained from the amalgamation of the three western zones, but not until the rise of the Federal Republic did the conditions for constructive co-operation exist once more.

1.62 Public Libraries

If the "Öffentliche Büchereien" of today are looked upon as a further development of the "Volksbüchereien", their history began in the 19th century. At that time, on the initiative of individuals and thanks to the influence of diverse political and other groups together with that of the two large Churches, the Protestant and the Roman Catholic, many small libraries came into being. Predominantly libraries serving particular communities, they were intended primarily for their own members. They soon however saw their mission in wider terms. Although their political and religious motives differed in detail, they all wished to offer citizens of the emergent industrial society a spiritual foothold or better opportunities in their careers. Faced with a general rise in literacy these libraries were intended to lead readers to what was then accepted as good and honest literature. Only in isolated cases in the 19th century were Volksbüchereien set up or maintained by towns.

The closing years of the 19th century brought new ideas. Under the influence of the USA and England there developed the "Bücherhallenbewegung" ("Public Libraries Movement") modelled on the Anglo-Saxon public libraries which, widespread in town and country, and supported by local authorities as a well-recognised obligation, served all citizens and all groups of society equally. Corresponding to this model was the pressure to unite the academic Stadtbibliothek and the Volksbücherei into one "Einheitsbücherei" ("integrated library"). Throughout the educational functions of libraries were recognised; but librarians were expected to be impartial and unprejudiced. In book selection only strict literary merit was to be the decisive factor. The problem of the "lower limit" of fiction, then hotly debated, has even today not yet completely disappeared from professional library discussions in Germany. Alongside fiction and general non-fiction the significance of more specialised literature was recognised. In the case of libraries of this kind demands were now made for professional staff, for financial support from the state and for library legislation.

The "Bücherhallenbewegung" influenced not only professional thinking but also evoked a response in the general public. After further libraries had been founded by voluntary organisations and industrial firms — among them the Öffentliche Bücherhalle der Patriotischen Gesellschaft in Hamburg and the Bücherhalle of the Krupp firm — numerous town libraries were founded in the first decade of this century and the expenditure of towns on libraries increased. The libraries maintained by and serving various groups also benefited from the increased attention now being given to librarianship; only the economic crisis after the First World War led to a definite retrenchment, until National Socialism put an end to any library work not controlled by the State and imposed severe restrictions upon the operations of denominational libraries.

It was by no means only the unwillingness of Gemeinden to assume responsibility for the Öffentliche Büchereien, which is what the Bücherhallenbewegung demanded, that prevented the development of the Anglo-Saxon type of public library in Germany during the following period. Much more decisive were the two decades of professional "Richtungsstreit" ("Controversy over Objectives"); as a result the Volksbüchereien in Germany sought their own particular path, which had the effect of alienating them from developments in other countries. The conflict led to autonomy for them and thereby made any rapprochement with the academic Stadtbibliotheken illusory.

Until the early thirties the "Stettiner Richtung" of Erwin Ackerknecht and the "Leipziger Richtung" of Walter Hofmann were in irreconcilable opposition to each other. Common to both movements however was the concept, then typical of contemporary thought, that the library had more of a duty to further the mental and spiritual development of readers than to achieve purely practical ends. Common to both also was the basic pedagogical standpoint, which led to strict criteria in book selection and to an intensive reader advisory service; this was in contrast to the "lending system for the masses" of the American public library, which adapted its book selection to reader demand and in which the librarian advised the reader only if asked. The small German Volksbüchereien, segregated as they were from the academic Stadtbibliotheken or the central academic departments, were represented as desirable, in contrast to the large American public libraries. The Volksbüchereien were simple to understand, a fact that was said to make it easier for them to carry out more effectively their educational function. The Thekenbücherei, a closed-access type of library with an open counter — as opposed to the completely open-access library — emphasised the role of the librarian as a mediator between the book and the reader. The movement led by Walter Hofmann, later Chief Librarian of the Leipzig Bücherhallen, wanted only the genuine, artistic, worthwhile book to be accepted into the library stock and was consciously content with the small circle of receptive readers, an elite from all strata of society, which would in turn influence others. These readers were to enjoy the librarian's unlimited help and guidance; such service was held to be vital.

Erwin Ackerknecht, City Librarian of Stettin, and other librarians based their movement on an expansion of the Bücherhallenbewegung. They rejected such a potential curtailment of service and such extensive paternalism towards readers. Subject interests and the need for recreation were recognised as justifiable desires. Ackerknecht even allowed a "temporary cultural value" to trivia, though not to sheer trash. He and his disciples were confident that many readers would find their way past the preliminary stage to the artistically worthwhile book; librarians saw that their pedagogical role lay in awakening and fostering the reader's desire for self-education through books and his willingness to respond to artistic influences. Individual "guidance" of the reader by the librarian was in this movement less pronounced than with Hofmann.

Much as we with hindsight may regret the course which German public librarianship followed during the Richtungsstreit, the theoretical findings and the practical experiences and achievements bore fruit in various fields. Ackerknecht made the library an organic part of the whole educational service and strove intensively and systematically for contacts with all cultural institutions. Walter Hofmann's Leipzig movement deserved praise especially for its contributions to librarianship as a profession, to the organisation and study of loans policy, to reader research and to the exploitation of stock by carefully constructed public catalogues.

The overall growth of librarianship from the twenties until 1933 was certainly hampered by the internal divisions among librarians; yet there were advances. The Gemeinden increasingly assumed responsibility for libraries, and the State began to set up Büchereistellen to advise Gemeinden, if they so desired, on the establishment and organisation of their libraries.

The first Staatliche Büchereistellen ("State Public Library Offices") opened in 1910 in Hagen and Elberfeld. Three Büchereistellen were set up during the First World War, 22 more in the years from 1919 until 1933. One factor common to them all was the purely advisory function; in spite of professional opinion and demand there was no systematic construction from a central office of a nation-wide library network. The Büchereistellen were mostly very inadequately staffed, and the state funds at their disposal for supporting library work were too small to make a fully effective library policy possible. The achievements under such circumstances are all the more noteworthy. For example, Ackerknecht built up on Scandinavian models an efficient library system in rural areas from Stettin outwards into the province of Pomerania. This stimulated others to expand especially in the border areas where the State for cultural and political reasons made more generous and recurrent grants. At that time the foundations were laid for what is still an outstanding library service in, among other places, the Saarland and especially in Schleswig-Holstein with the Zentrale für Nordmarkbüchereien ("Central Office for Public Libraries on the Northern Border"), situated in Flensburg under the distinguished leadership of Franz Schriewer.

Characteristic features of the independence for which the public libraries had striven were the founding of their own central organisations and the publishing of their own periodicals. In the first instance the librarians

47

were members of the Verein Deutscher Bibliothekare ("Association of German Librarians"), and the "Zentralblatt für Bibliothekswesen" ("Central Journal for Librarianship") as its official organ provided space for details of public library activities. From 1900 until 1903 it carried as a supplement the "Blätter für Volksbibliotheken und Lesehallen" ("News of Public Libraries and Reading Rooms"), which was subsequently published on its own. Whereas the pressure for public library independence was mounting, the Richtungsstreit delayed and overshadowed the formation of central organisations for public libraries. The attempt to establish a Deutsche Büchereigesellschaft ("German Public Library Association") failed. In the main, institutions were set up under the influence of one of the two Richtungen, and for a long time they were engaged in intense rivalry. In 1914 the Zentralstelle für volkstümliches Büchereiwesen ("Central Office for Popular Librarianship") was established in Leipzig; it was concerned with the advancement of public librarianship as a whole: the training and further education of librarians, the information and advisory service on library organisation and administration in co-operation with the Büchereistellen of the Länder, book selection and exploitation of stock, and the supply of technical library requirements. A central book bindery was attached to it, and in 1925 the Einkaufshaus für Volksbüchereien ("Supply Agency for Public Libraries") was added as a limited company. From 1926 onwards the Institut für Leser- und Schrifttumskunde ("Institute for the Study of Readers and Literature") took over as an independent organisation part of the functions of the Zentralstelle. The professional school of the Zentralstelle became in 1916 the first college to prepare public librarians for a state diploma. One publication of the Zentralstelle and therefore of Hofmann's movement was the series "Hefte für Büchereiwesen" ("Notebooks for Public Librarianship"), from 1916 onwards.

On the initiative of the other movement the Zentrale für Volksbüchereien ("Central Office for Public Libraries") was established in Berlin in 1915. It was followed in 1916 by the Büchereischule des Zentralinstituts für Erziehung und Unterricht ("Library School of the Central Institute for Education and Instruction"); this too was in Berlin. From 1919/1920 onwards there appeared the periodical "Bildungspflege" ("Encouragement of Education"), of which Ackerknecht was one of the founders. It was amalgamated in 1921 with the "Blätter für Volksbibliotheken und Lesehallen" and given the new title "Bücherei und Bildungspflege" ("Libraries and the Encouragement of Education").

Although adversely affected by the Richtungsstreit, there was founded in 1922 in Berlin the Verband Deutscher Volksbibliothekare ("Association of German Public Librarians") with which both movements co-operated for limited objectives. In spite of many difficulties it was active in professional, technical and policy matters.

The period of National Socialism from 1933 to 1945 brought fundamental changes. The whole of the publishing output was under control, books by "undesirable" authors were burnt in public and had to be withdrawn from libraries, all library work had to be placed at the service of the new ideology. To this end substantial financial contributions were made by the State and the Gemeinden, and with expert knowledge the organisational basis was created. In 1935 the Reichsstelle für das Büchereiwesen ("Reich Office for Public Librarianship") was established as the first central professional office and also the highest authority for public librarianship. It was in a position to direct the whole development of the German public library service in all the Gemeinden including the cities. The previously existing central authorities could hold their own only with difficulty. The Verband Deutscher Volksbibliothekare was severely hampered in its work. Of the Leipzig Deutsche Zentralstelle für volkstümliches Büchereiwesen and its Einkaufshaus für Volksbüchereien there remained the Einkaufshaus für Büchereien. It became the central supplier of technical material, which by this time had been standardised, and of books in library bindings, processed ready for issue; by this means it was possible to set up thousands of small libraries with largely uniform stocks, selected to a great extent from basic lists and all catalogued simultaneously. The contacts between public and school libraries in the small Gemeinden and the general concern to attract young readers led to the creation of many youth libraries.

Although on paper the Gemeinden retained their independence as well as their income from rates and taxes, in practice party political control left them few possibilities of going their own way. The "Richtlinien für das Volksbüchereiwesen" ("Principles for Public Librarianship") issued in 1937 laid down the duties placed upon them with regard to the public libraries. The same Richtlinien governed the competence and functions of the Reichsstelle für das Büchereiwesen and its subordinate Staatliche Volksbüchereistellen. Although according to their terms of reference they were expected to give systematic support to the expansion of public librarianship, they did not even then develop into a national controlling authority. Better staffed and better equipped than ever before, the

Büchereistellen thereupon gained a fresh lease of life, as a result of which the number of public libraries rose to around 20,000.

The combination of National Socialist politics and state dictatorship, characteristic of the growth of librarianship at this time, makes it hard to assess professional achievement objectively and has discredited institutions which in other circumstances might appear from a professional point of view thoroughly desirable. This affected decisions in the period after the collapse of the Third Reich; on the other hand certain aspects of professional progress in matters of organisation turned out to be fruitful in the reconstruction of public librarianship.

The first years after the end of the War were marked by taking stock, inspecting holdings, and searching for new concepts. Many of the libraries were destroyed or dispersed, book collections lost or left unsupervised. Staatliche Büchereistellen had to be re-established. Librarians who had remained behind and those who had returned set about saving what could be saved, removing National Socialist and militaristic literature and under the greatest external difficulties paving the way in town and country for the continuance of the public library service. A first set of statistics for 1949/1950 showed that within the territory of the present Federal Republic 77 per cent of the Gemeinden possessed no public libraries. Although these were almost entirely the smaller Gemeinden, they comprised 41 per cent of the population. Apart from the variations between town and country there were regional and local ones, affected by the consequences of the War but also by differing library traditions. After the stabilisation of the currency and the beginning of the economic recovery public librarianship made such progress that within two decades it left far behind the achievements of the past century.

FURTHER READING

In a publication entitled Die Bücherei in Gemeinde und Staat (Köln 1966) Heinrich Kaspers, Dietrich Oedekoven and Wilhelm Philippi have dealt with the legal form and status of the public library, outlines of the constitutional law relating to Gemeinden in North-Rhine-Westphalia and the budgets of the Gemeinden with special reference to public libraries.

The development and organisation of the book trade is described by Hans Widmann: Geschichte des Buchhandels vom Altertum bis zur Gegenwart. Wiesbaden 1952. Widmann has also revised Ernst Kuhnert's history of the book trade for the 2nd edition of the Handbuch der Bibliothekswissenschaft (Bd 1, Kapitel 10).

Details of book production in the Federal Republic are provided in the annual publication of the Börsenverein des Deutschen Buchhandels in Frankfurt am Main, Buch und Buchhandel in Zahlen.

Average book prices, related to book selection in public libraries, are also produced annually by the Arbeitsstelle für das Büchereiwesen and published in the Bibliotheksdienst, in the Handbuch der Öffentlichen Büchereien and in the Schnellstatistik (cf. the statistics in chap. 8.1).

The historical growth of German academic librarianship has been given an excellent exposition by Georg Leyh in the Handbuch der Bibliothekswissenschaft, Bd 3; for the Middle Ages and the Renaissance in the context of European development and for the period from the Enlightenment to the present day in the far-reaching chapter 8 (Bd 3,2, p. 1—491). Only the modern period from 1933 onwards is dismissed by Leyh in a few pages. The individual chapters in Band 2 on library administration also place their subject matter in historical perspective (cf. Further Reading at end of chap. 4).

An impressive testimony to the catastrophic situation of 1946 is supplied by Georg Leyh: Die deutschen wissenschaftlichen Bibliotheken nach dem Krieg. Tübingen 1947.

Another important contemporary document is the report on the first post-War librarians' conference in Hamburg in 1946: Probleme des Wiederaufbaus im wissenschaftlichen Bibliothekswesen. Hamburg 1947.

One of the first comprehensive accounts of reconstruction work since 1945 is given by Gisela von Busse: West German Library Developments since 1945. Washington 1962.

For the historial review of public librarianship we are particularly indebted to other authors.

An exhaustive account for the Handbuch des Büchereiwesens (Wiesbaden 1965—) was written by Johannes Langfeldt: Zur Geschichte des Büchereiwesens (1. Halbband, p. 57 ff.). In it the growth of public librarianship is investigated in its many aspects from its early beginnings in the Middle Ages onwards. The development of public librarianship in this century is treated also in other chapters of the Handbuch, especially in the contribution by

Rudolf Joerden: Das Büchereiwesen der Stadt (2. Halbband, p. 238—325), Wilhelm Hoppe: Das Büchereiwesen auf dem Lande (2. Halbband, p. 326—386),

Ludwin Langenfeld: Buchauswahl und Bestandserschließung (2. Halbband, p. 130—191),

Gustav Rottacker: Büchereigesetze und Verbände (2. Halbband, p. 192—237).

The history of public librarianship is discussed also in the book by Hans Hugelmann: Die Volksbücherei. Stuttgart 1952.

The beginnings of the popular library movement are treated in Karl-Wolfgang Mirbt: Stephani, Massow, Preusker. Pioniere des öffentlichen Bibliothekswesens. Wiesbaden 1969. (Beiträge zum Büchereiwesen. Reihe B Quellen und Texte. H. 2.)

Periods and questions that are typical of the development in Germany are treated in the works of Christel Rubach: Die Volksbücherei als Bildungsbücherei in der Theorie der deutschen Bücherhallenbewegung. Köln 1962, and H. J. Kuhlmann: Anfänge des Richtungsstreites. Arthur Heidenhain als Vermittler in den Auseinandersetzungen der Jahre 1909–1914. Reutlingen 1961.

Material on library theory and political attitudes during the period of National Socialism has been compiled and introduced by Friedrich Andrae: Volksbücherei und Nationalsozialismus. Wiesbaden 1970. (Beiträge zum Büchereiwesen. Reihe B Quellen und Texte. H. 3.)

Moreover, as a source of information on National Socialism and the early post-War period reference must be made to the professional journals, in particular the Zentralblatt für Bibliothekswesen, the Nachrichten für wissenschaftliche Bibliotheken, the Mitteilungsblatt Verband der Bibliotheken des Landes Nordrhein-Westfalen and Bücherei und Bildung.

2   Types of Library

Libraries can be classified by size, by the nature of their holdings, by type of reader, by the area they serve, or by the source of their funds. Here we have taken the primary function of each type of library as the distinguishing feature, with the addition, in some cases, of certain of the above characteristics. Separate types are not described in detail, but only sufficiently to show their essential features. Only in special cases are libraries belonging to any one type dealt with individually.

2.1   A "National Library" and Central General Libraries

There is no single national library in the Federal Republic today, just as there never was in the German Reich. An important part of such a library's functions is fulfilled by the Deutsche Bibliothek in Frankfurt. Beside it we should mention the Staatsbibliothek Preußischer Kulturbesitz in Berlin and Marburg, and the Bayerische Staatsbibliothek in Munich, as large, general central state libraries, not linked with a university, with more than regional responsibilities to all libraries in the country. They are supplemented in certain fields — technology, economics, agriculture, medicine — by appropriate central specialist libraries.

2.11   Deutsche Bibliothek

The Deutsche Bibliothek in Frankfurt, which was founded at the end of 1946 on the initiative of H. W. Eppelsheimer by an agreement between the city of Frankfurt, the West German book trade organisations and the American and British military authorities, is a repository and bibliographical centre for German-language publications. According to its charter, it has the task of "collecting as exhaustively as possible material in German and other languages issued since 8th May 1945 in Germany, and material in German issued abroad, to conserve it, to make it available for use, and to compile and publish the German [national] bibliography on scholarly principles". The obligation to collect was later extended to

53

literature on Germany published outside the country in languages other than German, and to translations of German works into other languages.

In the circumstances of 1946, a library with the same purpose as the Deutsche Bücherei in Leipzig had to be established in West Germany, to ensure the collection of new publications and their bibliographical control, and so to set in motion the work of the book trade and the libraries in the western zones. Later this decision, made initially for practical reasons, also proved to be right in principle. The Deutsche Bücherei, like other libraries in the DDR (German Democratic Republic), was incorporated into the structure of a unified Socialist library system and made subject to the Socialist party-line as applied there. This resulted, among other things, in restrictions on the use of politically undesirable works and information about them, and sometimes even in the suppression or alteration of unwelcome entries in the national bibliography. Moreover, the Deutsche Bücherei is still normally inaccessible to inhabitants of the Federal Republic, owing to the general restrictions on travel imposed by the DDR authorities.

The Deutsche Bibliothek is thus indispensable as a repository and bibliographical centre for the Federal Republic. Even so, there naturally remains a very unsatisfactory situation, in which two bibliographies are compiled and printed side by side in two different places — Frankfurt and Leipzig — each listing new publications from both parts of Germany.

From 1969 the Deutsche Bibliothek has been financed from Federal funds as a Federal licensed public corporation, and has received the right to legal deposit. Previously, the Bund, the Land of Hesse, the city of Frankfurt and the Börsenverein des deutschen Buchhandels supported the library between them. In 1952 it was given the status of a public foundation. In 1959 it moved into a specially-constructed new building, which has had to be altered and enlarged on several occasions because of the rapid growth of holdings and the increase of work.

Under the law for legal deposit the Deutsche Bibliothek now receives all books appearing in the Federal Republic. Its acquisition work, previously very complex, has thus been considerably eased: such regulations were previously in force only for the official publications of the Bund and of a few of the Länder. Commercially-published literature, on the other hand, was normally sent in voluntarily by the publishers. The library likewise receives the German-language publications of the DDR, Switzerland and Austria largely under voluntary agreements. The remainder

of the German-language material issued in other countries, and literature
about Germany, is procured by exchange or bought. Particular attention
is devoted to collecting the works of former German nationals who were
driven from the country under National Socialism. This collection —
"Exil-Literatur 1933–1945" — contains about 15,000 bibliographical
items; a selection was shown in an instructive exhibition in Frankfurt
in 1965, and later on several occasions in other countries. A catalogue
with the same title has been edited by Werner Berthold, keeper of the
collection (3. Aufl., 1967).

The other object of the Deutsche Bibliothek, that of rendering the collections bibliographically accessible, makes it the bibliographical centre
of the country. The full "Deutsche Bibliographie" appears in three
series:

A Publications of the book trade, except maps. (Weekly, with monthly
   and quarterly indexes).
B Material not issued through the book trade, except maps. (Two-
   weekly, with monthly index).
C Maps, whether or not issued through the book trade. (Two-monthly).

Entries in the Wöchentliches Verzeichnis (weekly list) are repeated in the
half-yearly list, and those in the latter repeated in the five-yearly list.
These cumulations are arranged by author and have detailed subject, as
well as title, indexes.

In addition, the Deutsche Bibliothek produces the following four special
bibliographies: a list of German periodicals (intermittent, to be discontinued after 1971); a list of publications by government authorities,
public bodies, institutions and foundations of the Federal Republic (two-
yearly); a two-monthly select list of the most important new publications
in the Federal Republic, "Das Deutsche Buch"; and the "Verzeichnis
deutscher wissenschaftlicher Zeitschriften" ("List of German scholarly
journals"), compiled by the Deutsche Bibliothek for the first time in 1965
to continue the issues compiled by B. Sticker and published by the Deutsche Forschungsgemeinschaft.

In 1966 the Deutsche Bibliothek took a decisive step in the rationalisation
of its bibliographical work: electronic data processing was successfully
used in the production of the Deutsche Bibliographie. The first issue
produced by this method appeared in January 1966 — an event which
aroused great interest in the library world, since the process had never
previously been applied to a national bibliography. One of the most

gratifying consequences was the faster publication of the half-yearly list: it now appears 2 $^1/_2$ months, instead of 15 months, after the end of the period covered. The Deutsche Bibliothek has a stock of 1,176,000 volumes, which increases by 80,000 volumes annually; it holds 24,000 current periodicals; its purchasing budget is DM. 175,000 and it has a staff of 291.

2.12 Staatsbibliothek Preußischer Kulturbesitz

The old Preußische Staatsbibliothek, which had its development into a German national library curtailed by the collapse of Germany (cf. 1.61), is now split into two parts: the Staatsbibliothek Preußischer Kulturbesitz in Marburg and West Berlin, and the Deutsche Staatsbibliothek in East Berlin. This separation is a result of political, not professional developments.

The end of the war found practically the entire stock of the library distributed to about 30 places scattered throughout the area of the Reich. The dispersed books could only be transported back to their libraries at the orders, and with the aid, of the military governments. The Soviet military administration had the books stored in its own zone brought back to the old, badly-damaged building of the Staatsbibliothek in the Soviet sector of Berlin, in the summer and autumn of 1945. The American military authorities had a large stock of about 1.7 million volumes, stored in their zone in Hesse, transported in the autumn of 1946 to Marburg, where the University Library building and rooms in Marburg Castle were available for it. The French occupying forces ensured that the valuable manuscript collections of the library stored in their zone were moved to Tübingen University Library. These actions were necessary in order to save and preserve the dispersed books, and to make them available for use again. The situation thus created was of a provisional nature.

The first firm ruling on the administration of former Prussian possessions was made by Law no. 46 of the Allied Control Commission of 25th February 1947. According to Article III, powers and obligations were transferred to the "participating Länder". These, according to Article II, were Länder formed from the area belonging to Prussia, or extended by the addition of parts of that area. Articles II and III could only be altered by the Allied Control Commission or "the future constitution of Germany". For the area of the German Federal Republic, the basis of the

1 Frankfurt: Deutsche Bibliothek, book tower

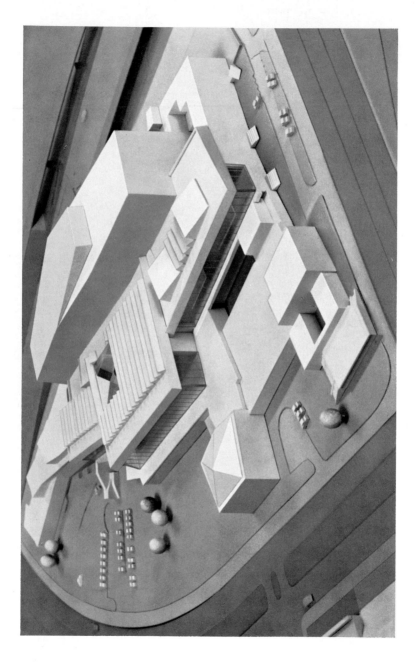

2   Berlin: Staatsbibliothek Preußischer Kulturbesitz, model of the new building, design by Hans Scharoun

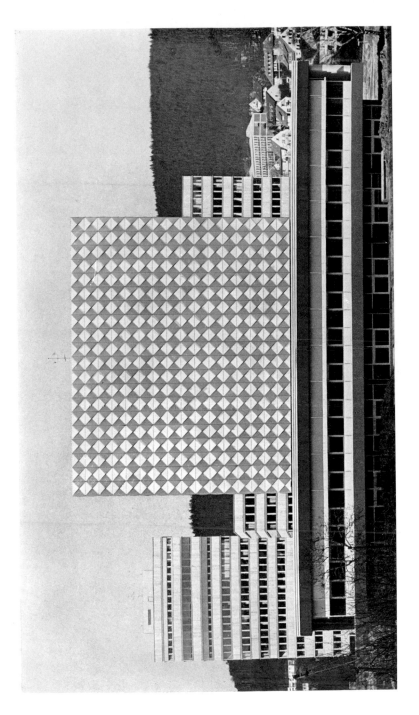

3　Marburg: Universitätsbibliothek Marburg

4 Berlin:
Amerika-
Gedenkbibliothek/
Berlin Central
Library

arrangements now in force was laid down by the law establishing the Stiftung Preußischer Kulturbesitz (cf. 1.4).

The government of the DDR has not accepted this as following from the abolition of Prussia. It regards those sections of the library situated in the Federal Republic as "illegally withheld" state property of the DDR, a claim supported by orders of the Soviet occupation authorities and regulations stemming from them. This interpretation is incorrect, since the former Preußische Staatsbibliothek was not a separate legal entity, and the title to the property of the books was hence affected in the same way as that to Prussian state property in general. The DDR itself, moreover, has never claimed to be the sole legal successor to the state of Prussia.

Only the western section, the Staatsbibliothek Preußischer Kulturbesitz, is described here. Its home is to be in West Berlin. Detailed plans are currently being drawn up for a bold, modern building designed by the architect Hans Scharoun: the foundation stone was laid in October 1967. The present accommodation arrangements, which hamper to some degree the running of a smooth and rational service, will continue for some years. Further sections of the library can only gradually be transported from Marburg to Berlin. The manuscript, music and official publications departments, and the international official publications exchange, have so far been entirely transferred to Berlin, while other special departments will follow in due course. The higher administration is in Berlin, the rest in Marburg. Acquisitions, cataloguing, local lending, inter-library loans and the technical department are divided between the two cities on the lines which offer the greatest efficiency. The bulk of the stock is still in Marburg and its neighbourhood.

The library is headed by a director-general. It has a staff establishment of 336; 47 of the staff belong to the administrative grade. It has a stock of about 2,240,000 volumes, of which 1,7 million are from the old holdings. 22,155 German and other periodicals were being currently taken in 1969. The purchasing budget (excluding binding and repairs) was DM 3,435,000 in 1969. Despite the fact that its holdings are scattered in several places, the library is subject to a heavy demand for inter-library loans (73,440 volumes issued in 1968).

In collecting, the humanities, social sciences and natural sciences are covered on a wide scale. In medicine, technology and agriculture, additions are largely limited to periodicals since central specialist libraries exist, or are being formed, for these fields. Emphasis in acquisition is

given to periodicals, official and parliamentary publications, and Oriental, East Asian and East European material. In its collecting on East Asia,
the library is supported by the Forschungsgemeinschaft under the co-
operative acquisition scheme (cf. 3.111). In the creation of separate departments for the Orient, East Asia, Eastern Europe, music, manuscripts
and maps, the tradition of the Preußische Staatsbibliothek is continued.
The new department for official publications and their international
exchange combines the work of the old Staatsbibliothek in acquiring
official publications, and that of the Reichstauschstelle as a central
exchange bureau. It thus provides a centralised service for the whole
Federal Republic. The library's general services to all German libraries
also include the compilation and issue of the Gesamtverzeichnis ausländischer Zeitschriften und Serien (GAZS), the Gesamtverzeichnis deutscher Zeitschriften und Serien (GDZS) (cf. 3.122) and the editing and
distribution of particulars of progress reports in the field of the humanities and social sciences (cf. 6.11).

The sixteen years from 1946 (the establishment of the stock in Marburg)
to 1962 (when the Stiftung began its work) were a period of continual
struggle for the basic necessities of the library's public function: sponsors
to ensure its maintenance, adequate finance for acquisitions and personnel, staffing, and space for librarians, books and readers. Since the
Stiftung assumed control, staff establishment has been increased by 273
(that is, more than tripled) and the budget for acquisitions from
400,000 DM in 1961 to 3,435,000 DM. The extreme shortage of space
has been alleviated by the removal of part of the library to West Berlin,
but really suitable working conditions will not be achieved until the
occupation of the new building.

2.13 Bayerische Staatsbibliothek

The Bayerische Staatsbibliothek in Munich celebrated its 400th anni-
versary in 1958. It has the good fortune to be able to function as before
as the central library of the Free State of Bavaria, in its old building
— now reconstructed and with modern premises attached. Despite considerable destruction in the war — the loss of about 500,000 volumes and
heavy damage to the building — it has been able, after overcoming the
initial wartime and post-war difficulties, to resume its old role as a
second general central library for the newly-formed area of West Ger-

many. Today it fills this role even more fully than before, owing both to the size and uniqueness of its collections, and to a range of supra-regional responsibilities which have in part been newly developed. With a stock of about 3 million volumes, it is currently the largest library in the Federal Republic. It receives about 12,000 current periodicals from Germany and elsewhere. The emphasis in acquisition lies on the humanities and social sciences, especially history, classical philology, Eastern Europe, music — subjects which it covers as special fields within the Forschungsgemeinschaft's co-operative scheme — and oriental studies. In addition, the valuable holdings of manuscripts, incunabula and early printed books are also being built up. All publications issued in Bavaria are received free under the legal deposit law. Official Federal publications are also supplied free. The budget for acquisitions amounted to 2,002,500 DM in 1969.

The library has special departments for Orientalia, Eastern Europe, manuscripts, incunabula, music and maps. It houses the library school for the administrative, executive and clerical grades for Bavarian academic libraries (cf. 7.3) and also the Bavarian union catalogue (cf. 3.121). It has a large general reading room with 500 places, and special reading rooms for the East European collection, Orientalia, music, the map collection, manuscripts and periodicals, with a total of over 200 places. Holdings are made freely available for inter-library loan, on the principle that the Staatsbibliothek should be approached first in order to ease the burden on the university libraries of the Land. In 1968, 80,525 volumes were despatched on inter-library loan.

One important establishment, unique in the country, is the Institut für Buch- und Handschriftenrestaurierung ("Institute of Book and Manuscript Restoration"). It originated during the war as a "repair shop" for burnt and damaged volumes saved from the great fire of March 1943, and is today an institute of international repute, using scientific methods and, since 1956, itself training restorers.

The Bayerische Staatsbibliothek has a staff of 308 including 42 in the administrative grade. It is also the seat of the administration for the state libraries of Bavaria.

The library is now housed in a building which is partly restored on the most modern lines, and partly entirely new, after several bombing raids had ruined six sevenths of Friedrich von Gärtner's great building — a feature of the classically-styled Ludwigstraße of King Ludwig I — a hundred years after its opening. From 1945 to 1965 the library suffered a period of difficult and often inefficient operation through lack of space and makeshift accommodation in various buildings throughout the city. It has only since then been able to embark on long-considered plans for improving operations by modern working methods.

The library has played an important part in resuming and maintaining relations with other countries after the war. Book exchanges were arranged as early as possible, and librarians from abroad were given work there. From 1958 to 1962 Gustav Hofmann, its first director-general after the war, was President of IFLA.

The Bayerische Staatsbibliothek has thus been able to carry out its postwar reconstruction, even if under very difficult conditions, at least under more favourable auspices than the Deutsche Bibliothek and the Staatsbibliothek Preußischer Kulturbesitz. Today it occupies a distinguished place among libraries in Bavaria, in Germany and internationally.

2.2 Staatsbibliotheken and Landesbibliotheken (State Libraries)

The Staats- and Landesbibliotheken form a highly varied group — in origins, historical development, size of holdings, intensiveness of use and size of readership. They may also assume the titles of Staatliche, Provinzial-, Regierungs- or Kreis-Bibliothek. There are 26 of them, if we include the Bayerische Staatsbibliothek (which has been treated in the previous section because of its supra-regional functions) and four libraries (Bremen, Hamburg, Göttingen and Darmstadt) which are also university libraries, as well as Kassel, where the city library has been joined with the Landesbibliothek. Other university libraries, besides those mentioned, act as Landesbibliotheken without this being explicit in their titles.

The average size is between 100,000 and 500,000 volumes. Fifteen libraries are in this range: SB Bamberg, SUB Bremen, LB Coburg, LB Detmold, LB Fulda, LB Hanover, Murhardsche Bibliothek der Stadt und LB Kassel, LB Karlsruhe, LB Kiel, LB Oldenburg, SB Passau, SB Regensburg, LB Speyer, LB Wiesbaden and the Herzog-August-Bibliothek Wolfenbüttel.

The following six Bavarian libraries have fewer than 100,000 volumes: Staatliche Provinzialbibliothek Amberg, Regierungsbibliothek Ansbach,

Hofbibliothek Aschaffenburg, Studienbibliothek Dillingen, Staatliche Bibliothek Eichstätt and Staatliche Bibliothek Neuburg.

There remain five libraries which stand out above the rest in size: the Bayerische Staatsbibliothek in Munich with about 3 million volumes; three institutions which are also university libraries — Göttingen with 2 million, Hamburg with over 1 million, and Darmstadt with 885,000 volumes, which will be dealt with in the next section — and the Württembergische Landesbibliothek in Stuttgart with nearly 1 million volumes.

For this group in particular, however, the value of their holdings should not be judged on their size alone. Excellent old accumulations of manuscripts and early printed books make not only the well-known collections in Munich and Stuttgart but also many of the medium and smaller ones, into outstanding fields for scholarship, such as Hanover for the study of Leibniz, Bamberg and Fulda for medieval manuscripts, and Wolfenbüttel for the Middle Ages and especially the 16th and 17th centuries.

The 26 libraries are distributed through the Länder as follows, in decreasing order of density: Bavaria 11; Lower Saxony and Hesse 4 each; Baden-Württemberg 2; Bremen, Hamburg, North Rhine-Westphalia, Rhineland Palatinate and Schleswig-Holstein 1 each. The standing and significance of these 26 libraries within their own Land varies a great deal. In Bavaria, the Bayerische Staatsbibliothek stands out as the chief library of the Land; some of the others are small provincial libraries, with holdings of historic interest, which have only very recently been awakened into new life.

The typical Staats- or Landesbibliothek is at present undergoing a transformation. It has not yet reached its definitive shape. Traditional and modern activities are mingled in it in different ways. Three points may be noted as characteristic of this group:

a) The first characteristic, common to all, which has always marked out the Landesbibliothek: it is a *deposit library* for the literature on its area, whether this is the Land in its present administrative or earlier historical form, a province, or a smaller local district. It is the library's task to collect comprehensively the entire published output of this area, or at least all that concerning the area, to preserve it and provide bibliographical access to it. By "literature concerning the area" is meant not only historical treatments, but also publications on political, legal and economic affairs. Acquisition is chiefly by means of obligatory deposit by the publishers. Bibliographical access may take the form of special catalogues, which also cover articles in journals and collections, and in many cases the issue of printed bibliographies. "Preservation" of such holdings includes repair and restoration work: they must, of course, be available to readers; but, as a source for later historical research, they must not be "worn out" but as far as possible kept in good condition and protected from wear and tear. Printed matter is often supplemented by the collection of manuscript material and writers' papers. These are frequently presented by well-known people in the area who feel a special relationship with the library.

b) Secondly, these libraries are *for public use* and not simply conservation; and indeed they often act at the same time as academic libraries for the inhabitants of their town. Acquisition policies and services to readers are adapted to this need. This means that these libraries must acquire scholarly and specialised publications, works on art and works of literature, but also manuals in physics and technology, and medical and legal publications. They are general libraries, often with the accent on the humanities following their tradition, but turning increasingly towards technology and the natural sciences. They have no need to go so far as the university libraries in acquiring scholarly publications, and can leave to them the very specialised journals and monographs. In general non-fiction and educational literature, they can exclude what is available in the municipal public libraries. Their collecting is gradually coming to concentrate on everything giving information on and introductions to matters of scholarship and science, such as large reference works, encyclopedias and bibliographies. In an effort to improve their periodical holdings, at present very inadequate, the Landes- and Stadtbibliotheken have combined to compile a recommended list of German scholarly journals (cf. 4.13). The acquisition principles mentioned have not yet been fully adopted because budgets are inadequate. The recommendations of the Wissenschaftsrat attempt to iron out excessive disparities (cf. 4.12), but are still unfulfilled in many places.

c) Like the Stadtbibliotheken, this group of libraries has especially substantial assignments in the field of *co-operation*, not only within the group but also with other types of library. Regulations for this are, in part, still being framed. Under this heading will come agreements with local university, special and public libraries on the efficient use of resources, the formation of regional organisations and the exchange of information.

Some of the major Staats- and Landesbibliotheken — like Munich and Stuttgart — act as centres for librarianship in particular Länder, but it is a function not exclusive to this type of library and hence cannot be designated as a special characteristic. Besides, this function has only developed in the Federal Republic in the last ten years, as a new role originating with the co-operative undertakings (union catalogues, interlibrary lending), and has not yet been fully defined. It plays an important part in regional planning (cf. 3.14).

2.3 University Libraries

2.31 Libraries of Universities and Colleges of University Status

The libraries of universities and higher educational institutions form a relatively homogeneous, closely-linked and easily distinguishable group, from which only the libraries of the Catholic and Protestant institutions — 16 in all — stand out as special cases. If we include libraries at newly-founded universities still in course of erection, there are 42 state-supported and 12 denominational libraries distributed over 50 towns (cf. the list in 1.222). 30 of them now have the title of Universitätsbibliothek; 7 that of Bibliothek der Technischen Hochschule, or Technischen Universität; one belongs to a medical and one to a veterinary institution, and three to Catholic philosophical-theological institutions. "Universitäts-" or "Hochschulbibliothek" has normally been used to denote the central library of a university. A change of meaning has been initiated by the new universities (see below).

The uniformity within the group is a matter of function and organisation, not of the size of holdings nor, hitherto, the size of budget or number of staff. A consensus on this last point has been felt by the Wissenschaftsrat to be needed (cf. model budget, 4.11). The great differences in holdings have historical causes. The university libraries proper are in some cases collections of centuries' standing — the oldest are Heidelberg (1386), Freiburg (1457) and Tübingen (1477); some have their origins in former princely libraries; some were founded ab initio as university libraries (Göttingen, 1737); a number are new foundations or re-foundations from the years between 1914 and 1919 (Frankfurt, Hamburg, Cologne) or after the Second World War (Berlin, Mainz, Saarbrücken); and finally, several have originated in the reform movements of the last few years and are still being built up (Bielefeld, Bochum, Bremen, Dortmund, Konstanz,

Regensburg and Ulm). Many of the older libraries, besides, suffered such heavy losses during the last war that their stock-building since 1945 is almost equivalent to a fresh start (Hamburg, Münster, Würzburg).

The following figures may give an idea of the size of libraries. It should be remembered that the total number of volumes belonging to any university is substantially higher, since stocks in institute libraries are not included. The number of volumes given refers to printed works, including dissertations. To these can be added, in some cases, very rich collections of manuscripts, music and maps, and, for libraries in technical universities, patent and report collections. In this survey, the libraries of recently-established universities and of denominational institutions are treated separately.

Holdings of about 1 million volumes or more:

12 university libraries: the largest is SUB Göttingen, with 2 million volumes, then StUB Frankfurt together with the Senckenbergische Bibliothek for natural sciences and medicine, with 1.8 million volumes. Also Bonn, Cologne, Erlangen, Freiburg, Hamburg, Heidelberg, Kiel, Marburg and Tübingen.

Holdings of between 415,000 and 900,000 volumes:

6 university libraries and one Landes- und Hochschulbibliothek: Berlin (Free University), Gießen, Mainz, Münster, Saarbrücken, Würzburg and LHB Darmstadt.

Holdings of between 290,000 and 415,000 volumes:

7 libraries of the former Technische Hochschulen, some of which have now been renamed "Technische Universität" or "Universität": Aachen, Berlin TU, Brunswick, Hanover, Karlsruhe, Munich, Stuttgart.

Holdings of between 80,000 and 260,000 volumes:

5 libraries of higher educational institutions which have a limited field of study — or had, and are now being expanded: Clausthal, Düsseldorf, Hanover (Veterinary Institution), Mannheim and Stuttgart-Hohenheim.

The university libraries take an average of between 5,000 and 8,000 current periodicals, with 2,500 as the lowest and 10,200 as the highest figures. The libraries of technical universities take between 2,500 and 4,800.

The libraries of universities recently founded or still in the planning stage are not comparable in figures with the older libraries because of their different structures (see below). Their growth has been unusually rapid, and statistics are continually being outdated. Bochum (foundation agreed 1961, teaching begun winter 1965–66) already had 525,000 volumes in 1969. Regensburg (founded 1962, teaching begun winter 1967–68) had over 620,000 volumes, and Konstanz (foundation agreed 1964, teaching begun winter 1967–68) over 274,000.

Many of the libraries in denominational institutions have significant collections, some of them old-established, with rich holdings of manuscripts and incunabula (cf. 2.61).

These points are characteristic of the group:

a) *Objectives and sphere of activity.* The primary task of these libraries is to serve their university — that is, to inform its members, the teaching staff and students, about the books they need and to make these available. This is not the limit of their functions, however. Their services go beyond the confines of the university, and are extended in some measure to the town where it is situated and also, to a great extent, to the surrounding region or the Land. In addition, each is linked with university and other academic libraries by co-operative activities — inter-library loans, union catalogues, the co-operative acquisition scheme (cf. chapter 3) — and to this extent has some responsibility to the Federal Republic as a whole. Its simultaneous function as a Stadt- or Landesbibliothek stems partly from historical causes — the amalgamation of formerly separate institutions (Frankfurt, Cologne, Darmstadt) — and partly from the present situation: some Länder (Saarland, North Rhine-Westphalia) have no Landesbibliothek of their own. The university libraries, being the major academic libraries in their areas, have in the past partially assumed this role, and are now faced with the need to agree on a practicable division of operations with the public library of their home town (cf. 2.51). The obligation of university libraries to participate in co-operative undertakings is a necessary consequence of the growth in published output throughout the world, which nullifies any attempt at independence by an individual library, and brings about mutual dependence which, though a burden, is in the interests of every participant.

b) *Library structure in the established universities.* The structure in a traditional university is often pictured as two parallel tracks, along which book provision for members of the university is carried on: on one side the central library, and on the other the large number (often 100 or more) of separate institute, seminar, hospital, laboratory and faculty libraries, sometimes themselves grouped into larger units. Both are heavily used by staff and students, one side being supplemented by the other. In order to assess the library situation, both must be taken into account.

The institute libraries are completely within the jurisdiction of their university. Their administration and finance are matters of academic autonomy and hence independent of the central library. Their director is normally the director of the institute, as a rule an Ordinarius (full professor). He may make a member of his assistant teaching staff responsible for the running of the library. The library staff proper belong to the institute, not to the central library. The funds for book-buying form a part of one budgetary item, along with funds for apparatus and equipment, in the university budget. The director of the institute is responsible for the acquisition of books.

The university library is a state institution which has been set up within the university. Its director is appointed by the Kultusminister, although with the approval of the Rektor and Senat (court or council) of the university. His participation in library matters which concern the whole university is provided for in differing degrees in the universities' constitutions. The funds for book acquisition are generally budgeted under the heading of institutes' costs, but as a separate item. Requests for funds and additional staff are made by the director, through the Rektor of the university, to the Kultusministerium.

Acquisition and cataloguing are usually carried out separately by the two types of library. In the central library, book selection is done by the Fachreferenten ("subject specialists"), who are responsible to the head of the acquisition department or to the director; in the institutes, by a designated member of the institute staff responsible to the director of the institute or by the newly established Institutsrat ("Council of the Institute"). The institute libraries are for reference only, accessible to members of the institute — and usually to them alone — until the late evening. Books can only be taken off the premises over the weekend. The central libraries are lending libraries: except for reading-room and reference collections, and certain other items, their entire stock is available for borrowing and inter-library loan.

The advantages and drawbacks of this system are closely connected. The advantages are a relatively clear division of functions, a large supply of material over the university's entire field of study, and few areas of friction between the two sides. The disadvantages are a gradual estrangement between the professors and the central library, since they rely as far as possible on their institute library; the uneconomic use of funds; and frequently the unsatisfactory administration of institute libraries, which seldom employ professional staff. The "double-track" system needs measures to counteract its inherent tendency to make institutes shut themselves off from each other and from the central library. It is not enough for both sides to keep within the areas of book acquisition which their functions dictate (something which, in any case, is not currently observed). Both must also realise that book acquisition in the university as a whole can only be done properly through mutual complementation, and they must be prepared for co-ordination and co-operation.

In recent years, measures against this divisive influence have been considered and recommended from several sides, and even attempted in practice: by the Forschungsgemeinschaft in a Denkschrift Instituts- und Hochschulbibliotheken ("Memorandum on Institute and University Libraries") (1955) and Empfehlungen für die Zusammenarbeit zwischen Hochschulbibliothek und Institutsbibliotheken ("Recommendations for Co-operation between University and Institute Libraries") (1970), by the Wissenschaftsrat in its Empfehlungen on libraries (1964), by the Arbeitsgemeinschaft der Hochschulbibliotheken, by verbal representations from 1965 onwards and by a formal resolution in 1968, as well as by the directors of some libraries. It has become clear that the division as such will have to be maintained in the established libraries. Proposals for reform are based on two points.

Firstly, an attempt is being made to set up lines of communication between the two sides. These include mutual consultation and agreement on book acquisition, especially for new periodical subscriptions; union catalogues of the periodical holdings of a university, even, in a few cases — Berlin (Free University), Münster, Marburg, Saarbrücken — union catalogues of the monograph holdings; cataloguing for the institutes by the central library; and the use in the institutes of staff employed by the university library and responsible to it.

Secondly, a structural assimilation is beginning here and there. The institute library is abandoning its isolation. Small libraries in related subjects are being amalgamated into larger units, sometimes into faculty libraries for law, theology or medicine. The central library, for its part, is breaking away from the notion of a self-contained entity. It may be placing its medical holdings near to hospitals or be planning to do so (Cologne, Frankfurt, Hamburg, Heidelberg, Kiel and Munich). It may be proposing to form a branch library near the faculty of natural sciences with its scientific and some of its medical holdings (Marburg). These are all steps towards rapprochement leading to more flexibility in a former rigid, unrelated, side-by-side existence. So far they have been taken mainly on the personal initiative of individual librarians and rest on the goodwill of both sides. The effect on university constitutions is slow to appear.

c) *Library structure in new universities*. In newly-established universities, where a development committee for each has designed an overall plan, the traditional library organisation has been much more radically approached. The new principle is that of a *unified university library system*. This means that, where the principle is consistently applied, both central library and institute libraries will give up their separate existences and combine. There are variations in how this is achieved, ranging from a moderate to a fundamental divergence from the old system. Here it must suffice to highlight the most important measures for unification and the shapes they result in — whether common to all these libraries or planned only for certain places — without going into detail in every case about the differences between universities.

Bochum, the first of the new foundations, stands somewhat apart, remaining closer to the traditional pattern. Here the bipartite structure has been retained, but a series of measures has been aimed at a constant interaction of the two sides. A "co-ordination office", set up in 1965, looks after their contacts. The central library has harmonised its acquisition policy with the institutes; the institutes may be called upon to lend; all collections are accessible to every member of the university, and are arranged in broad subject groups in the stacks of the central library.

In the other new foundations, the unified character of the library is laid down in the overall plan of the university. Instead of separate institute libraries there are Bereichs-Bibliotheken ("sectional libraries") in which related disciplines are brought together in a larger unit. These Bereichs-Bibliotheken do not exist in addition to the central library, but are themselves organic parts of it. The director of the central library is Librarian of the University: he is responsible for all library activity, wherever it is carried on. The central library remains the administrative centre, housing acquisitions, cataloguing and usually issue facilities or at least inter-library loans. It maintains a complete catalogue of all library holdings, which is produced in multiple copies where the use of a computer makes this possible, and distributed to some or all of the Bereichs-Bibliotheken. Apart from this, however, the position and functions of the central library in the library system as a whole, in the new universities, vary between its being a genuine centre for the university's entire book provision (Bremen), a central department with subject departments attached (Regensburg), a centre for information and administration with reading-room and a collection of general works (Konstanz), and lastly an information and administration centre pure and simple, with a bookstock of reference works only (Bielefeld). The unity of the library system is clearly demonstrated in regulations such as the following:

All collections in the university are freely accessible to every member of the university. Open access is envisaged everywhere for a large part, if not all of the holdings, even in the central library insofar as this has a stock of its own. Members of the teaching staff and librarians co-operate in various ways in the selection of new acquisitions, instead of each tackling it separately. The bulk of specialist material in those fields for which Bereichs-Bibliotheken exist is selected and housed at these points, with an academic librarian—attached permanently to the Bereichs-Biblio-thek as a subject specialist — playing an active part, and in particular attending to the co-ordination of overlapping requests. Interdisciplinary and general works, and literature in subjects not represented at the uni-versity, are selected by the central library in consultation with the Bereichs-Bibliotheken (except at Bielefeld), and are housed in the central reading-rooms and stack. Even where the central library is still actively building a stock of its own — not merely accumulating the residue of material not wanted by the institutes — its policy for specialist material is tailored to the institutes' acquisitions on lines similar to Bochum, where the central library buys works selected by its own subject specialists only after reference to the appropriate institute.

Thus a library structure differing from the traditional one is taking shape in the new universities. Everything about it is still in the melting pot and much may be changed in the course of practice. Only an extended period of practical experience will allow more to be said.

d) *Delimitation of selection responsibilities.* Selection of new acquisitions is according to known or anticipated demand. In the established uni-versities, the specialities of institute members determine the policies for the institute libraries: specialised material on certain limited topics predominates, with the addition of basic works indispensable to that particular field. The central university library, by contrast, builds up its collections steadily in general and interdisciplinary material as much as in specialist books and journals. This task, which involves keeping continuously abreast of current publications through national and specialised bibliographies, reviews, prospectuses, etc., is carried out by

Fachreferenten ("subject specialists" — academic librarians with subject qualifications), who are responsible to the head of the acquisition department or the director of the library (cf. 4.21).

It should not be regarded as invariably harmful that this division of duties gives rise to widespread duplication, either between institute libraries in related fields or between an institute library and the university library: multiple copies of heavily-used items are very desirable. Nevertheless, planned rather than fortuitous duplication should be the aim, not least in the interests of an economic use of resources. We have already remarked that libraries in the older universities are giving their attention to this. The new universities have only one general acquisitions programme, and a joint selection procedure in which academic staff and librarians participate.

Both systems have to come to grips with the problem of selecting "important" material from the great mass of what is published, and both are limited by the funds available. Even where a budget is generous — which can be said of very few university libraries today — the comprehensive acquisition of all important material is not possible. One means of alleviating this, introduced in libraries over 50 years ago and proposed for universities themselves in 1967, is to lay down areas of concentration for particular places — "special collection areas" for the libraries (cf. 3.11) and "special research areas" for the universities (cf. 1.222) — so that the specified areas are covered more intensively and comprehensively. The consequent restrictions on coverage in other areas can only be compensated for by a system of mutual assistance. In the case of libraries, this is the function of inter-library loans.

The co-operative acquisition scheme of the Forschungsgemeinschaft influences the acquisition policies of those university libraries participating, since the areas allocated to them have to be cultivated more intensively and with greater attention. How the "special research areas" will affect university libraries cannot at present be foreseen: this proposal has still to be worked out in detail by the Wissenschaftsrat and the Forschungsgemeinschaft.

University libraries which also have the status and functions of a Staatsbibliothek, Landesbibliothek or academic Stadtbibliothek (whether expressed in their title or not) are obliged to adapt their acquisition activity to this dual purpose.

e) *Text-book collections.* Text-book collections are a necessary component of the library provision in a university. In the Federal Republic they are of fairly recent date. Their beginnings — in many cases originating from the student body, in some places from individual institutes and seminars — were built up on a modest scale by the libraries of technical universities and some full universities under the pressure of the post-war increase in student intake. Thanks to generous initial and supplementary assistance from the Volkswagen Foundation in 1965, text-book collections now exist in all higher educational institutions. Although there are no fixed rules for the administration of these collections, a certain similarity in the running of them has grown up. The object of the text-book collection is to make available to students multiple copies of heavily-used books, particularly expensive ones, needed for their studies. It is assumed that students will themselves buy the text-books which they need most. The collection should "give them the opportunity of consulting additional text-books, including those on peripheral subjects, so that they can gain an idea of more distantly-related disciplines" (Wissenschaftsrat).

Their composition differs from one university to another. The largest collections in university libraries (Frankfurt, Göttingen, Cologne) contain 10,000 to 12,000 volumes, the smaller 2,000 to 8,000. Average figures for the technical universities are between 1,000 and 5,000; the largest are at Stuttgart and Hanover, with about 8,000 volumes.

Selection is done in consultation between teaching staff and librarians. Staff recommendations are welcomed and acted upon. Experience has shown that it is right to adjust each collection to the requirements of its particular university: the suggestion of standard lists for universities and technical universities has been abandoned. The collection will contain legal, scientific, medical and technical text-books, but not the large, multi-volume reference works, unless contributions to these are held separately bound, nor encyclopedias, whose place is in the reading-room. It will also include legal codes and commentaries, literary texts and grammars. Paperbacks and short introductory works are excluded. Dictionaries are treated in varying ways. The collections need constant renewal: old editions and superseded works require continual weeding-out.

The central library is regarded as a suitable site for the collection: only in a few exceptional cases are the text-books kept in institutes. In new buildings, a place easily accessible to students is found for them: Frankfurt, Hanover, Marburg, Clausthal and Stuttgart are good examples.

A separate catalogue in simplified, easily-scanned form is maintained for the collection — alphabetically arranged and broadly classified. Loan procedures, too, are made as simple as possible, usually with some form of book-card system like that used in public libraries. The average loan term is three months or a full semester; some places apply only the normal loan period of four weeks.

Exceptionally heavy use from the start has demonstrated the need for this arrangement: in university libraries it accounts for up to 25 per cent of all issues apart from inter-library loans, in technical university libraries between 30 and 40 per cent, and in the libraries of the medical and veterinary institutions up to 50 per cent.

It is to be hoped that the collections will be maintained after the funds from the Volkswagen Foundation have been used up: the Wissenschaftsrat repeated the need for this in 1967. The assistance has been provisionally renewed once more, under a plan for 1967—69 which envisages an increasing contribution by the universities, so that they alone may bear the running costs from 1970 onwards.

f) *Students' libraries.* Like the text-book collections, students' libraries are a form of library provision which have a special place in a university. Both are intended exclusively for student use. Both contain material which neither the central library nor the institute libraries provide -- the text-book collections "study" material, the students' libraries works of general cultural value. In their early days, which go back to the 19th century, the two were intermingled; in some universities (Heidelberg, Munich) they are still housed and administered together. There is, however, a trend towards separation. While the state is nowadays recognised as being bound to support the text-book collections, funds from other sources are employed for the students' libraries: donations from individuals or groups of "friends of the university", and contributions from the student body. This continues another earlier form of the students' library: the academic reading societies and reading-rooms of the early 20th century and the period after the First World War. These limited themselves initially to subscriptions to newspapers and journals financed from members' contributions.

The students' library of today is an educational library of similar type to the smaller public library. Its object is frequently described by the concept of Studium generale ("general studies"): the student is encouraged to read books on subjects other than his current field of study. Since requirements are unconnected with the demand for books for studies, consideration has been given to compiling a model stock-list for such a library for all universities. Indeed, the oldest students' library of the modern type, at Bonn (founded 1918) has frequently been taken as an example. In 1962 the Fritz Thyssen Foundation sponsored the compilation of a model list of stock, and presented four libraries based on the list to four universities (in two cases to hostels for academics and students which it had itself financed) (cf. 1.57).

The libraries generally contain works of literature (foreign literature often in German translations); art, history, current affairs and politics are given a certain priority, but religion, philosophy, education, law, government, economics and sociology are also included: the humanities and social sciences predominating, on the whole, over the natural sciences. Light literature is largely excluded, as are paperbacks, which students can buy themselves.

The principle of up-to-dateness applies here as much as in the text-book collections: obsolete and disused books are discarded. Accommodation is sometimes in the university library, sometimes in another building on the university site. Arrangement is usually by subject. Opinions are divided on whether or not lending should be permitted, the decision often depending simply on the space available. Issue routine is simple. Usage is very heavy. The rooms are furnished as invitingly as possible, to encourage readers to spend time there.

The students' library in Munich, by far the largest with a stock of 80,700 volumes and an annual bookfund of about 170,000 DM, is an exception to the overall picture. It is in practice an extension of the university library, and acquires chiefly books in demand for study purposes. It is run by the Studentenwerk (a welfare organisation for students). In Bonn, Cologne, Frankfurt, Heidelberg, and Münster the university library is in charge of the students' library. The Wissenschaftsrat has recommended the establishment of separate collections of general cultural interest in addition to the university libraries, though without going into particulars of their organisation. They are not yet provided at all universities.

2.32 Libraries of Specialist Institutions of Higher Education

There are libraries in all the specialist colleges or academies which exist alongside the universities — for fine arts, music (and theatre), teacher training and physical education (cf. 1.221). They are usually state-run institutions. The libraries concentrate on supporting the objects of their own college, acquiring material needed by the teaching staff for their theoretical instruction, and by students for their courses. They do not form a separate group of libraries with specific characteristics.

Libraries in these institutions are generally modestly equipped. Not all of them are professionally run, and only a few possess considerable collections. Libraries of the institutions for art and music have a stock rarely exceeding 20,000—30,000 volumes. The largest are the libraries of the two music schools in Berlin (120,000 volumes) and Cologne (about 90,000 volumes), (both chiefly sheet music), and the library of the Staatliche Hochschule für bildende Künste (State School of Fine Art) in Berlin, with 52,000 volumes. Noteworthy as a special collection is the library of the Sporthochschule (college of physical education) in Cologne, with 70,000 volumes. Several of these libraries have made their stocks available for inter-library loan, so as to benefit from it themselves and obtain additional books for their readers.

Those which have made the greatest progress in organising themselves are the libraries of the Pädagogische Hochschulen ("colleges of education"), which are also the largest sub-group in terms of numbers. Of the 55 colleges and institutes of education listed in the "Deutscher Hochschulführer" for 1970, three (one in Hamburg, two in Hesse) form part of universities, either as institutes or departments of education; their libraries have the character of "institute" libraries (cf. 2.31 b). The other 52 have their own libraries, which however — according to an investigation by the Arbeitsgemeinschaft pädagogischer Bibliotheken — do not meet the need for works of scholarship in a library for serious study. This type of library, which in most instances made its appearance in the years after the First World War, was especially badly affected by Nazi educational policies. A real start could not be made until after 1945, and not until 1962 were the function and significance of these libraries clearly stated in a report by the Arbeitsgemeinschaft.

The libraries' average holdings are today between 10,000 and 40,000 volumes, the largest being Dortmund (110,000 volumes), Berlin, Brunswick and Göttingen (about 70,000 volumes each).

The report stresses the need to concentrate stock-building on the chief objects of a library for teachers, "without descending to the level of introductory works, handbooks and concise encyclopedias": collecting adequate bibliographical and documentary resources; the maintenance of good catalogues; provision of an information service; and participation in the full range of relations between libraries, both academic and public. Standards are currently being worked out for finance, staff and space requirements (cf. 4.11).

In the general picture of German libraries, those of the specialist institutions of higher education belong in the context of their respective areas of study, rather than among libraries of general educational establishments. The libraries of colleges of education are a good example of this. One is forced to conclude that this group of libraries, if it intends to go beyond the simple provision of teaching material, will tend to assume the characteristics of special libraries.

2.4 Specialist Libraries and Special Libraries

Specialist and special libraries form a numerous and extremely varied group. Government, municipal and denominational libraries have a place there, besides the libraries of societies and associations, and large and small commercial firms. Their only common feature is their limitation to a particular field. To this extent, the libraries of specialist educational institutions and university institutions — from among the groups treated above — should be included here. We have, however, been guided by the present situation and have omitted both from the survey which follows. The former may so develop as to join the ranks of special libraries, but they have not yet done so. The institute libraries, on the other hand, will become further removed from special libraries as university reforms are carried out, and will probably operate more effectively in future within a co-ordinated unversity library system than in isolation.

The number of special libraries in the Federal Republic is estimated at about 1500; precise figures have not so far been available. A list published in 1965, "Verzeichnis der Spezialbibliotheken", enumerates 522 separate institutions, but is still incomplete, since it includes 125 central and institute libraries in universities, which are not reckoned as special libraries within the terms of this book. Nor have any criteria yet been established (size of stock, type of administration, staffing) to determine at what point a collection of books should be designated a library.

Central specialist libraries, parliamentary and government libraries can be separated, as special groups, from special libraries in the narrower sense. They are treated separately here, although the boundary between special libraries and government libraries is a vague one. Denominational and military libraries are treated below in sections of their own (cf. 2.6 and 2.7).

2.41   Central Specialist Libraries

The central specialist library, as a type, has been developed in the Federal Republic only in the last ten years. The four libraries now in existence, while in part of earlier date as libraries, were only given this new function in 1957 or later, and are the result of systematic planning. The basic concept was evolved by the libraries committee of the Deutsche Forschungsgemeinschaft.

The needs of scholarship, trade and industry for faster and more reliable information on the latest results of research — in whatever country, language or form they are issued — are easier to satisfy when there is greater certainty that material on a particular subject will be found in one place. The scattering of this information in many special and general libraries, from historical causes, and the establishment of areas of concentration in general libraries, which the Forschungsgemeinschaft had been supporting since 1949 — these things created a need for large specialist centres to supplement existing resources, in the first instance for those fields closely linked with practical work and applied studies: engineering, agriculture, economics and medicine. There could be no question, in the Federal Republic, of grafting these centres on to a general national library, since such a library does not exist there. Basic considerations, besides, do not favour this method: the material published in these fields is so varied, so copious and so rapidly outdated that only specially-planned libraries can control it. This has been proved by instances in the USA, the United Kingdom, France and the Soviet Union, where one or more central specialist libraries exist for medicine, agriculture and technology. The following points characterise the aims a) and activities b—e) of central specialist libraries in the Federal Republic.

a) *The library's responsibilities are to the entire Federal Republic.* The requirements of the subject field determine the structure of the collection and the services provided. Even if the library is part of an institute (like the Weltwirtschaftsinstitut in Kiel) or of a more general library (like the university libraries in Bonn and Cologne), or is closely linked with another library (like the technical university library in Hanover), these other institutions receive no preferential treatment. The needs of local users are catered for to the same extent as the requests from further afield.

b) The principles for *acquisition policies* are: thorough comprehensiveness for scholarly books and journals in the field; above all, coverage of report literature — particularly extensive here —, official and semi-official publications, information bulletins, preprints, statistics, conference papers and publications of firms and organisations; and careful attention to publications in "difficult" languages and from countries remote or difficult of access. In obtaining material, all possible channels must be used in addition to the book trade (which is of little use here), especially the exchange of scholarly and official publications, and personal contacts.

c) The *catalogues* demand particularly close attention in order that they may function as genuine aids to readers seeking information, and as useful tools for librarians supplying it. Existing information services in the field must be available in addition to the catalogues. Beyond this, as far as is necessary or practicable, the library should aim at an intensive exploitation of the stock through the indexing of articles in the major journals and collections. An imperative requirement is a comprehensible subject classification appropriate to modern developments in the field. Active information services, such as the compilation of book lists and special bibliographies, or the regular distribution of classified lists, are among the forms of information provision expected of these libraries.

d) A special form of assistance with the literature lies in making texts in less well-known foreign languages accessible by tracing available *translations*, in collaboration with the European Translations Centre in Delft, and the commissioning of translations by the library.

e) As regards *circulation*, these libraries are hybrids of reference and lending libraries, with variations according to the situation in each field. Circulation follows the principles of allowing serious users free access to the reading rooms, direct supply to distant borrowers, and generous use of photocopies in fulfilling requests for journals and collections.

These five points, some still plans rather than reality, imply a well-organised library administration and staff with a wide knowledge of the appropriate subject field.

The *Technische Informationsbibliothek in Hanover* (TIB, "Technical Information Library") is the first of the Federal Republic's central specialist libraries, founded in 1959 on the initiative of, and with financial help from the Forschungsgemeinschaft and transferred to a new building in 1965. It is closely connected, both physically and operationally, with the library of the technical university in Hanover. Both have the same director, but apart from this have separate staffs and budgets. The technical university library is financed by the Land of Lower Saxony, the TIB by the Ländergemeinschaft (cf. 1.4), which since 1966 has also taken on the greater part of the acquisition budget, which was initially borne by the Forschungsgemeinschaft. This amounted to 646,000 DM in 1969. There is a staff of 103. There is a stock of 92,000 volumes, 34,000 American dissertations on microfilm, and 61,000 American reports (on microfilm from 1966 onwards). It is supplemented by the stock of the technical university library in the same building: 414,000 volumes (including dissertations) and 1,230,000 patents. The two libraries together receive over 10,000 current periodicals.

The TIB carries out the five-point programme above, including the tracing and commissioning of translations, but for the present restricts the indexing of articles and the distribution of lists to literature in Eastern languages.

The library of the Weltwirtschaftsinstitut ("Institute of World Economics") in Kiel, which began as a small institute library in 1910 and was systematically built up as a comprehensive special library from 1924 onwards, has since 1966 been the central West German library for economics, with the emphasis on world economy and political economy. A new building is under construction. Both institute and library are financed by the Land of Schleswig-Holstein, but because of its supra-regional functions the Ländergemeinschaft contributes a regular subsidy. The Forschungsgemeinschaft has given the library financial support for special purposes since 1966. The library has a stock of 1,011,700 volumes; it receives over 21,000 current journals and annuals; its budget amounted to 475,000 DM in 1969 (including the contribution from the Forschungsgemeinschaft); it has a staff of 78.

Of the four points characterising the activities of a central specialist library, points b) and c) apply to an extent which may make the Kiel library a pattern for further central specialist libraries. "Report" literature, and other material issued by official bodies, international organisations and societies, now accounts for 63.7 per cent of acquisitions. The system of catalogues, with many subdivisions, much internal dovetailing and a plethora of instructive guide cards, offers very extensive access to the holdings, especially since journal articles are covered (cf. 4.41, 6.13). Catalogue cards are distributed to interested libraries in Germany and elsewhere under full or partial subscription arrangements. The catalogue is at present being published in volume form by the firm of G. K. Hall. A total of 207 volumes have already appeared. They consist of the catalogues for personal names, official organisations, corporate bodies and regional names (105 vols.), the subject catalogue (83 vols.), the title catalogue (13 vols.) and the location catalogue of periodicals (6 vols.). Thanks to financial help from the Forschungsgemeinschaft the supply of information has been intensified by the establishment of the library's own information office.

The *Zentralbibliothek der Landbauwissenschaft ("Central Agricultural Library") in Bonn*, set up in 1962 on the foundation of the agricultural section of Bonn University Library with the support of the Deutsche Forschungsgemeinschaft, is still in process of organisation. Its present accommodation, in an institute building of the Faculty of Agriculture, will shortly be replaced by new premises already designed. It is financed by North Rhine-Westphalia, the Forschungsgemeinschaft meeting half the annual acquisition budget. Provisional emphasis in acquisition has been placed on two countries, the USA and the Soviet Union. It is planned to establish a translation service for material in "difficult" languages. A particularly important function is expected to be close collaboration with information services for agriculture; these are currently being reorganised by the Forschungsrat für Ernährung, Landwirtschaft und Forsten ("Research Council on Food, Agriculture and Forestry"), which is based in the suburb of Bad Godesberg.

There is a stock of 176,000 volumes, and 2,200 current periodicals are taken. The acquisition budget amounts to 160,000 DM. The library has a staff of 14.

The *Medizinische Zentralbibliothek ("Central Medical Library")* for the Federal Republic has since 1968 been built up on the foundation of the medical section of Cologne University Library following a report made by the libraries committee of the Forschungsgemeinschaft at the end of 1967. It is being closely linked with the establishment of the Deutsches Institut für Medizinische Dokumentation und Information ("German Institute for Medical Documentation and Information"), for which firm plans have been made by the Federal Ministry of Health. The library and the institute are envisaged as complementary institutions, which will be accommodated close together from the beginning. The Cologne medical section, which has been supported by the Forschungsgemeinschaft for nearly 20 years as a participant in the co-operative acquisition scheme, is today the richest medical library in the Federal Republic, with a stock of 144,000 monograph volumes, 157,000 dissertations and 2,160 current periodicals.

As a central specialist library, it will retain the status of a department of the University Library, but with a greater degree of independence. Likewise, at least for the first stage of organisation, the Land will continue to bear its costs. The Forschungsgemeinschaft contributes substantially to the cost of acquisitions, staff and reprographic services. The objects of a central specialist library, as outlined above, have here been modified in some respects to take account of the close connection with information services and the special character of medical literature. The prime importance of journals has to be allowed for in acquisition policy: a rapid expansion of holdings to 3,000 titles is planned, corresponding approximately to the selection made for coverage by MEDLARS. Complete coverage of German medical literature is aimed at, for journals, monographs, dissertations and theses, and official publications. A reasonable selection is made of monographs from other countries. Thanks to the information activities of the institute, the catalogues will need no more than the library's previous normal treatment, but there are plans for a central cataloguing service for other medical libraries. A translation service for journal articles from "difficult" languages was set up recently by the Osteuropa-Institut at the Free University of Berlin, so the central library has avoided the need to embark on this activity itself.

The exceptionally intensive use made of medical journals has compelled the library to confine journals, on principle, to the premises, and fulfil all loan requests for single articles with Xerox copies. To keep costs low for the reader, the budget provides for a running subsidy of copying costs, shared by the Land and the Forschungsgemeinschaft.

2.42 Special Libraries

The group of special libraries in the narrower sense includes, in terms of their financial support, both public and non-public institutions. Among the former are the libraries of the research establishments of the Bund, the Länder, the Gemeinden and Gemeindeverbände, the learned academies and the Max-Planck-Gesellschaft, and museum, hospital and record office libraries. The latter include the libraries of industrial firms, economic and technical associations, and learned societies and organisations supported by the contributions of members. The group as a whole is numerically large, but lacking any unity, definite subdivisions or demarcation of functions. Its first characteristic is the libraries' isolation and confinement to their own field of activity. Here, too, there is a gradual move towards co-ordination and co-operation, but only on individual initiatives and a voluntary basis. This type of library is firmly organised only in countries where there is centralised state control and a nationalised economy and industry.

The following libraries may be noted as examples of unique special collections, the significance of which goes beyond their own institutions and has special importance for research in a particular field.

In the *humanities*:

Bibliothek des Zentralinstituts für Kunstgeschichte ("Library of the Central Institute for the History of Art"), Munich (92,000 vols.)

Bibliothek des Germanischen Nationalmuseums ("Library of the National Germanic Museum"), Nuremberg (330,000 vols.)

Ibero-Amerikanisches Institut ("Latin-American Institute"), Berlin (420,000 vols.)

Bibliothek für Zeitgeschichte ("Library for Contemporary History"), Stuttgart (158,000 vols.)

Bibliothek des Instituts für Auslandsbeziehungen ("Library of the Institute for Foreign Relations"), Stuttgart (204,000 vols.)

Bibliothek des Deutschen Literaturarchivs in the Schiller-Nationalmuseum, Marbach (130,000 vols.): special library for modern German literature from the Enlightenment to the present day.

Bibliothek des Freien Deutschen Hochstifts, Frankfurt (100,000 vols.): special library for German literature of the period 1750–1850.

In *law and the social sciences*:

Bibliothek des Hamburgischen Weltwirtschaftsarchivs ("Library of the Hamburg Archives on World Economy"), Hamburg (550,000 vols.)

The libraries of the two oldest Max-Planck-Institutes for law:

für ausländisches und internationales Privatrecht ("for Foreign and International Civil Law"), Hamburg (135,000 vols.),

für ausländisches öffentliches Recht und Völkerrecht ("for the Foreign

Law relating to Public Bodies and for International Law"), Heidelberg (150,000 vols.).

In *pure and applied science and technology:*

Bibliothek des Deutschen Museums, Munich (530,000 vols.): special library for the exact sciences and technology and their history.

Bibliothek des Deutschen Wetterdienstes ("Library of the German Weather Service"), Offenbach (92,000 vols.)

Bibliothek des Deutschen Hydrographischen Instituts ("Library of the German Hydrographical Institute"), Hamburg (79,000 vols.)

Bibliothek der Bundesanstalt für Bodenforschung und der Niedersächsischen Landesanstalt für Bodenforschung ("Library of the Federal and Lower Saxon Establishments for Soil Science"), Hanover (175,000 vols.)

Zentralbibliothek der Kernforschungsanlage ("Central Library of the Nuclear Research Establishment"), Jülich (281,000 vols., including reports)

Kekulé-Bibliothek, Leverkusen (352,000 vols.): special library for chemistry, physics, medicine and pharmacy.

Bergbau-Bücherei ("Mining Library"), Essen (148,000 vols.).

Numbers of volumes are intended only as a rough indication of the size of each collection. The value of collections is frequently enhanced by additional special materials such as slides, records, tapes, maps, manuscripts, report literature and microfilms.

In the field of *education,* a new development is under way. The following libraries, founded since 1945, are genuine special libraries of particular importance for educational research, owing to the nature of their collections and their information activities, notwithstanding in certain cases their small size:

Bibliothek des Instituts für Bildungsforschung ("Library of the Institute for Education Research") of the Max-Planck-Gesellschaft, Berlin.

Bibliothek des Internationalen Schulbuchinstituts ("Library of the International School Books Institute"), Brunswick.

Bibliothek des Deutschen Instituts für Internationale Pädagogische Forschung ("Library of the German Institute for International Educational Research"), Frankfurt.

Bibliothek des Unesco Instituts für Pädagogik ("Library of the Unesco Institute for Education"), Hamburg.

The educational libraries are in process of forming a group of their own which cuts across the classification we have made: the Arbeitsgemeinschaft pädagogischer Bibliotheken, founded in 1958, is endeavouring to set up a completely new organisation. Under this will be brought together all libraries concerned with educational research, teacher training and education in schools. A report by the Arbeitsgemeinschaft in 1967 outlines the "structure of library and information services for education" which is to be aimed at in the future.

To this group belong the libraries of colleges of education (2.32), school libraries (2.82), the Kreislehrerbüchereien (local teacher's libraries) — still at the start of their development — and another type of library still in its early stages, which has been designated a "central pedagogical library".

These latter have the characteristics of special libraries which we describe below, but have a special position to the extent that their acquisitions policy cannot be restricted in the subjects it covers, since educational studies have to concern themselves with all fields as "curricular subjects". A number of well-stocked, fairly large libraries is envisaged, distributed in a planned pattern over the country. Each will be closely linked with a "pedagogical centre" in the same region, which will have the triple function of research, instruction and practical work in education.

Seven libraries (in Berlin, Dortmund, Hamburg, Hanover, Koblenz, Munich and Stuttgart) appear suitable to act as starting-points for these central pedagogical libraries. Of these, Hamburg and Munich are based on older institutions founded by the teaching profession for its own benefit, while the rest have been founded by the state since 1945. Holdings are between 50,000 and 150,000 volumes, the largest being in Dortmund (library of the Pädagogische Hochschule Ruhr, Abteilung Dortmund — until 1965 the Pädagogische Zentralbücherei des Landes Nordrhein-Westfalen); Munich (Süddeutsche Lehrerbücherei); and Stuttgart (Pädagogische Zentralbibliothek Baden-Württemberg).

Despite their great variety, some common features can be identified as characteristic of special libraries:

a) The *purpose* and *functions* of a special library are normally determined by the larger institution of which the library is a part — research institute, society, museum, industrial concern, commercial association, etc. Hence it is not independent, but a component of a larger body, which it is its primary purpose to serve. Acquisition, cataloguing and circulation are adapted to the needs of this institution. An exception to this rule is the Bibliothek für Zeitgeschichte in Stuttgart, which is an independent organisation housed in the Württembergische Landesbibliothek.

In many cases, however, the basically internal orientation of a library's activities has changed to an external one, as a genuine specialist library has developed from the original small collection of books. Not only state-run libraries, but also those of industry, are opening their stocks and information services to the outside world (see e and f below). We may assume that this trend will continue as individual libraries come to feel the need to avail themselves of help from outside.

b) *Acquisition policy,* which is conditioned by the needs of the organisation, may in some cases aim at comprehensiveness as in a central specialist library — especially in a strictly limited subject field — and accordingly new publications may be collected systematically. A more normal thing, however, is to collect the material needed for the special projects and research currently under way, in a similar manner to libraries in university institutes. Report literature not issued through trade channels is generally of great importance to special libraries: exchange arrangements and personal contacts in other countries have to be made use of.

c) *Cataloguing,* which is bound to no formal rules and determined only by practical considerations, follows international usage in many respects — both in the alphabetic name catalogue (cf. 4.41), where mechanical word order is used and corporate authors are included, and in the subject catalogue, where UDC is frequently used. The analytical cataloguing of Festschriften, conference proceedings, report series and at least the most important journals in its special field, is recognised as a basic necessity and on the whole carried out as such.

d) *Documentation work* is often done in conjunction with cataloguing, or is planned, in fields where adequate and rapid documentation services are not currently obtainable (cf. 6.13).

e) *Dissemination of information* to its own users, about newly-received material in their special fields of interest, is the particular strength of a special library. Some libraries go beyond their ties to their own institution and provide an information service to outsiders.

f) It follows from the functions of a special library that it is a *non-lending library.* Exceptions include the library of the Ibero-Amerikanisches Institut in Berlin and the Bibliothek für Zeitgeschichte in Stuttgart, which participate in the national interlending service. A few are willing to lend to other libraries to a limited extent. Even where this is not the case, however, libraries do in practice help to meet the needs of readers outside by providing Xerox or microform copies and giving information. This is true of libraries belonging to research institutes and Federal establishments, as much as industrial libraries. Examples are the libraries of the Max-Planck-Institutes for foreign and international civil law in Hamburg, and for foreign public law and international law in Heidelberg; the Bibliothek und Kartensammlung der deutschen Landeskunde ("Library and Map Collection of German Topography") in the Bundesanstalt für Landeskunde und Raumforschung ("Federal Institute for Topography and Regional Planning") in Bonn-Bad Godesberg; the Kekulé-Bibliothek in Leverkusen; the Bergbaubücherei in Essen; the libraries of the Verein Deutscher Ingenieure ("Association of German Engineers"), the Verein Deutscher Eisenhüttenleute ("Association of German Iron-Workers") and the Verein Deutscher Gießereifachleute ("Association of German Foundrymen") in Düsseldorf; and of the Verband Deutscher Elektrotechniker ("Association of German Electrical Engineers"), the Gesellschaft Deutscher Chemiker ("Society of German Chemists") and the Glastechnische Gesellschaft ("Society for Glass Technology") in Frankfurt.

g) The internal structure of the libraries follows no fixed pattern. Many are one-man concerns: staff without professional training often have to learn their trade on the job and without any guidance. The result is that work cannot always be efficiently done. There are also, however, large libraries with a clearly-defined hierarchy of academically and professionally qualified senior staff. Two significant features mark the small collections as much as the substantial libraries: they must work as the needs of the moment dictate, and hence improvise rather than organise; and they have themselves to press for the status and legal position which they want in an administrative framework unfamiliar with libraries — these are not obtained as a matter of course at a library's inception. Many of the larger libraries are faced with the problem of the relationship between central library and branches, with which we are familiar on the university scene. Here, however, it is resolved by regarding the library as an undivided whole. The optimum utilisation of stock may in one case involve keeping books on the spot in laboratories and institutes (Leverkusen), and in another situation a high degree of concentration in the central library with a good service to outside users (the Nuclear Research Establishment at Jülich). As a rule, duplicate copies are avoided unless absolutely necessary, the central library carries out all the routine professional work, and a master catalogue of all holdings is maintained.

h) In the long run, special libraries can exist in isolation no better than the other types of academic library. Typically, they tend to associate on a subject basis, and to prefer the loose organisation of an Arbeitsgemeinschaft. These may be small groups of libraries, brought together solely by the requirements of subjects with which they deal, and of great value in professional work. Through the exchange of experience, information, publications — sometimes even catalogues — they are in close touch with each other and also (a new development) with similar libraries in other countries (those of nuclear research establishments, for example). There are also Arbeitsgemeinschaften formed for the purpose of documentation, or for purely professional activities in librarianship. Even the largest, all-embracing body, the Arbeitsgemeinschaft der Spezialbibliotheken, has grown from an organisation in a restricted subject field — of technical and economic libraries (cf. 3.21). There has so far been little action to establish firm links on a regional basis, either between these libraries themselves, or between them and other groups of libraries.

2.43 Parliamentary and Government Libraries

Parliamentary and government libraries today form a relatively well-defined group, as a result of the activity of the Arbeitsgemeinschaft der Parlaments- und Behördenbibliotheken (founded in 1957). They may be divided into the libraries of the Federal and Land parliaments, of the law courts, and of the Federal, Land and local administrative organs.

There are about 600 of these libraries, if we include only those with full-time staff and exclude the libraries of academic institutions run by the Bund and the Länder, as being special libraries. Many have only a small stock and few staff, but some make important contributions to the strength of German academic libraries as a whole by the size of their collections and their work for the community at large through loans, information and documentation services. Among these, we list the following as having holdings of over 100,000 volumes:

Bibliothek des Deutschen Patentamts ("Library of the German Patent Office"), Munich (532,000 vols.).

Bibliothek des Bundestages ("Library of the Lower House of the Federal Parliament"), Bonn (430,000 vols.).

Bibliothek des Auswärtigen Amts ("Library of the Foreign Office"), Bonn (160,000 vols.).

Bibliothek des Bundesgerichtshofs ("Library of the Federal Supreme Court"), Karlsruhe (170,000 vols.).

Bibliothek des Bundesverwaltungsgerichts ("Library of the Federal Court of Administration"), Berlin (130,000 vols.).

Bibliothek des Statistischen Bundesamts ("Library of the Federal Statistical Office"), Wiesbaden (135,000 vols.).

Bibliothek des Bundesverfassungsgerichts ("Library of the Federal Constitutional Court"), Wiesbaden (100,000 vols.).

Most of them have been founded since 1945. Only the libraries of the Patentamt and the Auswärtiges Amt were able to claim to succeed to former establishments of the Reich (three-quarters of the holdings of the Reichspatentamt were preserved; 60,000 volumes of the holdings of the Auswärtiges Amt, saved from the war, were returned to the Federal Republic after being confiscated by the American military government).

These seven libraries constitute an exception: in general, they show the characteristics of the big academic and special libraries, and only to a limited degree the following features which typify this group as such:

a) As with special libraries, the function of these libraries is primarily to serve their organisations (parliament, court, authority), of which they are adjuncts.

b) They are essentially practical libraries. It is important for them to have a stock that is up-to-date and suitable for daily use, where the cataloguing and arrangement allow quick access to material required at any moment.

c) Legal literature occupies an important place, besides specialised material dictated by the nature of the authority, e. g. politics, economics, sociology, physics, chemistry or technology. Perhaps to an even greater extent than in special libraries, the material needed here is composed of "minor literature" (especially the entire output of official publications, but also proceedings, programmes, memoranda, reports and statistics). Exchange is an important complement to purchase in acquisition work.

d) The stock is maintained, not only by additions, but also by the weeding-out of obsolete material no longer in use. Under the Reich, the disposal of unwanted publications by government libraries was regulated by a ministerial order and dealt with by the Reichstauschstelle in Berlin (cf. 8.4). Since such an arrangement no longer exists, the libraries of the Federal authorities help each other by conducting an exchange of duplicates among themselves.

e) The catalogues, intended for use by people in the course of their work, are arranged as simply as possible. The complicated nature of official publications places many obstacles in the way of simple presentation. After struggling along for years as best they could to meet their own needs, libraries can now turn to a code compiled by the Bundestags-bibliothek for this purpose, which is available to other interested libraries and takes into account the peculiarities of this material. The inclusion in the catalogues of material not separately published is almost universally necessary.

f) Indexing of the literature is done primarily for internal use, but in a few cases — in the larger libraries only — this has been expanded into a documentation service available to outsiders. The libraries of the Bundestag, the Bundesgerichtshof and the Bundesverfassungsgericht are examples (cf. 6.13).

g) The type of circulation follows from the function of the libraries. They are basically non-lending libraries; however, this does not mean that books are used in a reading-room, as normally, but at the place of work. Thus, a kind of issue on loan exists, which may in certain cases be extended to allow the removal of a book from the premises. Books are usually supplied immediately on request. Some libraries permit limited use by outsiders and participate in the inter-library loan system. Reference collections in divisions and departments of an office, and the circulation of journals and newspapers, require good organisation and constant attention.

h) The libraries of government authorities are often one-man organisations: most have been run for a long time by administrative officials. The assignment of professional staff to these posts has been accepted in the larger libraries, at least. Specially framed regulations on the training of librarians for posts under the Federal authorities were issued in 1964 (cf. 7.12). The necessary contacts between these libraries are fostered by the Arbeitsgemeinschaft mentioned above. Local Arbeitsgemeinschaften, such as those formed in some towns (Bonn, Hanover), have also proved useful.

2.5 Public Libraries and the Staatliche Büchereistellen

The public library scene is a varied one. It includes independent academic libraries, Einheitsbüchereien (an integrated system of popular and academic libraries) and the public library service in the towns as well as in the Landkreise. The Staatliche Büchereistellen are also dealt with in this context, since they are offices set up by the Länder to work with public libraries.

In the section which follows, we shall cover, among other things, wissenschaftliche Stadtbibliotheken (academic town libraries). However, since these institutions more often than not have the functions and standing of Landesbibliotheken or university libraries, a good deal has already been said about them in earlier chapters. Emphasis in this chapter is accordingly on local authority public libraries.

A glance at the statistics will show how impressively public libraries have developed since the war, and promise to develop further. At the same time, it will make clear how much is still to be accomplished. In 1968 more than 47 million people, about 79 per cent of the inhabitants of the Federal Republic, lived in communities served by public libraries. These libraries stocked over 30 million volumes and lent almost 80 million. The tables in the "Gesamtstatistik der kommunalen Öffentlichen Büchereien der Bundesrepublik" give a more detailed picture of the situation in separate Länder, Stadtkreise, Landkreise and Gemeinden of varying sizes.

The flourishing development of public libraries, which is also reflected in the statistics of individual libraries, was made possible by the internal transformation of the old "Volksbücherei" into the "Öffentliche Bücherei" (on the lines of the Anglo-Saxon "public library"), which has been going on for the last twenty years. Although the name of "Volksbücherei" has been retained here and there, the great majority now bear such names as "Stadtbücherei", "Gemeindebücherei", "Öffentliche Bücherei" or "Öffentliche Bibliothek".

The book stock of these public libraries presents a very different picture from that of the Volksbüchereien of former times. Democracy demands the freedom to form opinions which is guaranteed in the Basic Law of the Federal Republic. It is one task of the public library to provide the basis of published information which permits this. It regards the adult reader as a responsible person who must be allowed access to the whole of published literature. The influence of science in all spheres of life, and the changes in the structure of society, increase the need for orientation and for assistance to people in their careers and daily life. Public library holdings have been broadened accordingly: the proportion of non-fiction has grown markedly, and specialised scholarly material is also bought or obtained, where possible, by inter-library loan. The provision of multiple copies of selected works of fiction has become rarer, and the range of titles has been increased as it has in non-fiction. Nevertheless, attention is still paid to literary quality and a "lower limit", the more so because limited bookfunds compel restraint in any case. The most frequent cause of controversy is over the acquisition of some "best-sellers" and the preference to be given them. There is thus still a clear distinction between the public libraries and the commercial lending libraries.

The significance of journals in comparison with book holdings has increased markedly. In recent years, record libraries have also been established in many places. More rarely, series of slides have been added to the stock. One factor in this case is that film and pictorial material is collected by special Land and municipal picture bureaux and lent primarily to schools and further educational institutions. There are indications, though, that much attention will be paid by librarians to audio-visual material in the not-too-distant future.

Almost without exception the stocks of public libraries are accessible to readers on open shelves, and the advice of the library staff is now given mainly on request. Both these factors have helped to bring new classes of reader to the public libraries, so that they can now rightly claim to serve people of all ages and occupations. Other developments also indicate the abandonment of didactic attitudes in favour of a more effective service. Charges are being steadily abandoned, although this is still obstructed in many places by unconvincing financial arguments. In the move towards increased efficiency the old "Leseheft" is yielding to modern, often automated, issue procedures. (The "Leseheft" was a booklet of several pages serving as a means of identification, as an aid to readers' advisory work, in that it listed the books read and requested, and as a ticket for charging purposes.) Restrictions on the number of books that may be borrowed are being dropped, and so is the keeping of detailed statistics on occupational groups as a basis for research on readers' habits.

To meet modern conceptions of its function, the public library is widening the range of its services: it may offer an information service, publicity for cultural events, or a bibliographical service; but the focal point of the public library's work is still, by and large, the individual readers. There has been little attempt to develop a service for commerce and industry. A look at opening hours will also usually reveal that services might be much improved in this respect. Services to special groups of readers (old people, hospital patients, blind people, prisoners) have been developed to varying degrees, but on the whole fall outside the competence of the municipal public library. A great deal of attention has been devoted to libraries for children and young people, with appreciable success. Co-operation with schools and institutions for adult education leaves, on the whole, much to be desired.

The internal transformation of the public library has its external counterpart in the many modern library buildings in towns and Gemeinden of all sizes. These are also evidence of the public library's greater impact on the general public. Even so, the financial provision for public libraries shows that we have only made a beginning. Despite considerable increases, contributions by the Gemeinden are mostly still inadequate. Above all, the commitments of the Länder and the Landkreise will have to be raised greatly, if the provision of books is to be uniformly effective in town and country. The demand for laws on public libraries gains strength when taken in conjunction with regional library planning (cf. 3.14). In rural areas, forms of library provision, co-ordination and co-operation have grown up in some regions which might be components of this kind of overall structural planning.

In the co-operation which the public libraries have striven to establish with the academic libraries, as a consequence of regional library planning, a start has now been made by linking public libraries to the academic libraries' national interloan system, by separate regional systems and by co-operative acquisition agreements. The new functions of public libraries and their increase in size — especially in the big cities — are also bringing them closer to the academic libraries.

Now and for the future, society in the Federal Republic is setting tasks for the public libraries for which they are in many ways not yet fitted. Much that should already be taken for granted may, in the face of reality, still seem utopian for a long time to come. Nevertheless, the growth of German public libraries since mid-century, seen as part of a world-wide movement, encourages one to be hopeful of the future.

2.51 Public Library Service in the Towns

In comparison with library services in the towns of other countries, municipal public libraries in the Federal Republic frequently do not show up at all well, in spite of their remarkable growth since the end of the Second World War. There is no doubt that most German towns devote much smaller funds to libraries from their budget for cultural purposes than do comparable towns in the USA, Great Britain or the Scandinavian countries. Apart from this, the effectiveness of library services in the towns of the Federal Republic has been prejudiced considerably by the division between academic and public libraries.

There are historical reasons for the fact that a town's own academic library may exist side by side with its public library and be likewise supported entirely, or almost entirely, by the municipality (cf. also 1.6). The Stadtbibliotheken ("town libraries") are the older institutions: the first date from the time of the Reformation, and others grew up in the 17th, 18th and 19th centuries. There are today something over 20 of them in the Federal Republic, most of them in large towns which have a well-developed public library system in addition. No generalised picture of this type of library can be drawn from their historical development. Many, though not all, were founded by the citizens for their own use. Some have had their origins in former university libraries after the dissolution of the university (Mainz, Trier), whereas others, in this century, have been expanded from town libraries into university libraries (Cologne, Frankfurt, Hamburg, currently Bremen and Düsseldorf). Besides cases where a library has been transferred from the administration of the Land to that of the town (Düsseldorf, Kassel), there are instances of town libraries being taken over by the state (Hamburg, Bremen).

The majority of Stadtbibliotheken possess a stock of between 200,000 and 400,000 volumes. Düsseldorf (480,000) and Munich (500,000 vols.) exceed this figure. Only in very few cases have bookfunds reached the level recommended by the Wissenschaftsrat (cf. 4.12).

The Stadtbibliotheken participate in the co-operative activities of academic libraries in the Federal Republic: inter-library loans, union catalogues and staff training. The growing number of interloan requests in recent years shows that their holdings, now accessible through the regional union catalogues, contain material of considerable importance.

Like the Landesbibliotheken, and perhaps to an even greater extent, the Stadtbibliotheken are having to redefine their position in present-day conditions. Characteristic of them are two features which we noted in the Landesbibliotheken:

a) They are *deposit libraries* for material to do with their town, which has to be collected, preserved, specially catalogued and made available for research. The combination of library and archive collection under one roof or the same administration, which was formerly common, is still to be found in Brunswick, Bonn, Hildesheim, Lüneburg, Mainz and Trier.

b) They are *libraries for public use*, which must provide the citizens of their town with at least the basic works of scholarship, including science and technology, and must be able to obtain by inter-library loan the more specialised material which they do not acquire themselves. The emphasis is laid on works of reference used for answering enquiries — an activity which could with advantage be intensified in most cases.

From the function of the Stadtbibliothek as a library for public use there stems its overlapping with the municipal public libraries, which gives rise to suggestions for co-ordination and integration in the interests of the town and of professional efficiency.

Amalgamation is not possible in cases where the academic library in a town has assumed (or is assuming) the full functions of a Landesbibliothek or a university library, and is consequently supported wholly or partly by funds from the Land. Yet there are also many instances in which both academic and public libraries are financed solely by a town, where numerous obstacles oppose any move to integrate the two. Fully-formed organisations, each with its own strongly-marked peculiarities, are difficult to amalgamate. Besides, so long as separate courses of professional training lead to employment in academic libraries on the one hand and in public libraries on the other, apprehension will persist that amalgamation under a common administration might lead to the neglect of one side or other of the library's functions. All the same, widespread integration of library services in the towns is likely to be only a matter of time. The position of a town's special libraries, such as those of government authorities, will also be reviewed where possible in this connection.

The present situation varies greatly from town to town. In towns where an old-established Stadtbibliothek has become a university library also (as in Frankfurt, Cologne, recently Bremen and, rather differently, in Hamburg), the line of demarcation is relatively clear. Yet even here circumstances vary too much for any generalisation to be made. In *Cologne*, the Universitäts- und Stadtbibliothek has for some years been maintained by the Land alone. The expansion of the university and the rising number of students (currently around 20,000) compel the library to concentrate its efforts more and more upon the needs of the teaching

staff and students. The Cologne public library regards itself as being all
the more obliged to build up a large central library of its own. In *Frankfurt*, an agreement on the university, concluded between the city and
the Land in 1966, stipulates that the Stadt- und Universitätsbibliothek
is to remain under the city's administration. The Land contributes to its
running costs (up to one-third) and its capital expenditure (up to one-
half). The library regards itself as catering for the town as much as for
the university, and has regard to both in its stock-building, circulation
procedures and information service. Even here, however, the pressures
of university requirements and the needs of a large city have forced the
municipal public library system to expand its holdings of scholarly works
and develop an adequate central library. In *Bremen*, which is to become a
university town, part of the collection of the present Staatsbibliothek is
being transformed into a new university library. Another section of the
holdings is expected to be transferred to the present public library
system, which would then take over all the functions of a large Anglo-
Saxon public library within the framework of a unified library system for
the city. Therefore the libraries have changed their name from Volksbüchereien der Freien Hansestadt Bremen to Stadtbibliothek Bremen.

In *Hamburg*, the former Stadtbibliothek (now the Staats- und Universitätsbibliothek) is the main general academic library. It acts as a central
library for the city-state of Hamburg for purposes of book acquisition,
and as a seat for its union catalogue and library school. This alone
explains the fact that the Hamburger Öffentliche Bücherhallen (Hamburg
public library system) — the largest municipal system in the Federal
Republic, with the status of a private foundation although financed by
the city-state — has so far lacked a proper central library. It has, however,
been decided to establish such a library.

In *West Berlin*, the twelve Stadtbezirke ("wards") possess independent
public library systems, each with a main library and branches, and sometimes with mobile libraries and special libraries in addition. The Amerika-
Gedenkbibliothek ("American Memorial Library"), an Einheitsbücherei
("integrated library"), is subject to the direct authority of the Senate as
the central public library for West Berlin. In its relations with the Bezirke it confines itself to certain co-ordinating activities, e. g. in inter-
library loans and the provision of catalogue entries. The holdings of the
Amerika-Gedenkbibliothek in scholarly material are used on interloan
to supplement the book and journal stocks of the Bezirk libraries. Besides
this, the many services of the library can be used directly by anyone.

In some towns the two types of library have existed side by side without any real connection, as for many years in *Düsseldorf*, where the academic library has retained its traditional title of "Landesbibliothek" although now supported entirely by the city. At present the intention is to hand it over to the Land to function as a university library. In *Aachen, Mainz* and *Munich*, a common administration has been established as a first step towards integration. In *Dortmund* the Stadt- und Landesbiblio-thek — also a purely municipal institution — has been housed together with the central library of the public system in the "Haus der Biblio-theken" for a decade. Integration has made good progress in *Hanover*: here the public libraries in the different quarters of the city have been so much developed in recent years that a balanced relationship has been achieved between them and the existing Stadtbibliothek as the central library of the system. In the *Essen* public library system, planned from the start as an Einheitsbücherei, a separate academic section exists as a unit of the organisation within the central library.

Other variations could be quoted of the independent, parallel existence of public libraries and academic libraries still or formerly supported by the municipality — occasionally even without mutual interloan facilities. Again, other large towns could be cited where nothing but a unified library system has ever existed, or where a union of Stadtbibliothek and public library has evolved.

The smaller the town, the less likely one is to encounter this problem, since financial resources will not often permit the maintenance of two large municipal libraries. All the same, when we consider how much responsibility the large cities in particular have for the state of the public libraries, it is clear how unfavourable the overall situation remains. It also becomes obvious how fundamentally difficult it is to make a statistical comparison with library services in other countries.

On the whole, it is primarily in the large and medium-sized towns that the public libraries have been able to develop into effective organisations and put into practice many modern conceptions of a public library's functions. Although many towns provide much greater funds for opera-houses, theatres and museums, whose cultural attractions for the outside world are stronger, they are beginning to see their public libraries as a part of their general provision for citizens' needs, and hence to pay heed to the effectiveness of the service, to organisational models and to stand-ards for library stock and equipment (cf. 4.14). The standards laid down by the Kommunale Gemeinschaftsstelle für Verwaltungsvereinfachung

("Municipal Centre for Administrative Simplification"), and the development plans of some towns (Berlin, Bielefeld, Duisburg, Hamburg and others), set standards for comparison and give time-scales for public library development. In this they have partially assumed the functions of the legislation on public libraries which is still lacking.

The development of holdings and services is showing the public library in a new light. The introduction of Lektoren ("subject specialists") is evidence of the expansion and specialisation in holdings, and also of a close watch on the entire published output (cf. 4.3). The indexing of periodicals is growing more important. The bookstock of certain central libraries in big cities (like the Amerika-Gedenkbibliothek in Berlin and the Hanover Stadtbibliothek) can stand international comparisons. The work of Lektoren as subject specialists is of significance in the provision of readers' advisory services — to which library staff have always felt strong obligations — and in the growing provision of information services, which in a few large city libraries is now being made by a separate unit of the organisation (cf. 4.62). Some big towns now also have special staff for work with the public in the wider sense (e. g. the Amerika-Gedenkbibliothek in Berlin, Bremen, Dortmund, Duisburg, Düsseldorf, Frankfurt, Hamburg, Hanover); their work usually includes the preparation of special events and exhibitions, and the compilation of reading-lists. In medium-sized towns these activities often offer further opportunities for cultivating contacts with the locality, which all library staff must then make good use of.

Lending services are mostly well developed. In many of the larger towns, lending services within their boundaries are effectively improved by the use of vehicles owned by the town or the library itself.

The public libraries of large and medium-sized towns are today usually *library systems* of varying size and complexity. They also differ in their degree of centralisation. The organisation of public library systems, their central libraries and branches, will be dealt with in more detail in section 4.2. Libraries with special functions such as childrens' libraries, which have become an integral part of public library work, will be treated in one of the later sections of this chapter, along with certain types of special public library which exist in some systems: libraries in schools for vocational training, music libraries, hospital libraries and libraries for the blind.

In the space of only a few years, *mobile libraries* have acquired some importance in municipal public library systems. Only the third mobile library in Germany (which entered service in a Munich tram in 1928 with a stock of 3,000 volumes), was an urban venture, but the real development of this type of library after the Second World War has been, and still is, predominantly in the towns. By 1957 a total of 14 mobile libraries had entered service in the Federal Republic; twelve years later the number had risen to 82. Apart from the Munich tram library, which was discontinued in the spring of 1970, they were all motor vehicles, though with various names: Fahrbücherei, Autobücherei, Wanderbücherei or Überlandbücherei. 64 of the 82 mobile libraries were operating in 41 towns. 34 towns and 3 Bezirke in West Berlin possessed one mobile library each, 4 towns and 2 of the Berlin Bezirke two each, the cities of Hanover, Cologne and Berlin-Spandau three each, and Munich six. The number of stopping-points per vehicle runs from 4 to 33. About two-thirds of the mobile libraries were owned by towns of over 200,000 inhabitants, about one-third by towns of between 200,000 and 50,000 inhabitants, and only two by towns smaller than this.

Mobile libraries in the towns are used chiefly to provide library facilities in the more thinly-populated residential areas within the town boundaries. Bearing in mind that a well-knit community of at least 10,000 inhabitants is needed to justify the construction of a permanent branch library with a full-time staff, it can be seen that many opportunities remain for the use of mobile libraries in towns. Stopping-points may also be found in residential areas in the central part of towns, if there is no possibility of building a permanent branch there. For the rest, experience in Germany seems to bear out that from other countries: one of the advantages of mobile libraries is their flexibility which not only allows the most favourable stopping-points to be ascertained, but also suitable sites for any branch libraries which may be needed in the future. Compared with the smallest branch libraries, which likewise have limited opening hours, mobile libraries generally possess a larger total stock (at least 10,000 volumes per vehicle, according to present standards), and usually also have professional staff in addition to ancillary staff and drivers. For bringing books near to where people live, on a weekly round as far as possible, they will be welcomed by many, and for many reasons, even in these days of increasing car ownership — especially by young readers, who are among their heaviest users. An explicit offer to obtain books on loan from elsewhere, and the right to use other facilities in the library system with the same reader's ticket, go a long way towards overcoming the disadvantages of mobile libraries.

Besides their use in residential areas, mobile libraries are successfully used in some towns to serve old peoples' homes and industrial concerns (Munich) and schools (Berlin-Spandau and Munich). The bookstock of mobile libraries must cater for the high proportion of younger readers; on the other hand, experience everywhere has shown that a stronger representation of adult reading matter, particularly non-fiction, soon results in correspondingly heavier use.

Several types of mobile library have been developed by different firms in the Federal Republic in collaboration with librarians. Articulated vehicles and those with bus-style bodies are both available. Great attention has been given to their internal arrangements, and shelf capacity has been raised in the course of time to about 6,000 volumes. The external appearance of the modern mobile libraries is also appealing, and effective use is made of illuminated display cases and large lettering for publicity purposes.

Special aspects of public library work (chiefly in towns) will be dealt with in greater detail in the chapters that follow, and public library buildings in section 5.2. Details referring to individual towns will be found principally in the appendix, "Halts on a Library Study Tour".

Statistically measurable activities in Gemeinden of over 20,000 inhabitants can be found in the "Schnellstatistik kommunaler Öffentlicher Bibliotheken" and among the public library statistics in the "Statistisches Jahrbuch Deutscher Gemeinden". The following figures are reproduced from the "Schnellstatistik" as a yardstick of sorts for the situation in towns in different categories of size, as it appears in terms of bookstock and issues.

There are three cities in the Federal Republic with over 1 million inhabitants: the city-states of West Berlin (2.13 million) and Hamburg (over 1.8 million), and the city of Munich (1.36 million). Among these, the Amerika-Gedenkbibliothek and the 12 Bezirk public libraries in West Berlin had a bookstock of 2,181,082 volumes and 7,902,761 issues in 1969 (the Amerika-Gedenkbibliothek made about 612,000 issues, Berlin-Spandau 1,008,000 and Berlin-Steglitz 934,000). The Hamburg public library system reported a stock of 1,192,640 volumes and 4,821,136 issues, and the Munich public libraries 698,980 volumes in stock and 3,999,689 issues.

Eleven cities in the Federal Republic have a population of between 1 million and 400,000: Cologne (866,000), Essen, Düsseldorf, Frankfurt, Dortmund, Stuttgart, Bremen, Hanover, Duisburg, Nuremberg and Wuppertal (415,000). Hanover (525,000) stands out in this group, where the Stadtbibliothek and Stadtbüchereien had 775,008 volumes in 1969 and made 2,401,011 issues; so does Duisburg (460,000 inhabitants), with 1,802,562 issues from a stock of 414,743 volumes.

47 towns have between 400,000 and 100,000 inhabitants. Among this group, notable performances were shown by Ludwigshafen (176,000 inhabitants, 195,202 volumes, 811,907 issues) and Koblenz (107,000 inhabitants, 181,318 volumes, 478,613 issues).

The category of towns with between 100,000 and 50,000 population contains 57 towns. The most successful among these were Wolfsburg, home of the Volkswagen plant, which with 92,000 inhabitants had a stock of 96,813 volumes and issues of 369,659, Ulm (93,000 inhabitants, 198,739 volumes, 455,768 issues) and Rheinhausen (72,000 inhabitants, 66,695 volumes, 288,308 issues).

164 towns and Gemeinden belong to the category of 50,000–20,000 inhabitants. In twelve of them, more than 100,000 volumes were issued in 1969: 156,053 volumes in Rosenheim (37,000 inhabitants), and 119,356 in Uelzen, with 24,000 inhabitants, one of the smaller towns in this group.

In all, 11 public library systems achieved over 1 million issues each in 1969.

In comparing public library services in individual towns, a wide range of performance is evident within and between the size categories. Thus, according to the "Schnellstatistik", there were 286 towns with over 20,000 inhabitants in 1969: of those with a population of over 100,000, 14.8 % issued more than 3 volumes per inhabitant, 32.8 % issued 2–3 volumes, 50.8 % 1–2 volumes and 1.4 % less than 1 volume. Of the towns with between 50,000 and 100,000 inhabitants, 5.3 % issued more than 3 volumes per inhabitant, 31.6 % issued 2–3 volumes, 49.1 % 1–2 volumes and 14 % less than 1 volume. Of those towns with a population between 20,000 and 50,000, 8 % made 3 or more issues per inhabitant, 24.6 % issued 2–3 volumes, 33.7 % 1–2 volumes, and 33.7 % less than 1 volume.

New tasks for the future are falling to public libraries in the towns. Within their town, they may in many cases be the most suitable referral points for all library facilities and their holdings in, for example, periodicals. They are acquiring more than local functions within their region, and many already provide books and information, directly and indirectly, for users living outside the town in the same way as they do to their own

citizens. One's expectation that the towns will not refuse wider responsibilities is encouraged by the commitments of their local authority
associations and the initiative taken by their librarians in the discussions
on regional library planning. The Länder, for their part, will be expected
to facilitate these wider obligations of municipal public libraries through
increased financial assistance.

2.52 Public Library Service in the Landkreise

The public library service in the Landkreise covers the smaller Gemeinden and the kreisangehörige Städte (towns within the jurisdiction of a
Landkreis), and thus even medium-sized towns. The smaller the community the less, as a rule, are its financial resources, and hence its ability
to provide funds for cultural purposes — including public libraries. Thus
in the Federal Republic, as in most countries, the inhabitants of the
smaller communities and rural areas are still much less well provided
with library services than people in the larger towns. The need to even
out this disparity between town and country is strongly reinforced by
the general transformation in the rural social structure, changing it from
an agrarian to an industrial society. Industry is penetrating into the
country, and people living in the smaller communities often commute to
work in the towns. Universal access to motor transport has made the
distance between town and country meaningless. Even where the rural
population still works in agriculture, new methods of production and
marketing are forcing increased specialised knowledge upon them.
Modern means of communication like radio and television allow people
in the country to participate in events in just the same way as the urban
population, and act as a medium for all kinds of fresh stimuli.
All this results in totally new demands being made on public libraries'
stocks and services. Bookstocks need to be far larger than those which
the numerous small Gemeinde libraries can offer at present; they need to
contain very much more non-fiction and specialised material; and they
must be up-to-date and relevant to current life. Wherever the limits of
locally available holdings are reached, an efficient inter-library loan
system must be able to obtain books from other libraries. In the long run,
adequate library provision can be guaranteed only in a pattern of large
public library systems and regional networks, whatever shape the plans
for these eventually take, and in whatever way they are realised.

In most of the Länder such solutions are still a distant prospect even to-day. 51 per cent of the population lives in 23,308 Gemeinden with less than 20,000 inhabitants each. Of these, about 8,800 support independent permanent public libraries, and about 700 are visited by mobile libraries which they support jointly with other Gemeinden, or which the Land-kreis supports fully or partially. The rest of the Gemeinden are not served by public libraries. Denominational libraries, open to all, exist in many of these Gemeinden, but a large number are without any kind of library service.

Three major developments are now beginning gradually to reduce the number of independent library authorities: small country schools are being amalgamated into "central schools", and this is often linked with a more intensive deployment of mobile libraries; there are also the new boundary regulations and administrative reforms which have been in-troduced in the Länder and are leading to amalgamations of Gemeinden, Landkreise and Regierungsbezirke.

The formation of "central schools" for rural areas — usually fully-developed systems with nine or more classes and rooms for smaller groups — has in many parishes also removed the chief prop of the Gemeinde library: the smaller Gemeinde libraries were often run with the collaboration of the local school-teacher, who carefully selected and put into circulation the meagre bookstock, and added to this an educa-tional influence of great value in the intimate circle of life and reading in a village. Now that this circle can no longer survive, both schools and libraries are having to form larger units. The "centres for rural areas" designated under the reorganisation plans for the Länder, which are also to be educational centres, would appear to be suitable sites for permanent public libraries, while the smaller communities could be served by mobile libraries.

In the country, the *mobile library* offers the same advantages over per-manent "dwarf libraries" as it does in a town: a larger stock which can be rotated, and assistance from a qualified librarian. In addition to this, the rural population pattern — which varies so much from region to region and often even from Gemeinde to Gemeinde — gives even greater scope to the adaptability of mobile libraries. The number of stopping-points in a Gemeinde, lengths of stay, and the use of vehicles of different size and construction, offer plenty of room for experiment and allow an excellent degree of adjustment to local conditions. This has been out-standingly demonstrated in Flensburg and Rendsburg by the Bücherei-

zentralen ("regional library association headquarters" attached to the
Staatliche Büchereistellen, cf. 2.53). They have also developed vehicles
showing special features of construction: one of the Flensburg mobile
libraries, for example, is fitted with pneumatically-operated book-ends,
which at the touch of a button hold the books tight on the shelves and at
another touch release them. This is a great advantage for a mobile which
makes only short stops, often of only 20 minutes. The Büchereizentrale
Rendsburg has developed three different sizes of "Überlandbücherei",
for 1,000, 2,000 and 3,000 volumes, which may all be used in turn in the
same Gemeinde. There was considerable interest in other countries in the
construction of the "Überlandbücherei 3,000", which is in use in the
Landkreise of Rendsburg, Norderdithmarschen and Süderdithmarschen.
At stopping-points, the sides of the vehicle can be moved out to give it a
width of 4.40 m. (14 ft. 5 ins.). In this way, a library area of 25 sq. m.
(269.1 sq. ft.) is obtained from a total useable area of 32.5 sq. m.
(349.9 sq. ft.), and it is possible to install seats for readers in the centre.
The vehicle has proved its worth particularly in larger Gemeinden with
a genuine centre, where the number of users justifies a stay of at least an
hour. With slight modifications, this type has since entered service in the
Landkreise of Bamberg, Kronach and Uelzen. There are now Gemeinden
in 15 Landkreise which are served by mobile libraries carrying between
1,000 and 4,500 volumes. Two mobiles are in use in the Landkreise of
Rastatt, three in the area of the Landkreise of Rendsburg, Norderdithmarschen and Süderdithmarschen. Recognition of the fact that Gemeinden with less than 1,000–2,000 inhabitants are usually best served by
mobile libraries should lead to a continuing increase in the number of
these libraries in rural areas. This development is envisaged most notably
in the plans of the two Büchereizentralen at Flensburg and Rendsburg,
which serve their respective parts of Schleswig-Holstein. A move towards
the more intensive use of mobiles is also evident in Bavaria, where it is
being assisted by state grants.

The employment of mobile libraries, each serving several Gemeinden,
will at the same time partially solve the problem of staffing, which at
present is still a critical factor in the rural public library scene. The many
small country libraries can muster only a few full-time staff, and it is
most exceptional to find one run by a qualified librarian. This state of
affairs is a matter for concern, and not only from the point of view of
professional status: in practice, it causes considerable uncertainty, owing
for example to the increasing teaching and extra-curricular burdens on

the teachers who often act as honorary or part-time librarians. The development of public libraries in the Landkreise and the demand for quality in this service, are further reasons for establishing new staffing requirements. Professional librarians are needed for mobile libraries, for central public libraries in the Landkreise and for the larger Gemeinden with permanent libraries. Present thinking would regard one professional as essential for Gemeinden with over 5,000 inhabitants, while in Gemeinden of between 2,000 and 5,000 there should be one full-time professional looking after two Gemeinden. The shortage of professionally qualified librarians, and the situation in Gemeinden with under 10,000 inhabitants, have led to proposals for installing trained library assistants to run the libraries in these Gemeinden (cf. 7.23).

Efforts to make larger and more effective units responsible for library services in the Landkreise are based on the assumption that the Landkreise themselves will maintain and support public libraries to a much greater extent. At present only a proportion of the Landkreise maintain any library service: besides mobile libraries they may maintain or contribute to the upkeep of Kreisbüchereien ("libraries for the Landkreis as a whole") or Kreisergänzungsbüchereien ("supplementary libraries"), which lend sections of their stock or single volumes to public libraries and individual readers throughout the area of the Landkreis. Kreisbüchereien also act as the local public library for the chief town of the Landkreis, or vice versa. Many Landkreise make contributions towards the promotion and maintenance of the local public libraries. These contributions are sometimes regulated by library agreements between Gemeinden and Landkreise. The role of the Landkreise in library planning is particularly emphasised in Lower Saxony, where the "large administrative districts" (Großkreise), anticipated as a result of the overall administrative reforms, are seen as the future authorities for all rural public library services. In the other Länder, the Landkreise were regarded as an inadequate basis for public library systems, and the Regierungsbezirke are being taken as the appropriate units.

The draft development plan for public libraries in the Landkreise was presented in 1964 by a working party of the Arbeitsstelle für das Büchereiwesen and approved by the conference of the Staatliche Büchereistellen. The ideas it contained about areas of operation for services above local level, for mobile libraries and for permanent libraries, have become a permanent feature in the discussions on regional library planning, and will be further dealt with in this context later. The regional planning of public libraries, on which practical and theoretical work has already begun in the separate Länder, entered a fresh stage with the completion of the "Grundlagen für die bibliothekarische Regionalplanung" ("Basic principles for regional library planning") by the Deutscher Büchereiverband and its Arbeitsstelle für das Büchereiwesen. Nevertheless, despite the attention it is now receiving from both state and local authorities, the planning is only making a start. The reforms of the administrative structure and educational system now under way will have a decisive influence on the realisation of the plans (cf. 3.14).

The Länder, as well as the Landkreise, will have to assume greater responsibilities for the public libraries than hitherto, if an effective network of libraries is to be set up over the whole country. Their "Staatliche Büchereistellen" will play a vital part in developing this network.

2.53   Staatliche Büchereistellen

The network of Staatliche Büchereistellen ("State Public Library Offices") had to be reconstituted after the war, and adapted to the new administrative pattern. Today, a total of 29 Staatliche Büchereistellen are maintained in the eight territorial states and the city-state of Hamburg. They may bear different titles in some Länder: Staatliche Beratungsstelle für Volksbüchereien, Staatliche Volksbüchereistelle, Fachstelle für das Öffentliche Büchereiwesen, Staatliche Landesfachstelle für Büchereiwesen, Staatliches Büchereiamt, or Landesbüchereistelle.

The Länder finance the Staatliche Büchereistellen, with two exceptions: the Büchereizentrale Flensburg in Schleswig-Holstein, which is officially maintained by the Deutscher Grenzverein für Kulturarbeit im Landesteil Schleswig and also acts as Büchereistelle for the Schleswig part of the Land; and the Fachstelle of the Hamburg public libraries. In the Saarland the Staatliches Büchereiamt in Saarbrücken is responsible for the whole of the Land, and in Schleswig-Holstein the Landesbüchereistellen in Flensburg and Rendsburg cover the two parts of the Land; while in the other territorial Länder (i. e. excluding the city-states of Hamburg, Bremen and West Berlin) the work of the Büchereistellen covers one or more Regierungsbezirke. In these Länder the Staatliche Büchereistellen are institutions or offices within the administrative sphere of the local Kultusministerien, the head of the Regierungsbezirk administration being responsible for general administrative supervision and the Kultusministerium for professional supervision. Hence, instructions concerning the work of the Büchereistellen come direct from the Kultusministerien. The head of the Staatliche Beratungsstelle für Volksbüchereien in Munich is at the same time the ministry representative responsible for public libraries in Bavaria.

The emphasis on local self-government in the Basic Law of the Federal Republic has discouraged intervention by the Länder. The functions of most of the Staatliche Büchereistellen vis-à-vis the local public libraries were accordingly limited, initially, to advisory work and certain central tasks — excluding, however, the acquisition and processing of books. They have also taken on the distribution of funds from the Land for the promotion of local public libraries.

When looked at in detail, the list of functions is an extensive one. Advice is given to those who finance the libraries, as well as those who run them. It covers all aspects of the foundation and organisation of public libraries, their construction and equipment. It gives some emphasis to advice on publications, which is of crucial help in stockbuilding without constituting any attempt by the state to intervene in the librarian's freedom of choice. The Büchereistellen have varying resources and working methods for these purposes. The highest state of development in the use of subject specialists has been reached in the Büchereizentralen of Flensburg and Rendsburg; both, in different ways, have library staff in their area participating in the evaluation of books. All the Staatliche Büchereistellen issue select lists of recommended reading. In some Länder these lists are compiled by the Büchereistellen in consultation, and a number are published in their own journals. In Bavaria the subject specialists' work is linked with the editing of the journal "Die Neue Bücherei". Since 1968 booklists jointly compiled by the Staatliche Büchereistellen of the Federal Republic have been published twice a year under the title "Neue Bücher". They are important for small libraries and as a basis for stock control in the Einkaufszentrale für Öffentliche Büchereien ("Supply Centre for Public Libraries" — cf. 3.25).

Among these advisory duties we should include the further training of those in charge of the libraries by means of meetings of different sizes, which are organised by the Büchereistellen and at which professional and literary matters are discussed. Some Büchereistellen have also taken charge of the training and examination of ancillary staff. Internal communications with those who run and finance the libraries are linked with activities aimed at the general public with the intention of helping to improve general conditions for the planned development of public libraries. Both functions are assisted by the journals published by the Staatliche Büchereistellen in certain Länder: "Die Neue Bücherei" (Bavaria), "mb. Mitteilungsblatt des öffentlichen Büchereiwesens in Niedersachsen" (Lower Saxony), "Biblio" (North Rhine-Westphalia), and "Die Bücherei" (Rhineland Palatinate).

The centralised functions of the Staatliche Büchereistellen include the maintenance of supplementary collections to back up the loan service, and as a basis for the practice of sending different sections of the stock to other libraries for a limited period. By far the largest of these supplementary collections is that of the Staatliches Büchereiamt in Saarbrücken, with 120,000 volumes. Inter-library loans through the Staatliche Büchereistellen are becoming more and more important to the smaller public libraries which do not participate in the national inter-library loan system (cf. 3.131) or the Kommunaler Leihring ("Local Authorities' Lending Circle") in North Rhine-Westphalia (cf. 3.132). In some regions, this loan traffic is not only between local libraries within the area covered by the Büchereistelle, but access is also given through the Büchereistelle to the holdings of the bigger libraries, (cf. 3.13). In handling inter-library loans, great importance is attached to having available the catalogues of the bigger libraries, but above all to having central lists of the holdings of all local libraries in the area covered by the Büchereistelle. Not all Büchereistellen yet have complete and integrated union catalogues. In some places, on the other hand, modern technical aids are being employed to make fully effective use of these important tools for book provision (cf. 3.121 and 4.7).

Besides those centralised functions already enumerated, there are professional and administrative considerations in favour of the centralised acquisition and processing of books for loan, particularly in the case of rural public libraries, which depend so heavily on part-time and unpaid staff. After 1945 these functions were largely removed from the sphere of the Büchereistellen because the Länder felt them to be outside the province of state activities, and so different procedures had to be followed. The Einkaufszentrale für Öffentliche Büchereien in Reutlingen (cf. 3.25) established stocks of books with Staatliche Büchereistellen for examination and delivery purposes, which greatly simplified ordering. Books were supplied ready for issue, complete with catalogue cards. Other Staatliche Büchereistellen took the initiative in founding associations of local library authorities or their representatives, which undertook "practical work for building up the public libraries" in their area, and co-operated closely in this with the Büchereistellen and, in most cases, the Einkaufszentrale. These were, in Bavaria, the Staatliche Büchereistellen in Bayreuth, Nuremberg, Regensburg and Würzburg; in Lower Saxony, Lüneburg, Osnabrück and Stade; and in North Rhine-Westphalia, Hagen and Cologne. In Schleswig-Holstein, extremely effective Büchereizentralen were established in the same way, which opened up fresh dimensions for the activity of the Staatliche Büchereistellen there. They even created the conditions under commercial law which enabled them to take over the management of book acquisition themselves. The Staatliches Büchereiamt for the Saarland has attached to it a book-processing office supported by the local book trade, which works in collaboration with the Einkaufszentrale für Öffentliche Büchereien. In one or two Länder (Baden-Württemberg, North Rhine-Westphalia) the feeling has recently been gaining ground that the processing of books and production of catalogue cards are of great practical assistance to local library authorities, and that they could be done directly by the Büchereistellen of the Länder without going beyond the proper limits of the State's responsibility. The Einkaufszentrale in Reutlingen remains the chief supplier.

Their discretion in distributing state grants gives the Büchereistellen an important instrument for the shaping of the public library service in their areas, even if its effectiveness is usually restricted by the inadequacy of funds from the Land. Grants to the local authorities are made for different purposes according to principles laid down by the Länder, since no legal requirements exist: they may be for the establishment and expansion of the bookstock or for work on library buildings. The "Schnellstatistik kommunaler Öffentlicher Bibliotheken und Büchereien" contains a survey of expenditure by the Länder on public libraries.

Regular grants, which in several Länder are made to the public library authorities under contractual agreements, commit the parties to a specified sharing of costs over a sustained period. This makes them the best guarantee of a library's continuing effectiveness. This safeguarding of public library services by contract, to compensate for the lack of public library legislation, has been done in Schleswig since 1927 and in Holstein since 1948. Separate contracts are made between the Gemeinden, the Landkreise and the two Büchereizentralen. Their primary object is to fix the regular financial contributions of the three parties to the agreement; for libraries staffed part-time, these consist of fixed amounts per head of population. In Schleswig, for Gemeinden of less than 4,000 inhabitants, the Gemeinde and the Landkreise each contribute one-third of the total cost. Gemeinden with more than 4,000 inhabitants have to find the first 15 per cent themselves, and the remainder is then divided into three. In Holstein, all Gemeinden have to pay 50 per cent of the total cost. Different regulations on cost-sharing are applied to libraries with full-time staff. In Schleswig, the principle of allocation by thirds is retained, but the book budget of these libraries is determined differently, by a specially-designed formula which takes account of wear and obsolescence in the bookstock. A contribution from Land funds is to be made to public library authorities if certain conditions are met in a library's budgeting, following guidelines which have been worked out — and in part already put into operation — by the two Büchereistellen. These conditions are: a certain minimum expenditure on book purchases, and a staff appropriate to the size of the community. Contributions from the Land are fixed at different levels according to the financial resources of Gemeinden in the various size categories, and amount to between 30 and 60 per cent of the book budget and 40 to 50 per cent of the staffing budget. All funds are administered by the Büchereizentralen, which are for their part committed to providing certain centralised services and receive a contribution from the Land for this purpose. This is to be so calculated as to equal 40 per cent of the sum of all book and staff budgets for the libraries they deal with. In this way, finance for the Büchereizentralen will be made dependent on the level of development of public library services in their part of the Land.

The ultimate aim in the work of the Büchereistellen is to ensure the existence and planned development of the public libraries in accordance with principles which take account of local and regional conditions as well as professional expertise. A precondition for this is a detailed watch on progress, and statistics are an important aid which the Staatliche Büchereistellen employ. The statistics they compile on the public libraries in their area are the basis for the general statistics on municipal public libraries for the whole Federal Republic.

The Staatliche Büchereistellen do not, on the whole, have adequate resources for their extensive activities, which are so important for the public library service of the future. Clear exceptions are the Landes-büchereistellen in Flensburg and Rendsburg, in conjunction with their large Büchereizentralen, which have staffs of 37 and 69 respectively. Among the other Büchereistellen, the number of staff ranges from 15 in

Saarbrücken and Koblenz to 3 in Stade. Most have a full-time head. The good provision made for Büchereistellen in Schleswig-Holstein and the Saarland is partly attributable to the encouragement traditionally given to cultural institutions in these border areas. Apart from this, any judgement must bear in mind that the areas of responsibility of the Büchereistellen vary greatly in extent and in numbers of Gemeinden, of inhabitants and of libraries: 52 libraries in 306 Gemeinden for the Staatliche Büchereistelle in Aachen, for example, as against 696 libraries in 2,085 Gemeinden for the Staatliche Landesfachstelle für Büchereiwesen in Koblenz. The allocation of Gemeinden for which a Büchereistelle is responsible is done in different ways in each Land. Towns not under Kreis authority (kreisfreie Städte), and large towns with over 100,000 inhabitants, are usually excluded. In 1969, the 29 Büchereistellen in the Länder (excluding Hamburg, Bremen and West Berlin), were responsible for 23,627 Gemeinden with about 40 million inhabitants, and were serving more than 10,000 public libraries in about 9,000 localities with over 27 million inhabitants. Over and above their work for public libraries, the Staatliche Büchereistellen give support, in varying degrees, to other libraries — especially school libraries. For these wide-ranging activities, the Staatliche Büchereistellen in the Federal Republic possess a full-time staff of about 350, a good third of these being professional librarians.

The exchange of experience and co-operation between the Büchereistellen take place primarily within each Land, but also at the Fachkonferenz der Staatlichen Büchereistellen where representatives from every office meet once a year. The conference, for which each Büchereistelle in turn acts as a centre, may also state its opinion on important matters in public library development.

2.6 Denominational Libraries

The academic and popular libraries supported by the churches are treated here as a separate group, because common features in their history and present purposes make them a comparatively self-contained section of library activity as a whole. Just as with libraries controlled by central and local government, however, we find within this group two distinct types: the various kinds of denominational academic library and the denominational public library. The former include the earliest libraries of all:

the monastic libraries, which were important centres of scholarship in
the early middle ages. The latter are relatively late foundations, with
their origins only in the nineteenth century.

2.61 Denominational Academic Libraries

These libraries have been affected more than most by the vicissitudes of
history. The Reformation, and the secularisation of church property in
the early nineteenth century, were two great crises in the existence of
the monastic libraries: times at which they lost the bulk of their rich
manuscript and early printed book collections to the libraries of princes
or governments. After the mid-nineteenth century the Roman Catholic
Church did much to make good these losses, by founding new libraries
for religious orders and by more liberal provision for existing institutions. Nevertheless, the overall growth of denominational academic
libraries continued to be restricted and uneven. Both Catholic and Protestant libraries suffered almost continually from inadequate and often
unreliable funding. Interesting old collections – such as the Dombiblio-
thek in Freising, the Kirchen-Ministerialbibliothek in Celle and the
Bibliothek der Großen Kirche in Emden – have now been rendered usable, though their holdings have in fact hardly been added to at all. The
libraries of both churches suffered considerably from the anti-religious
actions of the National Socialist regime: some (chiefly the libraries of
religious orders) were confiscated, and the remainder more or less con-
demned to stagnation. Yet this very period of external oppression stimulated reconsiderations among the institutions affected. Within the churches – for example, in the Arbeitsgemeinschaft landeskirchlicher Archivare ("Study Group of Church Archivists") – discussion of their own
academic library services began as the need for these became more and
more widely recognised.

After May 1945 it became possible to develop such ideas and put them
into practice, and this fresh start was given its impetus by the Arbeitsgemeinschaften concerned. On the Roman Catholic side there was the
Arbeitsgemeinschaft katholisch-theologischer Bibliotheken ("Study Group
of Catholic Theological Libraries"), which was formed by a few libraries
in 1947 to cope with the most urgent problems then facing them, and
is now an association of some 90 libraries. On the Protestant side there
was the Arbeitsgemeinschaft für das kirchliche wissenschaftliche Bibliotheks-

wesen ("Study Group for Church Academic Libraries"), founded in 1956, which in 1960 amalgamated with the older Arbeitsgemeinschaft landeskirchlicher Archivare to form the Arbeitsgemeinschaft für das Archivund Bibliothekswesen in der evangelischen Kirche ("Study Group for Archives and Libraries in the Protestant Church"). Both of these — the Catholic body working as an association of institutions, the Protestant as one of individuals — have decisively influenced new library developments by fostering co-operation, encouraging staff training, and informing and advising the churches' leaders. Since 1962 they have maintained close contact, and joint undertakings have now bridged the gap which formerly separated them.

It is not at present possible to give an accurate account of all the denominational academic libraries, the nature and extent of their holdings or the services they offer. The "Jahrbuch der Deutschen Bibliotheken" (1969), which mentions 36 such Catholic and 22 Protestant libraries, covers only a fraction of those actually in existence. The "Handbuch der bayerischen Bibliotheken" lists 34 for Bavaria alone. Both Arbeitsgemeinschaften are producing accounts of these libraries: a handbook of academic library facilities for the Protestant Church is being compiled, and a guide for the Catholic Church is in preparation.

The types of library existing in both churches correspond to those under central and local government auspices:

(a) Libraries of educational establishments:
    higher educational institutions run by the churches, theological colleges and schools, seminaries and the colleges of religious orders.

(b) Regional libraries:
    in the Catholic Church — diocesan libraries;
    in the Protestant Church — libraries of the various constituent churches, provostries and deaneries.

(c) Special libraries:
    those belonging to denominational institutions, associations and services.

(d) Libraries attached to church administrative organs.

To these may be added

(e) in the Catholic Church only — libraries of religious houses and orders.

The distinctions between the different types, especially between (a) and (b), are not rigidly drawn. Just as libraries may be both Staats- and Universitätsbibliotheken, or as university libraries may simultaneously act as regional libraries, so some libraries of educational establishments may at the same time be diocesan central libraries, as at Paderborn and Trier. The division into four types makes the purpose of individual libraries fairly clear. Their acquisition policies show some variation within a common framework, with books on theology and religious studies forming a nucleus for material in related and peripheral subjects such as philosophy, history, politics, social studies, psychology, education, and even music and the fine arts. Use of the libraries is not restricted to members of the church concerned, or of its institutions; on the contrary, the libraries of both churches make it clear that they are at the disposal of anyone wishing to use them. Holdings are generally available for loan free of charge; but most of the special libraries, and some of those belonging to religious houses, do not lend.

Libraries of type (a) play a part in providing material for theological training, along with the libraries of university theological faculties and of the state-supported theological colleges (cf. 2.31). Those of type (b) are comparable in function to the Landesbibliotheken (cf. 2.2). Both diocesan libraries and those of the constituent Protestant churches collect theological and denominational material, including both works of general scholarly importance and literature published locally or of local interest. These will include publications produced, not by the book trade, but by local clergy, parishes, associations and church institutions. Book funds are usually smaller than those of Landesbibliotheken covering a comparable area; they vary widely, but among libraries of the Protestant constituent churches a figure of between 20,000 and 30,000 DM must be regarded as a good average. Among diocesan libraries, Cologne is in something of a special position as the library of an important centre of the Church — as is Hamburg, a former college library, among Protestant libraries.

Libraries of type (c) are special libraries in the true sense of the word (cf. 2.42). Those of type (d), which are mostly reference collections for the offices concerned, are of no significance for outside users and can to that extent be ignored here.

Libraries of religious houses and orders — type (e) — exist primarily to serve members of their order, but in many cases allow access to other research workers; some even participate in the inter-library loan network. Certain of them have now regained the status of centres for scholarly research.

The following important collections may be mentioned:

Type (a) — in part type (b) also:

Philosophisch-Theologische Hochschule St. Georgen, Frankfurt (300,000 vols.).

Erzbischöfliche Akademische Bibliothek, Paderborn (175,000 vols.).

Bibliothek des Priesterseminars, Trier (155,000 vols.).

Bibliothek der Theologischen Schule, Bethel (65,000 vols.).

Type (b) Erzbischöfliche Diözesanbibliothek, Cologne (140,000 vols.).

Bibliothek des Evangelischen Oberkirchenrates, Karlsruhe (65,000 vols.).

Landeskirchliche Bibliothek, Hamburg (90,000 vols.).

Bibliotheken des Landeskirchlichen Archivs, Nuremberg (75,000 vols.).

Type (c) Caritasbibliothek, Freiburg (c. 100,000 vols.), a specialist library for social welfare and related subjects.

Centralbibliothek der Inneren Mission, Berlin (60,000 vols.), a specialist library for charitable work and related subjects.

Type (e) Abbey of Beuron (260,000 vols.).

Benedictine abbey, Maria Laach (157,000 vols.).

Benedictine abbey, Ettal (c. 103,000 vols.), with a special library for the Byzantinisches Institut.

Bibliothek St. Albert, Walberberg (Dominicans) (c. 85,000 vols.).

The efforts made by both Arbeitsgemeinschaften to improve and modernise their libraries began in different ways, but are now coming to have more and more in common. The Catholic Arbeitsgemeinschaft has attempted since 1947 to make inadequate bookfunds go further by various kinds of mutual aid. These include, primarily, exchange of duplicates between member libraries and a special effort to fill gaps in periodical holdings. The library of an order at Oevertrop acts as a centre for this work, with the help of indexes of wants and offers. The Protestant Arbeitsgemeinschaft has at least temporarily alleviated the shortage of established professional staff by launching courses attended by unqualified library staff, including some from Catholic libraries. The separate interlending circles of the two churches have been linked since 1963, forming the "Innerkirchliche Leihverkehr" covering the libraries of both churches (cf. 3.131). A list of periodical holdings in Protestant libraries was published in 1962. A union catalogue of periodicals in Catholic libraries, at present in card form and limited to libraries in the Arbeitsgemeinschaft, is maintained by the diocesan library in Cologne.

The Protestant Arbeitsgemeinschaft has taken the initiative in the indexing of journal articles in the theological field (cf. 6.11). Both the Arbeitsgemeinschaften nowadays stress that all these efforts by their libraries
must have the support of the church leadership. In memoranda and
recommendations they have pressed strongly for increases in almost
universally insufficient bookfunds, and for more and professionally
qualified staff.

2.62 Denominational Public Libraries

After the war, "public" libraries run by the Protestant and Catholic
churches were extensively developed in the Federal Republic, side by side
with the municipal public libraries and in some cases with financial
support from the Länder and Gemeinden. The scale of denominational
library provision has wide regional differences. While in many Gemeinden denominational libraries either do not exist at all or suffer by comparison with the local library system, in other instances — especially in
the country — they are the only generally accessible library in a locality,
and as such are taking on the functions of general public libraries in
addition to their own characteristic work.

The churches' concern with libraries, which began in the 19th century in
parallel with public library development as a whole, found its expression
in early years — especially among the Catholics — in libraries for church
organisations; the chief purpose was to give their members access to
books. Around the turn of the century, a trend towards denominational
"popular libraries" set in, influenced by the growth of popular education.
This lasted into the 1930's, being more vigorous on the Catholic side
than the Protestant. During the period of National Socialism, strict limits
were set on the churches' library activities. Libraries had to be confined
to purely religious literature, and were allowed to lend only to their own
members. Millions of books were lost through government action and
the consequences of war. Today, the situation of 1933 has been not
only regained but even, in places, appreciably improved upon.

According to the Statistik der kirchlichen öffentlichen Büchereien in der
Bundesrepublik 1968, published by the Arbeitsgemeinschaft der kirchlichen Büchereiverbände Deutschlands, 2,298 Protestant public libraries,
in 1,730 Gemeinden with 232,070 readers and a total stock of 1,737,758
volumes, made 1,979,126 issues. In the same year there were 7,188

Catholic public libraries in 5,133 Gemeinden in the Federal Republic, which had 10,824,174 volumes available for 1,029,959 readers and recorded 13,168,662 issues.

Nearly all denominational public libraries are now run as parochial libraries, administered and financed by the Protestant or Catholic communities. This results in a widespread distribution of libraries, but also in a small average size for the individual library. Work is now in progress to supplement the network of local libraries with regional organisations which can improve the overall availability of books and satisfy specialised needs — for example, in connection with adult education projects. Among special forms of library work, both churches have a particularly strong tradition of providing services to homes for the young, the old and the sick and to hospitals.

With a few exceptions, denominational libraries are dependent on unpaid or part-time staff. Both churches maintain central or regional offices staffed by professional librarians to provide advice, guidance and training. The seminars which both instituted some years ago to build up a large pool of trained staff, and many other central and regional courses and separate events, have been attended by a high proportion of the unpaid staff.

Special, centrally-compiled guides to publications and library routine have a particular significance in the staffing structure and character of work in denominational libraries. Reviewing journals are published — for the Protestants "Der Evangelische Buchberater" by the Deutscher Verband Evangelischer Büchereien, and for the Catholics "Das Neue Buch" by the Borromäusverein and "Buchprofile" by the St. Michaelsbund — and introductions and other material on technical matters are drawn up or adapted to the special requirements of denominational library work.

On the Protestant side there exist associations of Protestant libraries at the level of the member churches of the Evangelische Kirche Deutschlands ("Protestant Church of Germany"). These member churches, with a few exceptions, maintain the offices which advise and support Protestant libraries. On the Catholic side, the dioceses, again with exceptions, have established offices for Catholic public library work with the same functions.

The central Protestant organisation is the Deutscher Verband Evangelischer Büchereien, which has as members the library associations of the member churches and some other associations with specialised functions.

115

Its own office acts simultaneously as a centre for book and library matters for the Protestant Church in Germany.

Among the Catholics, the central organisation for Bavaria is the St. Michaelsbund, the association of Catholic public libraries, whose central
office also acts as a professional advisory office for the whole of the
Land. For the other Länder, the Bundesarbeitsgemeinschaft der katholisch-
kirchlichen Büchereiarbeit is a joint body representing both the professional advisory offices and the Borromäusverein. The Borromäusverein
is a registered society to which the Catholic public libraries belong; it
also maintains a central office in Bonn which carries on much work above
the regional level. The Arbeitsstelle der Katholischen Büchereiarbeit in
Deutschland is responsible for information, co-ordination and liaison
work at Federal level. The Arbeitsgemeinschaft der Kirchlichen Büchereiverbände Deutschlands was formed as a joint organisation for denominational library work in the Federal Republic.

The objects of denominational libraries were re-examined after the war
in the light of developments throughout the fields of education and
librarianship. In a period of social change and theological reconsideration,
this sphere of work is likewise in a continual state of flux, influenced by
the dynamism and receptiveness to future needs shown in other areas
of educational work. Hence the denominational public library regards
itself as a separate educational medium maintained by the churches, not
merely as an amenity intended for "internal" use by members of the
churches themselves. The actual choice of books offered by these libraries
should therefore neither be governed by narrowly sectarian considerations nor be entirely devoid of moral value.

When in 1964 the function and educational responsibilities of the public
library in modern society were discussed by a meeting of librarians from
local authority and denominational public libraries, the result was the
so-called "Tutzing Declaration". In this it is affirmed that a society of
mixed religious convictions needs the publicly-supported libraries, which
make educational facilities available to all and "in their function as forums
for intellectual encounter and dispute, are institutions for society as a
whole". There is also a need for independent libraries, "in which those
groups committed to a particular view of life may present a full picture
of their own intellectual world and state critically their own concern for
the intellectual, cultural and political problems of the world at large.
They represent an important aid for the work of education in these
groups — important not for them alone, but for society as a whole". The

Tutzing Declaration not only affirmed the value of the libraries' respective special functions; it also expressed the desire for meaningful co-
operation, based on mutual goodwill, within the framework of the German library system as a whole. The internal development of the
denominational libraries is today decisively determined by the Tutzing
Declaration: all in all, it has also contributed to a better understanding
between the partners, and thus created conditions for the desired co-
operation — even if at present situations of rivalry exist in some localities and regions.

In the Essener Gesprächskreis (Essen Discussion Group), which was
established in 1969 and meets twice a year, the Arbeitsgemeinschaft
Öffentliche Bücherei and the Arbeitsgemeinschaft kirchlicher Büchereiverbände discuss professional matters of common interest.

2.7 Libraries of the Armed Forces

The libraries of the Bundeswehr ("Federal Armed Forces") form a group
of their own. Many valuable old collections in military libraries, some
dating from the 18th century, did not survive the Second World War:
the important Heeresbücherei ("Army Library") in Berlin, with holdings
of about 425,000 volumes and 256,000 sheets of maps, was totally
destroyed. Arrangements were made for sections of former military
libraries which were saved, but then confiscated, to be handed over to
new Bundeswehr libraries. The most notable of these is a rich collection
from the former Bayerische Armeebibliothek ("Bavarian Army Library")
in Munich, of around 70,000 volumes, which was passed on to the present Wehrbereichsbibliothek VI. Generally speaking, however, the
foundation of the Federal Republic and the building up of the Bundeswehr necessitated the creation of a modern library system for the Bundeswehr which would meet its new functions and requirements. A clear and
firmly-established organisation, which is obviously needed here, also
makes its outlines easier for the outsider to comprehend. The division
into academic libraries and soldiers' libraries reflects a firm distinction of
functions within this group.

2.71 Academic Libraries of the Armed Forces

The Bundeswehr, including the Bundeswehrverwaltung ("Armed Forces Administration"), currently has 102 academic libraries with total holdings of more than 1,000,000 volumes. As with such libraries run by central and local government and by the churches, these may be divided into three main types:

(a) regional libraries

(b) libraries of training establishments

(c) libraries of special institutes and offices of the services.

Type (a) comprises the six Wehrbereichsbibliotheken ("Military District Libraries") in Kiel (I), Hanover (II), Düsseldorf (III), Mainz (IV), Stuttgart (V) and Munich (VI). That at Düsseldorf also serves as a central library for the Bundeswehr as a whole. The largest libraries are those at Düsseldorf and Munich, each with about 125,000 volumes, followed by Hanover (70,000 vols.). The rest have holdings of between 20,000 and 35,000 volumes. These six libraries have been allotted special-collection fields, by language or by subject, thus forming a co-operative unit. Collecting policy is determined by the needs of Bundeswehr personnel for scholarly material from Germany or other countries. However, their reading-rooms, and the information and lending services, are available for civilian use — which may be heavy, especially where the library participates in the interloan service, as at Hanover and Düsseldorf.

Type (b) includes the libraries of the military academies: the Führungsakademie der Bundeswehr ("Armed Forces Staff College") at Hamburg, the Stabsakademie ("Staff College") at Hamburg, the Akademie für Wehrverwaltung und Wehrtechnik ("Academy for Military Logistics and Technology") at Mannheim, the Technische Akademie der Luftwaffe ("Air Force Technical Academy") at Neubiberg, and others. It also covers the libraries of the so-called "military schools", for example the training schools of the army, navy and air force for officers, the training schools for non-commissioned officers, and technical schools.

The most important library of type (c) is that of the Federal Defence Ministry, the highest Federal defence authority (about 70,000 vols.). Also of this type are special libraries such as that of the Militärgeschichtliches Forschungsamt ("Military History Research Office") in Freiburg; the library of the Wissenschaftliches Institut für Erziehung und Bildung in den Streitkräften ("Research Institute for Training and Education in the Armed Services") at Heide near Siegburg, now under construction;

and libraries of offices and establishments, down to the reference collections at medical posts and staff headquarters.

Libraries of types (b) and (c) are, on the whole, non-lending reference libraries, intended for specialised use and restricted to serving their parent institution. Nevertheless, there are exceptions — libraries which also grant access to qualified outsiders, such as the Defence Ministry's library and that of the Forschungsamt at Freiburg.

In matters of organisation and basic approach, all these libraries come under the control of the section for military science, libraries and documentation in the Führungsstab der Streitkräfte ("General Headquarters of the Armed Services"). The section also exercises professional supervision over all military libraries, in part directly and in part through the Wehrbereichsbibliotheken. Libraries are each responsible for their own acquisitions, making their own decisions on the purchase of books and journals according to their particular function and to local requirements. In 1968 the overall total of loans was 850,000. Of the 102 libraries, 52 have qualified staff of the administrative or executive grade who have completed the usual courses of professional training.

All the libraries provide information and answer enquiries as far as they are able. The central library in Düsseldorf and the library of the Defence Ministry have assumed special responsibilities in this respect: the former has a union catalogue of holdings in all Bundeswehr libraries, and has issued since 1963 "Militärwissenschaftliche Quellenkunde" ("Sources in Military Science") every two months, the latter lists new publications in the Defence Ministry's "Ministerialblatt" ("Official Gazette").

2.72 Soldiers' Libraries

Besides academic military libraries, the Bundeswehr maintains Truppenbüchereien or Soldatenbüchereien ("soldiers' libraries") for recreational and educational purposes: there are no separate officers' libraries. Under the "general directions for armed forces' libraries and gramophone record collections" laid down by the Federal Defence Ministry in 1965, all these libraries are subordinated to a special section in the Ministry. Organisation is decentralised, however: each batallion, or other unit at the same level, maintains a soldiers' library, for which it is itself responsible. Operational supervision is exercised by the commanding officer of the unit, and professional supervision by the head of the appropriate Wehr-

bereichsbibliothek. A supervisor administers each library. The Federal
Defence Minister issued special instructions in 1968 to assist book selection, at the same time emphatically recommending the formation of links
with public libraries and Staatliche Büchereistellen.

2.8 Special Fields of Public Library Work

2.81 Libraries for Children and Young People

Unlike any other special field of public library work, libraries for children and young people are today a universally-accepted part of the service.
These libraries must accommodate themselves to the psychological and
intellectual circumstances of the child and the adolescent. At the same
time they are dealing with the adult reader of tomorrow; and now, after
the intensive development of youth library work since the 1950's and the
rise of a new generation, the fruits of those exertions are being
gathered.

We use Jugendbücherei ("youth library") here as an inclusive term,
covering libraries for children with readers aged up to 13, 14 or 15, as
well as libraries for adolescents with readers ranging from 14 or 15 up to
16 or 18 years old: there is no uniformity about the age limits. It should
be noted, however, that in the Federal Republic Jugendbücherei may also
be used in a narrower sense to mean a library for adolescents — something which has received such other titles as "Bücherei der Jugend" or
"Bücherei für junge Menschen".

In the belief that the young reader should experience library services as
an integrated whole, and that it is important to be able to fall back upon
the resources of an adult library — especially in the case of non-fiction —,
it is nowadays in the Federal Republic generally felt desirable that a
library for young people should be housed in the same building as an
adult library, though in a separate room. The Amerika-Gedenkbibliothek
in Berlin, which has a childrens' library and an adolescents' library next
door to the sections for adults, is regarded as a model for this practice.

This layout is often not adopted because of the greater expenditure which
would be incurred by the necessary duplication of sections of the stock,
and by increased staffing requirements. On the other hand, the physical
separation of childrens' library from adult library is very common. In

these cases, the adult section often possesses a special collection for 14- to 16- or 18-years-olds which is kept, if not in a room of its own, at any rate in a special area. In some towns, however, there are youth libraries which are independent in both accommodation and organisation. This situation is frequently the result of necessity or chance, but in other cases arises from co-operation with schools or centres for young people. There is a planned basis for the network of separate youth libraries run by the Bremen public library service, which are also assuming the role of school libraries. The network already has more than 20 of these libraries, with an average stock of 5,000—6,000 volumes, and is being extended.

Special attention is paid to achieving a friendly and inviting effect in the appearance of libraries for children and young people. Shelves are lower than in the adult library. Picture-books are usually placed in a special area, where they can be properly read by the smaller children at book-troughs and specially-designed reading tables. Sometimes there is also an inviting "reading carpet". Separate reading-rooms for children are not common; instead, seats for reading and writing are provided in the lending area, usually with a special corner containing a collection of reference works. There have been recent demands for at least 30—35 seats, so that it will be possible to introduce an entire class to the use of a library. A special situation in Hildesheim resulted in a very successful combination of reading-room, waiting-room and library in the station building, for children travelling to school.

Today, the stock is on open-access shelves. The educational potentialities of the librarian's job do partly lie in advising the children, but reside principally in the selection of stock. An aid to childrens' librarians in this work are the reviews in the journals "Bücherei und Bildung", "Jugend-schriftenwarte" or the "Bulletin Jugend+Literatur". To these may be added the "Jahresbestlisten" of the Arbeitskreis für Jugendschrifttum and some good and well-tried select lists from libraries. In the selection of books, not only appearance and subject-matter are considered, but also, for example, whether and in what way works of fiction set moral standards, stimulate an aesthetic sense or arouse a child's imagination. In selecting for adolescents, to whom part of the adults' reading matter is already accessible, titles are examined for their compatibility with adolescents' intellectual development.

Within the limits of a stock chosen on this basis, children and young people are given the freedom to read without restriction or supervision. The fiction stock in childrens' libraries is divided into broad groups to help them find their way about: picture-books, legends and fairy-tales, stories for small children, and stories for boys and girls. Many libraries also group books by subject either on the shelves or in select catalogues — for example, adventure stories, historical tales and animal stories.

The non-fiction stock may, according to size and coverage, be arranged in a simple classified order or on a system corresponding to or adapted from one used in adult libraries. Thus the "Systematik für Kinder- und Jugendbüchereien", developed by the Arbeitskreis Kinder- und Jugendbüchereien, which was established by the Arbeitsstelle für das Büchereiwesen, is derived from the "Allgemeine Systematik für Büchereien" (cf. 4.42). This classification provides for the possibility of a clearer differentiation by adopting the letter notation of the "ASB" or by limiting the notation to 9 numbered groups. The classification can thus be used in libraries for children as well as for adolescents, and can also be easily adapted to the size of the stock.

The non-fiction stock for adolescents consists largely of titles which also appear in the adult library. The fiction stock is necessarily of mixed character, since it contains selected recreational and serious material from the stock of the adult library besides novels for the young. For the exploitation of the stock libraries for children and young people usually have a title catalogue as well as author and classified catalogues; alphabetical subject catalogues have recently become more common.

Some children's libraries have long kept up the practice of story-hours and reading-hours for their young readers — and sometimes puppetshows and amateur theatricals too. Book exhibitions are arranged in youth libraries to support programmes of lectures and discussions. Quiz games and how to find out contests are also popular. All these events, like the guided tours arranged for school classes, serve ultimately the purpose of leading the child towards books and introducing him to using and profiting from the printed word.

Although all library schools include library work with children and young people in their teaching for public library service, only the Süddeutsches Bibliothekar-Lehrinstitut in Stuttgart has so far offered an additional, specialised course culminating in a special examination; but this is not obligatory for those working in, or in charge of such libraries. The public library systems of large towns often have a librarian with special responsibility for and overall charge of youth libraries and the development of their stocks.

Librarians participate in the work of the Arbeitskreis für Kinder- und

Jugendbüchereien of the Arbeitsstelle für das Büchereiwesen. Besides the "Systematik für Kinder und Jugendbüchereien" already mentioned, this body has produced a memorandum about work with children and young people in public libraries, which compares the real requirements in a youth library with current practice. This is to be the basis for further work on different aspects of the problem.

An Arbeitskreis für Jugendschrifttum, which is supported by public funds, is open to all institutions and individuals interested in books for young people. One of the tasks of the Arbeitskreis, which has children's librarians among its members, is the selection of books for the Deutscher Jugendbuchpreis ("German Prize for Children's and Young People's Books"), which is awarded annually by the Federal Ministry for Youth, Family and Health. The work of judging entries produces the "Jahresbestliste", which every year lists about 50 commended books with short appreciations.

The attempt to provide a statistical survey of the condition and achievements of youth libraries has been undertaken by the Arbeitsstelle für das Büchereiwesen. The survey, which after an interval of 10 years was again published in 1968, covers the children's and young people's libraries controlled by the Gemeinden in the Federal Republic. According to these figures, the incompleteness of which is emphasised, between 12.6 and 17.2 % of children and adolescents between the ages of 6 and 18 are registered as readers in these libraries.

The Internationale Jugendbibliothek, Munich

The Internationale Jugendbibliothek ("International Youth Library"), founded in 1948, deserves special mention here: it is a centre for study and information unique in the world, with a stock in 1968 of over 110,000 volumes. It collects books for children and young people in all languages; there are 10,000 volumes of older German children's literature. The various catalogues giving access to the collection are to appear as a published series. Besides books for young people, the library collects relevant secondary literature on the theory and history of books for young people and their illustrations — all on an international scale.

The research library has attached to it, for field work, a lending stock for children in four languages. This children's library of 6,000 volumes is chiefly used for practical investigations by students at colleges of education and other specialist institutions. Story-telling, reading sessions, discussions (sometimes in foreign languages), and similar programmes are arranged in efforts to obtain data on the reading behaviour of children. A painting studio is also attached, in which information is obtained about the development of the pictorial imagination in children.

The staging of book exhibition is one of the most important activities of the Internationale Jugendbibliothek (a quarterly programme of events is published). There is an annual display of a cross-section of recent publishing around the world; two or three single-nation surveys; international comparative exhibitions on special themes; exhibitions in honour of outstanding authors and illustrators, and so on. Catalogues in several languages are compiled for some of these displays.

The information service is used mainly by advanced students and by publishers who are considering works for translation, looking for material to incorporate in new editions of classic children's books, or wishing to produce non-fictional works for the international market.

The library is maintained by a group, among which the chief sponsors are the Bund, the free state of Bavaria and the city of Munich. Publishers of childrens' books from all over the world show their recognition of the library's services by presenting their new publications free of charge. The Rockefeller Foundation gave substantial initial assistance to the library, which is a UNESCO "associated project".

Main themes for further expansion include, besides the growth of the collections, the publication of select catalogues in several languages on a variety of topics of international interest, a reprographic service for old journal articles hard to obtain, and participation in inter-library lending. A special programme of scholarships allows eight visitors from other countries every year to spend three months studying in the library.

2.82 School Libraries

Libraries for teachers and pupils in all kinds of schools form part of the educational library service. There are, however, a number of links with public libraries, especially insofar as these are intended to be used by schoolchildren. This prompted the Deutscher Städtetag in 1961 to make its "recommendations on co-operation between schools and public libraries". Although there are numerous concepts of the school library, especially in relation to the reform of teaching methods, they have not yet been fully realised. No comprehensive statistics are available.

School libraries can be divided into class libraries, central school libraries, and a combination of these two, in which the class library is no more than a small collection for teaching purposes. There are a number of different approaches and models for the organisation of school libraries. For example, in Duisburg, a school library office, run full-time by a teacher, has been set up as a department of the teachers' library serving that district. It establishes school libraries in the form of lending libraries, resembling in their composition youth libraries on a small scale, and supplies them with ready-processed books, furniture and equipment. It also gives guidance to those supervising the libraries, and maintains a card-index of helpful information on practical problems affecting schools. The person in charge of each library has complete freedom in his book selection. Bremen has its Staatliche Jugendschriftenstelle ("State Office for Childrens' Books"). This functions similarly to the office in Duisburg but exercises no influence on the form of the school libraries. It arranges exhibitions, and makes efforts to combat undesirable literature.

Other towns show many different forms of co-operation between school libraries and public libraries. In Hilden, the school libraries are run by teachers (who are not paid for this service), but are otherwise serviced by the municipal public library in the same way as branches. Co-operation in Oberhausen is even more thoroughly integrated. Here, an office organises and co-ordinates the school libraries, and carries out the technical work involved. A committee of childrens' librarians and teachers-in-charge of libraries works on the composition of stocks, on the basic assumption that the school library is to play a part in the teaching programme. In some towns — such as Dortmund, Bremen, Bonn, Mannheim, Hanover and others — youth libraries run by professional staff have been installed in school buildings, in agreement with the public libraries. They have assumed the functions of school libraries, with the advantage of being well-stocked and open for longer hours. The remoteness of some schools in Munich has led to a different solution here: their younger classes have been provided with libraries on the premises, while the older pupils are given a fortnightly service by mobile libraries.

Public libraries in some towns, which have centres of vocational schools, have set up professionally-run branch libraries specially designed to cater for those attending. Towns which have followed the successful example of Bremen in this respect include Cologne, Düsseldorf, Duisburg, Dortmund, Hanover, Mannheim and Wanne-Eickel.

In the smaller rural communities there is often a particularly close relationship between the local public library and the school library, both of which are frequently run by teachers in an honorary capacity. As a result, both will be in contact with the Staatliche Büchereistelle. The Büchereizentrale in Rendsburg has a separate school libraries department, which carries out the necessary technical and professional processes and the replacement and repair of stock. The Büchereizentrale Flensburg serves the school libraries in the rural areas by means of an "exchange library" for young people, which has its own vehicle. The Gemeinden share in the costs of this arrangement, which gives school libraries the opportunity of exchanging their stock wholly or partially every six months, and thus becoming more effective.

Examples like these, of successful school library services and fruitful contacts between public and school libraries, cannot disguise the fact that school libraries in the Federal Republic as a whole are underdeveloped.

This is confirmed also by a project carried out by a team from the Institut für Jugendbuchforschung ("Institute for Research into Juvenile Literature") of the University of Frankfurt. The team investigated the situation in 55 schools in the Federal Republic and in West Berlin which were held to be progressive and well equipped. The research revealed standards considerably lower than those in other countries (USA, USSR and Scandinavia). The team demonstrates how the gap can be bridged by means of a model based upon 9 propositions. The school library must occupy a central place in school life; must be equally accessible to pupils and teachers; must, since it serves primarly as a reference library, have sufficient seats for readers; must be the responsibility of a full-time school librarian; must be the co-ordinating centre and main clearing house for the pedagogical functions of the school; and, by means of its standard routines, train the pupils to use other libraries.

2.83 Music Libraries

Music libraries have grown up as a special feature of the general public library service, intended for performers at all levels and for those with an interest in music. They encourage the playing of music, thus serving the aims of both general education and musical training. It is this which determines the character of their stocks, laying more emphasis upon the practice of music than an academic collection. Music libraries nearly always possess their own stock of books on music, separate from the holdings of the general public library, major music journals and scores, the choice of the latter depending on suitability for performance as well as aesthetic considerations. Here too, there are an upper and a lower limit to what is acceptable. Most music libraries nowadays also have a record collection. Owing to high costs and the priority given to book acquisition, only a few have so far taken the decision to issue records on loan; instead most offer various kinds of listening facilities in the library to individuals and groups.

The music library is usually physically separate from the general public library. In the lending area, books are frequently on open access, scores more rarely. Next to it there will be rooms to accommodate many types of musical event, and listening booths for records. Some libraries also have tape-recording studios. They often possess musical instruments of their own.

Special instructions have been compiled for the difficult cataloguing problems of music scores, but these are being replaced by a German version of the "Full Code", which has resulted from international collaboration on the initiative of the Association Internationale des Bibliothèques Musicales (AIBM). A basis for the classification of books on music has recently been provided by the "Systematik der Musikliteratur und der Musikalien für Öffentliche Musikbüchereien" ("Classification of Musical Literature and Musical Compositions for Public Music Libraries"), compiled as a supplement to the "Allgemeine Systematik für Büchereien" by the musical classification committee of the Arbeitsgemeinschaft für Musikbüchereien ("Association for Public Music Libraries"), the German section of the AIBM. One aid for music libraries since 1967 has been the "Zeitschriftendienst: Musik" issued by the Arbeitsstelle für das Büchereiwesen. This compilation of the Bremen public library service indexes articles from music journals. A bibliography of music scores under the title "Musikbibliographischer Dienst" began publication by the Deutscher Büchereiverband in 1970 (cf. 6.12).

The origins of German music libraries date from the work of Paul Marsop, whose own library formed the foundation of the Städtische Musikbibliothek in Munich. This library, with 111,200 volumes, is the largest of the 54 music libraries (including separate music departments of public libraries) in the Federal Republic. According to the special list in the "Handbuch der Öffentlichen Büchereien 1970", there are major music libraries in Berlin, Hamburg, Saarbrücken, Hanover, Nuremberg, Essen, Wuppertal, Bochum, Frankfurt and Bremen. The music libraries usually have an important place in the musical life of their town; nearly all help to put performers in contact with each other.

The music libraries of the Federal Republic are joined together in the Arbeitsgemeinschaft für Öffentliche Musikbüchereien, which was founded in 1951 and is at the same time the country's section of the AIBM. Its former journal, "Die Musikbücherei", which until 1967 was a regular supplement to "Bücherei und Bildung", has since the summer of 1968 been incorporated into the journal "Fontes Artis Musicae".

Since 1955, the Süddeutsches Bibliothekar-Lehrinstitut in Stuttgart has offered music librarians the opportunity of taking a special examination (cf. 7.21).

In 1961 the Deutsche Musikphonothek was established in Berlin as a foundation financed by the Federal Ministry of the Interior, the Federal Länder and the Land of Berlin. It collects gramophone records, tapes and other media recording serious music, folk music, jazz and a selection of popular music. Two copies of each record are received free from the industry. Its functions are the accumulation of experience in this field, cataloguing, the co-ordination of small collections by means of a union catalogue, the evaluation of academic and popular contributions and co-operation with other countries.

2.84 Works Libraries

By works libraries are meant libraries for recreation, general education and further training, serving the employees of any type of firm — though primarily industrial concerns. They are institutions maintained voluntarily by the management, and to this fact they owe their variety of forms and sizes.

The history of works libraries begins with those founded around the middle of the nineteenth century. They originated in the patriarchal attitude of the factory owner — partly maintained out of a genuine sense of social responsibility, and partly intended as a defence against the influence of socialist ideas. Later, as firms' welfare facilities increased, the libraries were also expanded. The spirit of the "Bücherhallen" movement gave rise to large libraries such as those of Krupp's, the Farbfabriken Bayer A. G. in Leverkusen, the Zanders Stiftung in Bergisch-Gladbach, the Carl-Zeiss-Stiftung (which was to become the public library of Jena) and others. Membership was usually not restricted to factory employees. Besides the libraries of the large concerns, which generally had several full-time staff, many smaller libraries were founded. These varied in quality and in the level of their users, and were mostly run by part-time staff.

After the Second World War, half of all the works libraries were started from scratch. The publication, "Deutsche Werkbüchereien heute", published in 1969, identified 326 works libraries in the Federal Republic. The total number should be higher. The libraries covered by these statistics served 1.3 million employees. They possessed nearly 1.8 million volumes and in 1968 made 4.15 million issues. Again, according to these statistics, 13 works libraries in 1968 had over 20,000 volumes, and 38 less than 1,000 volumes. 39 per cent of the libraries had a full-time head.

A works library is usually financed entirely by the firm. In isolated instances, gifts of books are made — a practice of questionable value — or regular contributions are made by employees, supposedly to encourage a sense of involvement with the library. According to the statistics mentioned above, 213 libraries may count on a regular book budget.

Loan procedures are of many kinds. According to the enquiry previously referred to, 79 per cent of the libraries have open access. In the others, closed access, with issue from a counter, is in force, or "works access" which is used chiefly by the Siemens works in Berlin. There, the reader orders books from catalogues displayed in the departments of the works, using special order cards, and the books are then brought to his place of work by messenger. A number of concerns also serve readers through small branch libraries in outlying parts of their organisation, or by means of small mobile libraries. Some large works have set up their own youth libraries.

The proportion of employees making use of a works library varies greatly. With a good library, and under favourable conditions, it may reach 80 per cent. The works library benefits here from its proximity to the place of work and its ability to suit opening hours entirely to the needs of its readers, who can for example borrow books during a break period.

Not many instances are known of co-operation between public libraries and works libraries. There are libraries in some towns which fulfil both functions: in Cologne and Munich the public library service has its mobiles visiting certain firms under special agreements. Some factories have recently closed their works libraries, and have continued to run only their research libraries. In some cases the stock of general books was offered to the local public library. The reasons for this action have been moves towards rationalisation, and the running-down of voluntary social services in the face of deteriorating business conditions. The number of firms involved has so far been insignificant, but they have included the well-known Krupp library.

Since 1956 there has existed an Arbeitsgemeinschaft Werkbüchereien für das Bundesgebiet und Berlin e. V. ("Association of Works Libraries for the Federal Republic and Berlin"), with groups in each Land, which concerns itself particularly with the training of works librarians. It publishes its own information bulletin, "Werkbüchereiarbeit".

2.85   Hospital Libraries

We use the term "hospital libraries" to denote general libraries for the use of patients, as distinct from the special medical libraries. According to figures in the "Deutsches Krankenhausadressbuch 1966", there were 3,600 public and private hospitals in the Federal Republic in 1964, with a total of 19,000 beds. 10 per cent of publicly-supported hospitals, 42 per cent of Protestant institutions and 51 per cent of Catholic institutions possessed a library. Private hospitals are not covered by the statistics. The number of hospital libraries should not be allowed to obscure the fact that German hospital library services are in a very unsatisfactory state. With few exceptions, they have no full-time staff, or even any with professional training; they are inadequately housed; and bookstocks are insufficient.

According to the 1969 annual statistics for 7 large, professionally-staffed hospital libraries (the figures are supplied by the Arbeitsstelle für das Büchereiwesen) only 4 towns have hospital libraries with about 5,000 volumes and upwards: Bremen, Düsseldorf, Hamburg and Munich. In Munich 10 hospital libraries in all come for organisational purposes under the care of the central office of the Stadtbüchereien. The above-mentioned 7 libraries achieved on an average 24.4 issues per bed per year out of a stock of 5 volumes per bed per year.

Although the majority of hospital libraries still exist in isolation and thanks to the initiative of individual hospital administrations, a number of central organisations have in recent years given such libraries increasing attention. For example, the Arbeitskreis Krankenhausbüchereien

("Hospital Libraries Committee") has been established under the auspices
of the Arbeitsstelle für das Büchereiwesen, and the Beratungsstelle für
Krankenlektüre und Krankenhausbüchereien ("Advisory Office for Sick
Persons' Reading and Hospital Libraries") at the Medizinische und
Nervenklinik of the Justus Liebig University, Giessen. Both have had
some success in their efforts to resolve special problems and foster
hospital library development.

The work of the Arbeitskreis has resulted in the "Richtlinien für Krankenhausbüchereien" ("Guidelines for Hospital Libraries"). The Richtlinien,
having regard to conditions in Germany and international standards,
recommend a stock of 4 volumes per bed for general hospitals, and 5
volumes per bed for institutions with long-term patients, small hospitals
with under 200 beds, and childrens' wards. The library should have
separate accommodation, and when catering for over 700 beds should
employ a qualified librarian and a junior. The service should concentrate
on a personal bedside loan service once a week, besides lending on its
own premises to hospital staff and patients able to walk.

A hospital library is recommended to aim it issues of at least 15 volumes.
and as high as 40 volumes, per bed per year. The Richtlinien recommend,
as the best solution, that the hospital administration should place the
local public library in charge of the establishment and operation of the
hospital library, while itself retaining responsibility for the service and
meeting the costs. At the very least, there should be an attempt to work
closely with the public library and to take advantage of its inter-library
loan facilities. This connection already exists in some towns, for example
Düsseldorf, Mannheim, Munich and Saarbrücken. Munich has so far gone
furthest towards fulfilling the requirements of the Richtlinien.

Book selection is of special importance in hospital libraries, since the
books are intended not only for recreation, education and passing the
time, but also as something to complement and reinforce the hospitals'
treatment: the term "bibliotheraphy" has been used. The Beratungsstelle für Krankenlektüre und Krankenhausbüchereien in Giessen is
conducting research into the effect and significance of reading. It compiles
lists of recommended reading for sick persons, which are published in
several journals. The Arbeitskreis Krankenhausbüchereien has also
compiled stock lists for hospital libraries.

Despite the high demands made on a hospital librarian, no special training for the work is yet available in the Federal Republic.

2.86 Prison Libraries

The ministries of justice of the Länder have responsibility for the carrying out of court sentences; hence the establishment and maintenance of prison libraries is also a duty of these Land authorities, and they have issued instructions for the purpose. All prisons now have libraries for the prisoners. These libraries, run by teachers, prison staff or clergy — sometimes with the assistance of inmates — vary in size and quality, but are rarely adequate in either respect. They are better developed in prisons for men serving longer sentences. Stocks are quite often supplemented by gifts from prisoners' aid organisations. There are no special regulations about book selection.

Only a few public libraries have any links with prison libraries. Co-operation with the Staatliche Büchereistellen has not yet progressed very far, even where — as in North Rhine-Westphalia — it is recommended in the instructions of the Ministry of Justice.

In Hamburg, where the Fachstelle der Hamburger Öffentlichen Bücher-hallen has ever since the fifties been giving professional advice to institutions for young offenders, there is now a definite pattern of professional oversight of the libraries in penal institutions, which do not belong directly to the public library sector. This consists of reorganising and standardising the existing arrangements in the 11 penal institutions, linking their libraries with the internal interlending system of the Bücherhallen, supplementing their book stocks with the aid of annotated reading lists compiled by the Fachstelle, and arranging for their books to be centrally processed by the staff of the Fachstelle. Since 1970 there has been a special section at the Fachstelle concerned with the work involved in the administration of the libraries in the penal institutions, for example, the compilation of a union catalogue for all such libraries.

2.87 Libraries for the Blind

There are a number of libraries in the Federal Republic with the special task of providing books for its 40,000 or so blind people. In a few cases these are special libraries belonging to the public library system of large towns, but the bigger libraries are institutions of more than local coverage. Some still work exclusively with books in the dotted script developed by Louis Braille, while others depend wholly or partly on the new means of communication represented by sound recordings, and are hence described as "listening libraries for the blind". The predominant means of lending books and tape-recordings is by post, the more so since there are no postal charges for material for the blind.

Marburg is a centre for the education of the blind. Blind people can obtain a secondary education at the Marburger Studienanstalt, and there is also an advisory office there for blind students. The Marburger Hochschulbücherei, with a stock of about 50,000 volumes, specialises in books for the blind which are of scholarly value or in other languages than German. The Studienanstalt has a publishing-house for the blind attached to it, which issues books in Braille.

Hamburg has the Centralbibliothek für Blinde with a stock of over 40,000 volumes and a noteworthy music section with more than 25,000 scores. It lends its stock free of charge inside Germany and to other countries. Libraries with books in Braille also exist in Essen, Karlsruhe, Cologne, Münster, Stuttgart, and Hanover — where there is, besides, a special centre for the procurement of musical scores for the blind. The Roman Catholic Borromäusverein in Bonn also maintains a central library for the blind.

The development of tape-recording techniques led to the establishment of "listening libraries for the blind" in Marburg (1953), Münster (1955), and later in Berlin, Hamburg, Saarbrücken, Stuttgart and Munich. These seven libraries each serve as central libraries for the blind in a particular region. They are maintained by registered associations, which depend for support on organisations for the blind, local authorities and state contributions. In addition to the seven tape libraries, which form the Arbeitsgemeinschaft Deutscher Blindenhörbüchereien ("Association of German Listening Libraries for the Blind"), the library for the blind attached to the Essen public library also possesses a "listening library".

The question of copyright has created certain problems in the work of the "listening libraries". Under an agreement with the Börsenverein des Deutschen Buchhandels, only 30 copies of a work can be recorded, and these may only be used by the totally blind — in other words, not by the partially-sighted. Each library will therefore have, on average, only four or five copies. Of the seven libraries, those in Munich and Saarbrücken have so far produced no book recordings of their own. The rest agree among themselves on which of them should record a particular title. The Münster library records, besides books, the weekly paper "Die Zeit" and two bimonthly special journals for the blind.

2.9   German Libraries in Other Countries

To end this chapter we must look briefly at a number of German libraries in other countries. There are two distinct types of library in question: the strictly academic libraries, dealing in the manner of special libraries with archaeology, history, the history of art, or Oriental studies; and the cultural establishments entitled *Goethe-Institut* or *Kulturinstitut*, which most nearly resemble public libraries.

The first group is a small one, consisting of the following: the libraries of the seven branches of the Deutsches Archäologisches Institut in Athens, Baghdad, Istanbul, Cairo, Madrid, Rome and Teheran; the library of the Kunsthistorisches Institut in Florence; the library of the Orient-Institut in Beirut, belonging to the Deutsche Morgenländische Gesellschaft zu Mainz; the Bibliotheca Hertziana in Rome (for the history of art); and the library of the Deutsches Historisches Institut in Rome, with a separate musical department. Of the two libraries for art history, that in Rome forms one of the institutes of the Max-Planck-Gesellschaft, and that in Florence is maintained by an association. Some of the other libraries come under the Federal Ministry of the Interior, some under the Federal Ministry for Education and Research.

The four Italian libraries are the oldest, all dating from the nineteenth century. Thanks to the intercession of Italian and other foreign scholars, they were returned to German hands after the war and financed by Unesco from 1948 to 1951. All have the characteristics of specialist academic libraries. Their special position is a result of their location in another country: the emphasis of their acquisitions policies is on links and points of contact between scholarship in Germany and the country in question, in archaeology, the history of art, history and Oriental studies. They thus become places where German and other researchers work together, or meet regularly. They normally have a classified arrangement, allow free access to books and catalogues, and, in principle, do not lend.

The second group of libraries — those of the *Goethe-* and *Kulturinstitute* — are, on the contrary, basically intended for use by the host country's own citizens. Their essential reason for existence is to act as a means of contact with the whole intellectual and cultural life of the Federal Republic, and it is for this purpose that the activities of the institutes are mounted — and with the libraries as their most important instrument.

The needs of scholarship are not forgotten, but they are not strictly academic institutions.

All these libraries have been founded since the last war. They fall ultimately within the sphere of the Foreign Ministry, which did in fact establish the first institutes, but later placed them under the control of the Goethe-Institut in Munich and transferred the care of the libraries to Inter Nationes. There are at present about 180 of these institutes (60 in Europe, 48 in Asia, 40 in South and Central America, 20 in Africa and 11 in North America); about 20 more are being established. There are in addition a large number of libraries belonging to societies and associations of Germans living abroad, set up and run in collaboration with the people of the country concerned, with similar aims; but these are only mentioned in passing.

The character of their stock is on much the same basic lines everywhere, with individual modifications to meet the special requirements of the country and the local library situation. Only recently (April 1968), a list of about 3,000 books in German, with a total value of about 75,000 DM, has been prepared by Inter Nationes. It is intended for the new Goethe-Institut in Manchester, but also simultaneously as a kind of model list which can be altered according to local circumstances. It contains a varied selection of books from all fields of the humanities and social sciences, bibliographical aids, a full range of literary works and a limited number of mathematical, scientific and technical publications.

The majority of the libraries cater for reading on the premises and loans in the immediate locality; some do not lend at all. It is taken as a matter of course that they should have a comprehensible classified arrangement with appropriate accommodation, clear catalogues and simple issue procedures — all modelled on public library practice. Their librarians must be good linguists and well acquainted with cultural affairs (especially library matters) in the Federal Republic. An important part of their job is to provide reference and information services. The Bibliotheka-rische Auslandsstelle (cf. 3.22) counts it as one of its functions to maintain and strengthen these libraries' contacts with the library scene in Germany.

Further Reading

Much has been published about all the types of library dealt with in this chapter and about many individual libraries. We have restricted our citations to a limited number of items published after 1945, giving preference to those which offer comprehensive surveys of their field.

Academic libraries

For information on the various types of academic library, their present state and desirable development in the future:

Empfehlungen des Wissenschaftsrates zum Ausbau der wissenschaftlichen Einrichtungen. Teil 2. Wissenschaftliche Bibliotheken. Bonn 1964.

To supplement this, there are the statements made by representatives of the various types of libraries at the Bibliothekarstagung ("Conference of Librarians") in 1964, all of which are printed in the Zeitschrift für Bibliothekswesen und Bibliographie (ZfBB) 11 (1964): university libraries (Fritz Redenbacher, p. 252—263); technical university libraries (Paul Kaegbein, p. 263—271); Landesbibliotheken and municipal academic libraries (Wilhelm Totok, p. 271—275); and special libraries (Norbert Fischer, p. 287—290).

Central general academic libraries

The postwar development of the three great libraries in Frankfurt, Berlin/Marburg and Munich, has been treated in a few general accounts, as well as in short reports and, to some extent, in annual reports.

Frankfurt

Die Deutsche Bibliothek 1945—1965. Festgabe für Hanns Wilhelm Eppelsheimer zum 75. Geburtstag. Frankfurt 1966 (ZfBB, Sonderheft 3).

Bibliographie und Buchhandel. Festschrift zur Einweihung des Neubaus der Deutschen Bibliothek. Hrsg. vom Ausschuß für Bibliographie und Bibliotheksfragen beim Börsenverein des deutschen Buchhandels. Frankfurt 1959.

Berlin/Marburg

Wilhelm Witte: Die Staatsbibliothek. In: Jahrbuch der Stiftung Preußischer Kulturbesitz 1962. Köln und Berlin 1963. p. 264—293.

Munich

Heinrich Middendorf: Die Bayerische Staatsbibliothek 1945—1964. In: Buch und Welt. Festschrift für Gustav Hofmann zum 65. Geburtstag. Wiesbaden 1965. p. 7—61 (with a detailed table of statistics);

Irmgard Bezzel: Bayerische Staatsbibliothek München. Bibliotheksführer. Geschichte und Bestände. München 1967. A second part, intended as a practical reader's guide, is in preparation.

Staatsbibliotheken and Landesbibliotheken

Basic problems connected with the Landesbibliotheken are examined in:

Heinrich Ihme: Landesbibliothek und Landesgeschichte. In: In Libro Humanitas. Festschrift für Wilhelm Hoffmann zum 60. Geburtstag. Stuttgart 1962. p. 94—111.

Die Landesbibliothek und ihre Aufgaben im Bibliothekssystem des Landes was the title of two papers given by Hans M. Meyer and Lorenz Drehmann at the annual conference of the Verband der Bibliotheken des Landes Nordrhein-Westfalen, which were published in the Mitteilungsblatt of the Verband, 20 (1970), p. 16—31, 31—39.

University libraries

University and institute libraries have been the subject of many lively discussions in the last 15 years. The two memoranda of the Deutsche Forschungsgemeinschaft have been referred to in the text. They are:

Instituts- und Hochschulbibliotheken. Deutsche Forschungsgemeinschaft 1955. Empfehlungen für die Zusammenarbeit zwischen Hochschulbibliothek und Institutsbibliotheken. 1970.

The former was preceded by:

Gerhard Reincke: Gutachten über die Lage der Institutsbibliotheken und ihr Verhältnis zu den Universitäts- und Hochschulbibliotheken. Im Auftrage der Deutschen Forschungsgemeinschaft 1953.

The present shape of the dual university library system is traced from its origins by:

Carl Wehmer: The Organization and Origins of German University Libraries. Library Trends 12 (1964), p. 491—512.

The working of the system in practice, and possible ways of improving it, are outlined and examined in:

Wilhelm Grunwald: Kooperation Universitätsbibliothek — Universität. Mittellungsblatt. Verband der Bibliotheken des Landes Nordrhein-Westfalen 17 (1967), p. 131—141.

On the special question of *selection policies*, there is an interesting comparison between German and American libraries:

J. Periam Danton: Book Selection and Collections: a Comparison of German and American University Libraries. New York & London 1963 (cf. the review by Gisela von Busse: Buchauswahl und Aufbau der Bestände in deutschen und amerikanischen Universitätsbibliotheken. Libri 14 (1964), p. 62—75).

Discussion has been sparked off afresh by the *new universities*, and is still being carried on. A report on the differing status of the main library within the university, according to newly-established or drafted university laws, is given by Günther Pflug: Die Stellung der Hochschulbibliothek in den Gesetzen, Entwürfen und Empfehlungen zur Hochschulreform. ZfBB 16 (1969), p. 245—

262. Some insight into the controversy about the proposals for Bielefeld may be gained from the Mitteilungsblatt des Verbandes der Bibliotheken des Landes Nordrhein-Westfalen. In this, a supporter of the planned Bielefeld structure appears in print with detailed explanations (Günther Pflug, Mittbl. 17 [1967], p. 141—157), as does an opponent (Hartwig Lohse, Mittbl. 18 [1968], p. 39—50). The latter number also contains a counter-statement based on deliberations of the Direktorenkonferenz der Hochschulbibliotheken ("Conference of University Librarians") of the Land and the committee of the Verband der Bibliotheken des Landes Nordrhein-Westfalen:

Werner Krieg: Zu den Plänen der Struktur der Universität Bielefeld. p. 14—39. The arguments for and against are finally summed up by Joachim Stoltzenburg: Zentralisierung und Dezentralisierung in Entwurf und Gegenentwurf für ein Bibliothekssystem der Universität Bielefeld. Mittbl. 18 (1969), p. 93—111.

The Arbeitsgemeinschaft der Hochschulbibliotheken has been foremost in its efforts to clarify the situation. The first reflections on the topic as a whole have been:

Friedrich Adolf Schmidt-Künsemüller: Um die Zukunft der Universitätsbibliothek. ZfBB 15 (1968), p. 107—115.

Guidance on the subject of *text-book collections* and *students' libraries* is provided by:

Clemens Köttelwesch: Die Lehrbuchsammlung in deutschen Bibliotheken. ZfBB 14 (1967), p. 73—82;

Werner Schulz: Studentenbüchereien in Deutschland. ZfBB 7 (1960), p. 110—126.

Libraries of colleges of education

These are dealt with by Nikolaus Koch in:

Das pädagogische Bibliothekswesen in Deutschland. Hrsg. N. Koch und R. Renard. T. 3. Bibliotheken an Pädagogischen Hochschulen. München 1965.

Central specialist libraries

An account of the central specialist libraries is given in connection with the measures taken by the Deutsche Forschungsgemeinschaft to foster their growth:

Martin Cremer: Zentrale Fachbibliotheken. In: Fünfzehn Jahre Bibliotheksarbeit der Deutschen Forschungsgemeinschaft 1949—1964. Frankfurt 1966 (ZfBB, Sonderheft 4), p. 71—77;
Dieter Oertel: Der Aufbau zentraler Fachbibliotheken in der Bundesrepublik Deutschland. ZfBB 13 (1966), p. 322—330.

Special libraries

Special libraries are one of the few forms of academic library which receive a special chapter in the Handbuch der Bibliothekswissenschaft:

Norbert Fischer: Die Spezialbibliotheken. Bd 2, p. 555—632.

General discussions on special libraries take place chiefly at the meetings of their own Arbeitsgemeinschaft. We may mention:

Günther Reichardt: Die wissenschaftlichen Spezialbibliotheken im Rahmen des deutschen Bibliothekswesens. In: Arbeitsgemeinschaft technischer und wirtschaftlicher Bibliotheken. Bericht über die 8. Tagung. Essen 1962. p. 29—54.

Two recent works on *educational libraries* have been referred to in the text. Besides the book mentioned above — Das pädagogische Bibliothekswesen in Deutschland, edited by N. Koch and R. Renard — the following is significant for future developments:

Gutachten zur Struktur des pädagogischen Bibliotheks- und Dokumentationswesens. Arbeitsgemeinschaft pädagogischer Bibliotheken. Dortmund 1967.

Parliamentary and government libraries

This type of library is among those covered in the chapter by Norbert Fischer on special libraries, already mentioned. The following is devoted exclusively to the subject:

Fritz Prinzhorn: Eigenart und Bedeutung der Parlaments- und Behördenbibliotheken. In: Aus der Welt des Bibliothekars. Festschrift für Rudolf Juchhoff zum 65. Geburtstag. Köln 1959. p. 293—307.

Public libraries and the Staatliche Büchereistellen

The Festschrift for Rudolf Juchhoff, cited above, contains a fundamental article on the function of the academic Stadtbibliotheken:

Wolfgang van der Briele: Die wissenschaftliche Stadtbibliothek heute. Probleme und Erfahrungen. p. 308—324.

A look at future developments is given by:

Jürgen Busch: Die wissenschaftliche Stadtbibliothek — heute und morgen. ZfBB 11 (1964), p. 276—286.

It was being pointed out as early as 1955 that the Stadtbibliotheken, like the Einheitsbüchereien and the local authority public libraries, will face new tasks in meeting the demands of the population in large industrial areas:

Wilhelm Bayer: Aufgaben und Probleme der allgemeinwissenschaftlichen Bibliotheken in Industriebezirken. ZfBB 2 (1955), p. 292—307.

The most recent survey on the state of integration and organisational structure of the local authority library services in large towns is Alois Klotzbücher: Die sogenannte Einheitsbücherei. Formen der Integration und Zentralisation der wissenschaftlichen Stadtbibliothek und der öffentlichen Bücherei. Untersuchungen zur Entwicklung und Organisationsstruktur der sogenannten Einheitsbücherei. Köln 1969. (Arbeiten aus dem BLI des Landes Nordrhein-Westfalen, H. 33.)

On *public libraries*, essential contributions appear in the Handbuch des Büchereiwesens (2. Halbband. Wiesbaden 1965), which have already been mentioned in connection with the historical survey in Chapter 1:

Ludwin Langenfeld: Buchauswahl und Bestanderschließung;

Gustav Rottacker: Büchereigesetze und Büchereiverbände;

Rudolf Joerden: Das Büchereiwesen der Stadt;

Wilhelm Hoppe: Das Büchereiwesen auf dem Lande.

Recent contributions (Festschrift Wilhelm Schmitz-Veltin. Die Öffentliche Bibliothek. Auftrag und Verwirklichung. Berlin 1968):

Hansjörg Süberkrüb: Die Öffentliche Bibliothek. Aufgabe, Politik, Zukunft (p. 31—56), and

Adolf von Morzé: Wird es eine Öffentliche Bücherei von morgen geben? Institut und Beruf in der Perspektive von gestern und heute (p. 57—84).

Current conceptions of the shape of public library services in large towns are expressed in:

Rolf Kluth: Strukturmodell eines voll ausgebauten großstädtischen Büchereisystems. Kulturarbeit 13 (1961), p. 36—40.

The establishment of the Amerika-Gedenkbibliothek, the central library of West Berlin, was a milestone in the history of city public library services in the Federal Republic. A full account is given in:

Fritz Moser: Die Amerika-Gedenkbibliothek Berlin: Entstehung, Gestalt und Wirken einer öffentlichen Zentralbibliothek. Wiesbaden 1965 (Beiträge zum Buch- und Bibliothekswesen 13).

Individual towns and Staatliche Büchereistellen publish their own annual reports. Examples are given in Chapter 8.

A very attractive comparative study, with many pictures, statistics, plans and a brief text is:

Büchereien in Dänemark und Schleswig-Holstein, published in 1966 in connection with an exhibition.

A complementary account is:

Erik Wilkens und Volker Weimar: Das Büchereiwesen in den Landkreisen Schleswig-Holsteins. Flensburg — Rendsburg 1963.

Written from the viewpoint of the Land of Lower Saxony is:

Karl-Heinz Schulze: Die Kreisbücherei und ihre Aufgaben. In: mb. Mitteilungsblatt des öffentlichen Büchereiwesens in Niedersachsen, Heft 10 (1967), p. 2—20.

In chapter 3.14 we examine more closely the Modell eines Aufbauplanes für Landkreise.

This forms appendix 11 in the publication:

Grundlagen für die bibliothekarische Regionalplanung. Wiesbaden 1966 (Beiträge zum Büchereiwesen. Reihe A. Bd 5).

On mobile libraries in town and country, there is a standard account, supplemented with tables and illustrations, in:

Horst Buschendorf: Fahrbücherei. Begriff — Aufgabe — Arbeitsmethode. Berlin 1967 (Bibliotheksdienst, Beiheft 25/26). Technical and organisational data in this publication were brought up to date in: Fahrbüchereien 1969. Technische und organisatorische Daten von 79 Fahrbüchereien in der BRD. Berlin 1969. (Bibliotheksdienst, Beiheft 45).

The work of the *Staatliche Büchereistellen*, dealt with in Wilhelm Hoppe's contribution to the Handbuch des Büchereiwesens (cited above), is described also in a series of articles:

Carl Jansen: Die Staatlichen Büchereistellen der Bundesrepublik. In: Bücherei und Bildung 19 (1967), p. 470—478; 20 (1968), p. 204—209, 621—628; and 21 (1969), p. 345—349. So far the Länder of Bavaria, Lower Saxony, Rhineland Palatinate and the Saarland have been treated.

Denominational libraries

Comprehensive reports on the history and present state of *denominational academic libraries* are given by

Ernst Wolf: Kirchliches Bibliothekswesen. In: Die Religion in Geschichte und Gegenwart. I (1959), p. 1255 f.

Hermann Erbacher: Schatzkammern des Wissens. Ein Beitrag zur Geschichte der kirchlichen Bibliotheken. Neustadt a. d. Aisch 1966.

Library problems and activities from the viewpoint of the Roman Catholic Church are treated in the Mitteilungsblatt der Arbeitsgemeinschaft katholisch-theologischer Bibliotheken. Selbstverlag; we mention especially: Wilhelm Schönartz: Notwendigkeit und Aufgaben eines eigenen kirchlichen Bibliothekswesens. 17 (1970), p. 71—119.

The most complete information will be contained in the Handbuch des kirchlichen Bibliothekswesens. Hrsg. von Hans Werner Seidel. In preparation, to be published in 1971.

Standard accounts of *denominational public library* work are the contributions to the Handbuch des Büchereiwesens:

Leo Koep und Alfons Vodermayer: Die katholischen Volksbüchereien in Deutschland. (2. Halbband. p. 421—490).

Rudolf Rüppel: Das evangelische Büchereiwesen. (2. Halbband. p. 387—420).

Important for Catholic libraries are:

Werkhefte zur Büchereiarbeit. Hrsg. vom Borromäusverein;

Beiträge zur katholischen Büchereiarbeit. Hrsg. von der Bundesarbeitsgemeinschaft der katholisch-kirchlichen Büchereiarbeit in Verbindung mit dem Borromäusverein;

Werkhefte für die katholischen Volksbüchereien des St. Michaelsbundes.

Protestant library practice is described in:

Leitfaden für die Verwaltung evangelischer Büchereien. Hrsg. vom Deutschen Verband Evangelischer Büchereien. 2. Aufl. Göttingen 1966.

Also in:

Herbert Reich: Die Gemeindebücherei. Gütersloh 1968.

The papers presented at the Tutzing meeting, with their accounts of denominational library work, are to be found in:

Der Bildungsauftrag der Öffentlichen Bücherei. München 1965.

Libraries for children and young people   ˎ

Of fundamental importance is the memorandum by the Deutscher Büchereiverband and its Arbeitsstelle für das Büchereiwesen:

Büchereiarbeit mit Kindern und Jugendlichen. Berlin 1964. (Druckschriften der Arbeitsstelle für das Büchereiwesen 3).

The survey in the Handbuch des Büchereiwesens is:

Friedrich Andrae: Jugendbüchereiwesen. (2. Halbband. p. 491—539).

In the same contribution, the author also deals with school libraries.

Papers of two conferences on childrens' literature and library work with children were published by the Deutscher Büchereiverband and its Arbeitsstelle für das Büchereiwesen: Jugendliteratur in der Bundesrepublik Deutschland. Berlin 1969. (Bibliotheksdienst, Beiheft 41);

Jugend und Buch. Berlin 1968. (Bibliotheksdienst, Beiheft 39).

School libraries

The state of school library services and their problems are described in two works already cited:

Das pädagogische Bibliothekswesen. München 1965;

Gutachten zur Struktur des pädagogischen Bibliotheks- und Dokumentationswesens. Dortmund 1967.

An evaluation of practical experiences in Germany and other countries is:

Ulrich Mallmann: Theorie und Praxis der Schulbüchereien. München 1966.

The recommendations of the Deutscher Städtetag on co-operation between schools and public libraries are printed in Bücherei und Bildung 13 (1961), p. 356—360.

The survey of school libraries in the Federal Republic carried out by a team from the Institut für Jugendbuchforschung at the University of Frankfurt culminates in a number of suggested standards for a model central school library. It has been published under the title: Die moderne Schulbibliothek Bestandsaufnahme und Modell. Gütersloh 1970.

Music Libraries

The contribution on music libraries in the Handbuch des Büchereiwesens covers their nature and functions, history, organisation, construction and working methods:

Alfons Ott: Die Musikbücherei. (2. Halbband. p. 568—576).

More recent are papers contained in:

Alfons Ott: Probleme der musikbibliothekarischen und musikbibliographischen Arbeit. Berlin 1967 (Bibliotheksdienst, Beiheft 23).

A. Ott, M. Willfort und E. Maschat: Musikbibliothekarische Arbeit und Arbeitsplanung. Berlin 1969. (Bibliotheksdienst, Beiheft 44).

Works Libraries

One book is of fundamental importance as a scholarly study of the development and significance of the works library:

Ulrich Birkholz: Geschichte und Probleme der Werkbücherei. Stuttgart 1959.

The first general survey of works library operations from the viewpoint of one running them is:

Kurt Busse: Handbuch der Werkbüchereien. München 1955. Its principal contents, still relevant today, deal chiefly with the position of a works library in a concern and outlines its special functions.

The article in the Handbuch des Büchereiwesens is:

Maria Gabriel: Werkbüchereien. (2. Halbband. p. 695—714).

Latest statistical data as well as addresses of 326 works libraries are to be found in Deutsche Werkbüchereien heute. Statistik, Anschriften, Büchereileiter. Bergisch-Gladbach 1969.

Libraries of the armed forces

Information on academic military libraries will be found in professional journals; we mention here:

Erwin Latzel: Der Aufbau der militärischen Fachbibliotheken ZfBB 7 (1960), p. 14—27;

Olof Wendt: Das Bibliothekswesen der Bundeswehr und die Behördenbibliotheken. Arbeitshefte. Arbeitsgemeinschaft der Parlaments- und Behördenbibliotheken. 20 (1966), p. 29—55;

Hermann Heidegger: Militärwissenschaft, Bibliothekswesen und Dokumentation. In: Taschenbuch für Wehrfragen. 1966/67. Frankfurt 1966. p. 249—254.

The article on soldiers' libraries in the Handbuch des Büchereiwesens gives an outline of their history and present state, and also of the recommendations on the subject by German public librarians in 1954:

Guido Geyer: Die Truppenbücherei. (2. Halbband. p. 653—672).

Hospital libraries

The contribution in the Handbuch des Büchereiwesens is:

Gertrud Gelderblom: Die Krankenhausbücherei. (2. Halbband, p. 589—627).

The Deutscher Büchereiverband and its Arbeitsstelle für das Büchereiwesen have published:

Richtlinien für Krankenhausbüchereien. Berlin 1967 (Bibliotheksdienst, Beiheft 20).

Basic discussions and accounts of the present position appear in the proceedings of the 3. Öffentliche Arbeitstagung für Krankenhausbüchereien ("3rd Open Conference on Hospital Libraries"), held in Düsseldorf in 1967:

Büchereiarbeit im Krankenhaus. Berlin 1967 (Bibliotheksdienst, Beiheft 29/30). On questions to do with "bibliotherapy", besides journal articles there is:

Karl Friedrich Euler: Krankenlektüre. Erfahrungen — Folgerungen — Ratschläge. Stuttgart 1964 (Schriftenreihe zur Theorie und Praxis der Psychotherapie).

Prison libraries

The article in the Handbuch des Büchereiwesens outlines the basic problems and the situation in Germany:

Gertrud Gelderblom: Die Gefängnisbücherei. (2. Halbband. p. 628—652).

Libraries for the blind

Libraries for Braille material and for tape-recordings are both covered in the article in the Handbuch des Büchereiwesens:

Hans Thiekötter: Die Blindenbücherei. (2. Halbband. p. 577—588).

Statistics

These are issued both as separate publications and in the various professional journals. Readers should refer to the survey in Chapter 8.

3 Library Co-operation and Central Organisations

3.1 Special Projects

All over the world today, especially in countries with highly-developed research, industrial and economic resources, plans are being drawn up for the effective unification and co-ordination of all library services. This has been forced upon us by the amount of material being published, the splitting-up of academic disciplines, their interaction to produce fresh fields of study, and the dependence on science shown in all aspects of life. In our short look back into history, we showed that the peculiar situation of German libraries, their disparity and variety, and the lack of a comprehensive national library, was by the beginning of this century already giving rise to such measures among academic libraries. Today, co-operation is being practised in acquisition schemes, cataloguing and inter-library loans over the entire area of the Federal Republic and for individual regions. Public, as well as academic libraries, are participating in some projects. Some regional schemes are based exclusively on the public libraries. More comprehensive proposals for co-operation in public library systems and library regions have been put forward, and their practicability is currently being studied.

3.11 Co-operative Acquisition Schemes

3.111 Co-operative Acquisition Programme of the Deutsche Forschungs-gemeinschaft

The co-operative acquisition programme of the Deutsche Forschungs-gemeinschaft, drawn up in 1949, is based on the tradition of the Not-gemeinschaft der deutschen Wissenschaft (cf. 1.52). The programme is intended to provide a planned supply of foreign publications to academic libraries and to ensure that there is at least one copy in existence and available in the Federal Republic of anything with significant research interest. 25 state and university libraries are participating in it, each of which has assumed responsibility for intensive coverage of one or more of the 117 subject fields into which the scheme is subdivided. The allocation scheme treats the whole sphere of research purely from the point of view of the practical convenience of libraries; a classification of knowledge is not intended. Some major disciplines, such as theology, medicine, geology and geography, have each been designated as a single special-collection field, while others — primarily the applied sciences and engineering — have been extensively subdivided. In the humanities and social sciences, a large group for "languages and cultures" has been designated, with numerous subdivisions. As a result the subject field of history, with some exceptions, excludes material related to a specific country or region.

The co-operative acquisition programme is a joint undertaking of the Forschungsgemeinschaft and the participating libraries. The expenditure involved is divided between the parties, on the basis that the libraries pay for the acquisition of German publications and the fundamental journals and monographs from other countries which are required everywhere, while the Forschungsgemeinschaft makes annual contributions, according to estimated requirements, for specialised journals and monographs from outside Germany. In 1965 the programme was confirmed in its present form by the libraries committee of the Forschungsgemeinschaft, after a thorough re-examination. Between 1949 and 1969 the Forschungsgemeinschaft has put up about 17 million DM for this purpose, to which should be added exchange material from other countries with a value equivalent to about 2 million DM. Annual contributions were 1,400,000 DM in 1969.

The libraries bear sole responsibility for the selection of monographic literature obtained with funds from the Forschungsgemeinschaft. From 1970 onwards the same principle has been adopted for periodicals, the selection of which had previously been decided by a subcommittee of the libraries committee. The only general criterion is that material should be acquired which is of importance for research in that particular field. Instructions have been drawn up to define the limits of each subject field. Acquisition is at present restricted to monographs and journals. Consideration is now being given as to whether, and to what extent, other types of material (e. g. newspapers) should be included in the programme. The large category of report literature is causing particular concern to the central specialist libraries, which supplement the co-operative acquisition programme in the more "applied" fields of technology, economics, agriculture and medicine (cf. 2.41). The programme covers all fields of knowledge, and material from all countries and in all languages. It has only been made fully comprehensive with the establishment of the central specialist libraries. Following the re-examination, however, certain fields (e. g. foreign law, meteorology, regional geology and recent military history) have been excluded because special libraries are now able to provide all the services required: those of the five Max Planck Institutes concerned with law, the Zentralamt des Deutschen Wetterdienstes ("Central Office of the German Meteorological Service") in Offenbach, the Bundesanstalt für Bodenforschung ("Federal Establishment for Soil Science") in Hanover, and the Bibliothek für Zeitgeschichte ("Library for Contemporary History") in Stuttgart.

From the outset, a condition for participation in the programme has been the willingness to make available the material acquired under it, quickly and without restrictions. In principle the participating libraries are general academic libraries taking part in the inter-library loan service.

The fact that the Forschungsgemeinschaft has provided central finance for the scheme is one of the reasons why it has been carried on in the same spirit for nearly 20 years, why the libraries feel a commitment to it, and why the intention of giving them a sense of community has been realised. This arrangement makes it easier for an individual library to take on an obligation above the regional level — and to justify this to the body maintaining it — and helps considerably in giving unity of form to the project. Scholars using any library benefit from the scheme, since the collections which it helps to build form a great pool of carefully selected scholarly material, on which anyone engaged in academic work can draw through his own library, regardless of whether or not it is taking part in the scheme.

3.112 The Co-operative Acquisition Scheme of the Large Town Public Libraries in North Rhine-Westphalia

The idea of a rationally organised pattern of library services in a single region is at the root of the Federal Republic's second co-operative acquisition undertaking: the co-operative acquisition scheme of the large town public libraries in the Land of North Rhine-Westphalia, founded in 1956. More than 20 municipal libraries have now joined the scheme. The material acquired is limited to German monographs in all fields of study, including fiction and musical scores. The intention is primarily to cover standard works and textbooks of scholarly value, while excluding highly-

specialised works. The allocation of special-collection fields is based on
the subject classification of the Deutsche Bibliographie; fiction is subdivided into language groups. Plans are being made to obtain coverage of
German learned journals.

Participating libraries are obliged to provide the bulk of the necessary
funds from their own budgets. Since 1960 the Land has made an annual
contribution to this enterprise undertaken by municipal institutions for
the benefit of all, and this money is distributed in accordance with the
proposals of the Verband der Bibliotheken des Landes Nordrhein-Westfalen ("Association of Libraries in the Land of North Rhine-Westphalia"). Catalogues of the material in special subject fields are being printed,
also with the financial assistance of the Land.

The purpose of this co-operative acquisition scheme is the systematic
building of holdings in scholarly material, which is a crucial precondition
for inter-library loan services between municipal libraries. The scheme
forms an important stage in the Land's plan for regional library development now taking shape. It has permitted a fruitful test of co-operation
between the Land, the municipal authorities and libraries — who in this
case took the initiative.

3.12 Union Catalogues

3.121 Regional Union Catalogues

The holdings of academic libraries in the Federal Republic are today
recorded in these seven regional union catalogues:

Zentralkatalog Baden-Württemberg	in Stuttgart (LB)
Bayerischer Zentralkatalog	in Munich (SB)
Hessischer Zentralkatalog	in Frankfurt (StUB)
Niedersächsischer Zentralkatalog	in Göttingen (SUB)
Norddeutscher Zentralkatalog	
(for Hamburg, Bremen and Schleswig-Holstein)	in Hamburg (SUB)
Zentralkatalog Nordrhein-Westfalen	in Cologne (UStB)
Berliner Gesamtkatalog (for West Berlin)	in Berlin (UB
	der Freien Universität)

The libraries in the Rhineland Palatinate and the Saarland are covered by
the catalogues in either Stuttgart, Frankfurt or Cologne.

The catalogues were started from scratch after the war: only the Hessischer Zentralkatalog could be continued from the older "Frankfurter Sammelkatalog", dating from 1891. They were begun partly on the initiative of the libraries themselves, partly due to initial help from the Forschungsgemeinschaft, which was given to all seven catalogues from 1956 to 1958 and was renewed, as development assistance, from 1965 to 1968.

The first phase — the compilation of the catalogues from the separate catalogues of the libraries taking part — has now been largely completed. The method used has been microfilming, followed by re-enlargement. New acquisitions, as they arrive, are notified by libraries to their union catalogue, on catalogue cards. This means that a union catalogue, like any ordinary library catalogue, requires constant maintenance. The second phase was begun in 1962 with work to fit the union catalogues for their main function — the routing of inter-library loan requests. The new inter-library loan regulations of 1966 have laid down the precise role of the union catalogues.

There are some practical reasons, among others, why a single, all-embracing union catalogue was not established in the reorganisation after 1945 — corresponding to the earlier Preußischer (subsequently Deutscher) Gesamtkatalog. The regional principle was preferred, firstly, since the same principle was being made the basis of the new interlending arrangements; secondly, there was reluctance to tackle the mammoth task which a single catalogue would soon present; and finally, it was easiest to ensure long-term financing at the level of the Länder.

There have been initial successes in the regional recording of public library holdings in North Rhine-Westphalia and in the areas covered by individual Staatliche Büchereistellen. In North Rhine-Westphalia, in conjunction with the co-operative acquisition agreements and the Kommunaler Leihring ("Lending Circle of Local Authority Libraries"), catalogues are published annually listing the material acquired under the scheme. Full lists are also published of material in the special-collection fields of individual libraries. Efforts are at present being made to get these holdings in special fields recorded in the Land union catalogue, so as to make them accessible to a wide circle of libraries outside the Kommunaler Leihring, and thus bring about their more intensive use.

Probably the majority of Staatliche Büchereistellen possess duplicates of the card catalogues for public libraries in their area. In the Büchereizentralen of Flensburg and Rendsburg there are also union catalogues, which give a complete picture of the entire stocks in the municipal libraries served by them; public libraries of the large towns are not included. In addition, the Büchereizentrale of Flensburg some years ago published a printed union catalogue for non-fiction, and has since kept it up-to-date by cumulations and supplements.

3.122 Other Union Catalogues and Union Lists

There are certain categories of material for which catalogues exist giving the holdings of all the academic libraries in the Federal Republic. We list these below.

The *"Gesamtverzeichnis ausländischer Zeitschriften und Serien (GAZS)"* ("Union list of foreign journals and series") is compiled by the Staatsbibliothek Preußischer Kulturbesitz. It contains an alphabetical list of journals from other countries received currently by West German academic libraries since 1939. The number of regularly contributing libraries is around 130; the holdings of many smaller libraries are also included to some extent. The main body of GAZS, for the years 1939–1958, has just been completed; it lists about 53,000 different journals. Work is in progress on supplements. The enterprise has been supported from the outset by the Forschungsgemeinschaft.

A similar list, the *"Gesamtverzeichnis deutscher Zeitschriften und Serien (GDZS)"* ("Union list of German journals and series"), likewise compiled by the Staatsbibliothek Preußischer Kulturbesitz, has been in course of preparation since 1969. It will contain the holdings of German periodicals in West German libraries from the beginning up to the present day.

The next two union catalogues, which were founded to meet the needs of the immediate post-war period, and were for years important sources for the identification and location of material, have now been discontinued.

"Verzeichnis von Zeitschriftenbeständen und Serienwerken aus den Gebieten: Technik, Naturwissenschaften, Medizin, Wirtschafts-, Rechts- und Staatswissenschaften (TWZ)" ("List of journal holdings and series in technology, science, medicine, economics, law and political science"). Six volumes published in duplicated form in 1956 by the Arbeitsgemeinschaft der technischen und wirtschaftlichen Bibliotheken ("Association of Technical and Industrial Libraries").

"Zentralkatalog der ausländischen Literatur (ZKA)" ("Union catalogue of foreign literature"). A monthly list of books published abroad since 1939, acquired by German libraries since 1945. Cologne, 1951–1959;

also the two multiannual catalogues: Zentralkatalog ausländischer Literatur (ZKA). 1. Erwerbungen 1945–1950. Bd 1–4. Göttingen 1951; and 2. Erwerbungen der Jahre 1951–1954. Bd 1–3. Köln 1955. This catalogue was at first compiled by the Staats- und Universitätsbibliothek Göttingen with assistance from the Forschungsgemeinschaft, and subsequently as a self-supporting venture of the union catalogue in Cologne, edited under the supervision of Rudolf Juchhoff.

The *"Gesamtverzeichnis russischer und sowjetischer Periodika und Serienwerke (GRP)"* ("Union list of Russian and Soviet periodicals and series") records the holdings of 305 libraries, up to and including the year 1956. It is being compiled by the Osteuropa-Institut of the Free University in Berlin, with the support of the Forschungsgemeinschaft. Publication of this catalogue, which has been appearing in fascicules, is now almost complete.

A *"Zeitschriftenverzeichnis westdeutscher Kunstbibliotheken"* ("List of journals in West German art libraries") — planned by the Arbeitsgemeinschaft der Kunstbibliotheken ("Study Group of Art Libraries") — is ready for printing. Editorial headquarters are at the Kunstbibliothek in Berlin. The holdings of journals on the history of art in about 40 libraries are recorded in their entirety. The list is to be published, and is being supported by the Forschungsgemeinschaft.

An *"Auswählendes Standortverzeichnis deutscher Zeitungen"* ("Select location index of German newspapers") in preparation since 1965 is in the press, as a project of the Kommission für Zeitungsfragen ("Committee on Newspapers") of the Verein Deutscher Bibliothekare, with assistance from the Forschungsgemeinschaft. It covers the period 1700–1966. Selection is restricted to important newspapers, taking into account places of publication. Editorial headquarters are at the Staatsbibliothek Bremen.

A *"Verzeichnis der Nachlässe in deutschen Archiven und Bibliotheken"* ("List of collections of personal papers in German archives and libraries") lists the manuscript collections of personal papers held by archives and libraries in the Federal Republic. It is a joint undertaking by archivists and librarians, compiled by W. Mommsen (Bundesarchiv, Koblenz) and L. Denecke (Murhardsche und Landes-Bibliothek, Kassel) and financed by the Forschungsgemeinschaft. Teil 1, archives, was published in 1970, Teil 2, libraries, in 1969. This list is being supplemented by an index to all autograph material in the collections, including entries for the authors of correspondence contained in the collections of personal papers. This

Zentralkartei der Autographen, which will be only in card form, has been established at the Staatsbibliothek Preußischer Kulturbesitz with the support of the Forschungsgemeinschaft.

3.13 Inter-Library Loans

3.131 The National Inter-Library Loan System

Before co-operative schemes for libraries are drawn up, a natural form of practical mutual assistance usually already exists: that of one library lending books from its stock to another library for the use of the latter's readers. In Germany, this procedure was being regulated as early as 1893, although then only in Prussia. The first Prussian "Leihverkehrs-ordnung (LVO)" ("Set of loan regulations") of 1893 was expanded in 1910 and replaced in 1924 by new regulations applying to the whole ter-ritory of the Reich. These remained in force, in their altered form of 1st January 1931, until May 1945.

The present regulations for the inter-library loan system in the Federal Republic (Leihverkehr der deutschen Bibliotheken) took effect in 1966. They replace the LVO of 1951, which already contained some of the trends now established. The 1966 regulations, like all their predeces-sors, were drawn up by librarians. Drafting was done by two committees of the Verein Deutscher Bibliothekare — for reader services and for the union catalogues respectively — and the membership as a whole was involved in the question through circulars, reports and discussions at the annual meetings. Approval was given at the assembly of the Verein Deutscher Bibliothekare in 1965; the Ständige Konferenz der Kultusmini-ster (cf. 1.54) recommended them to the Länder for acceptance in January 1966; and the regulations were put into force in each Land separately in the early months of 1966.

The purpose of the national inter-library loan system conforms to an established tradition: it is to serve "the advancement of research, teaching and other activities of scholarship". The scholar should be able to carry on his work wherever he is, and the libraries must see that he can do so. The general reader is referred to the public libraries and the interloan facilities which they offer under regional arrangements.

The purpose of the loan system for scholarly material has implications both for the type of libraries participating and for the kind of material

9 Hanover:
Stadtbüchereien
Hannover, Branch
library
at Hannover-
Ricklingen

10 Bremen:
Volksbüchereien der
Freien Hansestadt
Bremen, Youth and
School Library in
Graubündener
Straße

11 Bad Friedrichs-
hall: pop. 9,800,
Kreis Heilbronn,
Stadtbücherei

12   Wolfenbüttel: Herzog-August-Bibliothek, converted modern exhibition room

to be lent. The system is operated by those libraries open to the public whose holdings are primarily of a scholarly nature; by special libraries not open to the public; and by municipal public libraries "if they are administered by qualified staff". This last group was included for the first time in the new regulations of 1951, and with its inclusion the old basic principle of complete reciprocity, well established for inter-library lending in Germany, was abandoned: the municipal public libraries are preponderantly recipients, not lenders of material under the system. Their incorporation into the system met with criticism, but was necessary in view of the social and economic changes after 1945. Not every library within these categories can join the system unconditionally: formal acceptance is required, and must be sponsored by another approved library before being granted by the Kultusministerium in the Land concerned. Each of the Länder maintains an official list of institutions participating in the system; these lists and amendments to them are published in the "Zeitschrift für Bibliothekswesen und Bibliographie" and the "Jahrbuch der deutschen Bibliotheken".

A series of restrictions has been laid down about the material which may be sent on inter-library loan. This is to ensure that the services of the lending library are called upon only for scholarly purposes and to a reasonable and justifiable extent. Excluded are works at an elementary level; recent travel guides; paperbacks and smaller works available through the book-trade at a low price; and works held by the requesting library (or another local library open to the public or willing to lend), which are only temporarily not available. Complete volumes of journals or newspapers have now also been excluded, where only a short paper or article is being requested, on the principle that these should be supplied in the form of a reproduction (usually a Xerox copy). Works which are heavily used in their home library, or which may only be consulted there, loose-leaf publications, and books unsuited through size, weight or other reasons — all these may likewise be excluded from the material available for loan. Finally, there are certain classes of material which may not be sent on loan outside the immediate "loan region", for example works of reference and German books still in print "which the requesting library, or another library in the same region, may be expected to acquire".

The regional union catalogues occupy a key position in the 1966 regulations. The rule is that a library should send request forms for scholarly material not in stock to the appropriate union catalogue, having verified them bibliographically. The function of the union catalogue is to find locations in the region and, where there are several, to specify the route for the form to follow. If no copy can be traced in the region, it must pass on the request to the next union catalogue or, in certain cases, direct to a library (e.g. to one with a particular special-collection field, to a special library, or to the Staatsbibliothek Preußischer Kulturbesitz, whose holdings are not recorded in any union catalogue). Only in specified exceptional cases is it envisaged that the holding library shall be approached direct by the requesting library (e.g. for foreign periodicals listed in the GAZS).

The simplest possible rule about postage costs has been made, requiring no complicated accounting. "All costs arising from inter-library loans are met by the library incurring them. There is no accounting between libraries." Exceptional costs are reimbursed by the receiving library to the lending library on request; they may be charged to the reader if they have been incurred with his consent. A special case of costs incurred is the supply of Xerox copies in place of originals, which has been made standard practice for journal articles. The practical testing of this still novel procedure in a large number of libraries, and the working out of a unified set of instructions for guidance, was made possible by a contribution from the Forschungsgemeinschaft towards the cost of materials used from 1965 to 1967. It turned out from this that libraries on average incur no extra expense if, instead of sending often heavy journal volumes through the post, they provide Xerox copies at a charge of DM 0,50 per article. The advantages in service provided, both to the requester and the library, are obvious. Dispatch is faster, more requests can be met because the original volumes are constantly accessible, and much unproductive work is avoided.

By means of the new inter-library loan regulations, the mutual assistance, to which academic libraries are committed today more than ever before, has been brought into a system for the whole Federal Republic, rationally planned and suited to existing conditions. Some of the chief defects connected with interloans, which led to frequent complaints by readers — long delays in receiving a requested item, often when it was no longer of use, and many requests not satisfied at all — have now been mitigated, if not eliminated. In 1968, out of 832,736 request forms from the Federal Republic received by the national inter-library loan system, 517,775 were routed via the union catalogues. Of these, 61,2 per cent were answered positively, that is, by the tracing of the book. A further 75,000 requests from the DDR and from other countries may be added to this figure. The average delay between handing in the request and receiving the book is now between two and three weeks. This performance is still not satisfactory. Improvements are continually being worked on — by all the participating libraries, and especially by the two committees of the Verein Deutscher Bibliothekare, for the union catalogues and reader services. The possibilities of using technical resources in this connection are being examined, and experiments made. Among these are the timetabled running of small vans between the libraries in a region. This is being tested over four trial routes with financial aid from the Forschungsgemeinschaft: experience to date encourages one to hope that the services will be continued and extended.

The academic libraries of the Roman Catholic and Protestant churches formed a joint interlending circle of their own in 1963; interloan regulations applying to member libraries were one of the first achievements of the two Arbeitsgemeinschaften concerned (cf. 2.61). In its expanded form since 1963, this interlending circle is still intended to supplement and relieve pressure on the national inter-library loan system. It helps to satisfy loan requests from participating libraries quickly and directly, without calling on the services of the national system, and is all the more essential because the denominational libraries are at present only meagrely represented in the regional union catalogues.

3.132 Regional Inter-Library Loan Systems

Public libraries in both town and country are facing increasing demands from their readers for the supply of genuinely scholarly publications, and they naturally regard as unsatisfactory the strict conditions for admission to the national inter-library loan system, besides the many limitations placed on individual requests. For example, the rule that only one library in any town should take part in the national system has forced some public libraries in the larger cities to find alternative solutions — as most public libraries have found it necessary to do all along. As a result, regional inter-library loan systems for the separate Länder are being developed, to supplement loan facilities within town public library systems, Landkreise, and the areas served by individual Staatliche Büchereistellen. Their aim is partly to reduce the pressure on academic libraries, but also to give public libraries not admitted to the national system access to more specialised and scholarly material.

One example of such a system is the *Kommunaler Leihring in Nord-rhein-Westfalen* ("Lending Circle of Local Authority Libraries in North Rhine-Westphalia"), a co-operative enterprise by the municipal libraries of the Land to help them in procuring German-language material in all subjects. Its function goes beyond that of lending purely scholarly material, in that it can fulfil serious requests not only for research purposes, but also in pursuit of professional or personal further education.

All municipal libraries employing full-time professional staff can join the Kommunaler Leihring. Libraries with full-time non-professional staff require special permission. Libraries with part-time or unpaid staff can participate through the Staatliche Büchereistellen or through professionally-staffed Kreis supplementary libraries. Moves are now under way to replace the Kommunaler Leihring by a Regionaler Leihring ("Regional Lending Circle"), which is to help improve further the inter-library loan facilities of those public libraries in the Land not within the national system. If the same conditions for a request are observed as obtain in the national system, then it would be possible for the smallest municipal public library to obtain material from academic libraries in the Land through a multi-stage loan procedure.

The *Bayerischer Leihverkehr* ("Bavarian Interloan Service"), which became operational in 1966, has already linked the public and the academic libraries in this Land. Its intention is to help the former to obtain scholarly works and other non-fiction which they do not hold themselves. Requests are to be met which are for purposes of research, or professional or personal further education. All public libraries may take part without special permission. There is a prescribed route for requests, running from within one of six regions, via its Staatliche Beratungsstelle für Volks-büchereien ("State Advisory Office for Public Libraries") to the appropriate main library of the Regierungsbezirk, and thence to the Bavarian union catalogue. As the main library for Upper Bavaria, and through the medium of the union catalogue, the Bayerische Staatsbibliothek is thus in principle linked with every public library in the Land.

In some of the other Länder, too (Lower Saxony, the Saarland and Schleswig-Holstein among others), interloan routes lead — with differences of detail — from small public libraries via the large public libraries and Staatliche Büchereistellen to the academic libraries of the Land. In other Länder, similar developments are on the way.

3.14 Regional Library Planning

We have taken a regional library plan, in the wider sense of the term, to mean an organised framework into which public libraries and academic libraries in all fields are fitted. In some places, first steps have been made towards plans of this kind, based on practical requirements. In others, preliminary schemes have been drawn up after consideration and discussion, and here and there a start has even been made on reorganising library services in a region. However, the course these developments will take is still in no way fixed.

Important components of these plans are the arrangements just dealt with, which originated from the initiative of librarians and are leading towards joint action by libraries — at present following the division between academic and public libraries: acquisition schemes, union catalogues, interloan systems and "lending circles". Here it is the regional union catalogues, above all, which exert pressure towards systematisation within their region.

Regional systems are already being set up in North Rhine-Westphalia and Bavaria. In North Rhine-Westphalia, the activity of the local Verband der Bibliotheken led the Kultusministerium in 1966, in agreement with the Städtetag, to commission a plan for the co-ordination and extension of library services. This is being drawn up by a commission established by the ministry on which are represented the ministry itself, the associations of local authorities (cf. 1.55) and the Verband. The co-operative undertakings already in existence will be incorporated into the plan.

In Bavaria, the directorate-general of the Bavarian state libraries and the Kultusministerium together formulated a regional plan, in which the first element of the system was supplied by the Land's great centre of library resources: the Bayerische Staatsbibliothek, with its union catalogue and library school. Two further arrangements have been newly made for the plan: the Bayerischer Leihverkehr already mentioned, and the linking of different types of library by designating certain libraries as liaison points. The ten regional Landesbibliotheken, which serve public libraries as transmission channels for interloans and as bibliographical information centres, also link public libraries directly with academic libraries, and have at the same time been given a fresh lease of life. Similarly the libraries of colleges of education, which had previously been outside the library system, are being linked to the academic libraries through the university library or, again, the regional Landesbibliothek in their own town.

The first document on regional library planning for the whole Federal Republic was presented in 1965 by the Arbeitsstelle für das Büchereiwesen of the Deutscher Büchereiverband, and published in 1966 under the title "Grundlagen für die bibliothekarische Regionalplanung" ("Fundamentals for regional library planning"). It arose from model proposals for the establishment of a properly-organised public library system, commissioned by the conference of the Kultusminister. Public libraries, for which detailed organisational proposals are made, serve as a point of departure, but the planning is directed towards a system to embrace all types of libraries. The report is based on experience in Germany and elsewhere, which has shown that only public libraries of a certain size, which can give their readers access to sources of help from beyond their own town or region, can provide the services demanded of them. Recognition of this fact shows the need to raise the standard of provision of books and information, in rural areas and the smaller municipalities, towards the standard of public library services in the larger towns. The report proceeds from this to set out the following stages of the plan:

The basis for the provision of material in the future is to be the *public library system*, which is no longer to be an organisational unit restricted to large towns. Instead, such systems will be created above Gemeinde level to amalgamate the libraries of rural Gemeinden, Landkreise, towns, and perhaps also Stadtkreise. The optimum size for such systems is stated to be an area with about 500,000 inhabitants.

The systems are to use permanent and mobile libraries in carrying out their tasks. Mobile libraries are to be employed in areas with a scattered population, villages with less than 1,000 inhabitants, and thinly-populated suburbs of towns. Large libraries should act as central libraries for these higher-level systems, and should be open for direct use as well as lending within the system. A central office would have to see to it that every library in the system had adequate working conditions, and that its working methods, area served and bookstock were compatible with those of the other libraries, without encroaching on the initiative and responsibility of individual libraries. The centre would have to oversee the development of the system and to assume certain functions for all member libraries. The report envisages that the systems would be set up by corporate bodies composed of the authorities supporting the libraries

— that is, chiefly the Gemeinden, Landkreise and associations of local authorities.

The next stage is the *library region*, which is generally taken to be the territory of a single Federal Land or an inter-library loan region. Inside it, the public libraries are to be linked to each other, and to the academic libraries, to form a library network, which should be capable of meeting most of the demands of library users within the region.

The initiative, planning and co-ordination within the library region, and the region's links with the Land authorities and supra-regional organisations, are to devolve upon a top-level committee, on which all types of library would be represented — the academic libraries especially.

The report of the Deutscher Büchereiverband and its Arbeitsstelle für das Büchereiwesen aroused intense discussion in professional circles, in the Länder and in the municipalities. The reactions of the Staatliche Büchereistellen have taken the form of amendments to the report. In them, the part played by the state is more strongly emphasised and the significance of the Büchereistellen pointed out, as being a vital means of reorganisation in the regions. It is regarded as absolutely necessary that the central offices of public library systems should be supported by the state or by regional associations. There are certain precedents for this, for example the collaboration of Staatliche Büchereistellen with associations of municipal library authorities, which is a solution already tested in practice.

For further investigation of the problems a working party on regional planning was set up by the Arbeitsstelle für das Büchereiwesen. On this, library specialists from the Land administrations, representatives of the associations of local authorities and librarians from all the Länder are working together.

Intensive deliberations within this working party and contacts with many bodies then led to the first draft of the "Bibliotheksplan" ("Library Plan"), which was presented by the president of the Deutscher Büchereiverband to the conference of the Kultusminister and to the public at large at the beginning of 1969. This draft proposal for a comprehensive network of general public libraries represents a further extension of the "Grundlagen für die bibliothekarische Regionalplanung". The proposal is less concerned with institutional factors and, by laying its emphasis upon functional requirements, leaves more scope for future development. The optimum effective range of library systems is left more flexible. The first part of the Bibliotheksplan argues the necessity for an efficient library network in town and country and lays down general standards

159

for the provisions to be made for public libraries. The second part contains the plan. The appendices comprise: a list of references on librarianship in the Federal Republic as a whole and similar references and statistical information on the individual Länder; calculations for a model telex network; standards for the space requirements of public library buildings; costing figures for mobile libraries; a development plan for the Arbeitsstelle für das Büchereiwesen; suggestions and proposals for a regional interloan service; and costing figures for basic reference collections and documentation material on the education and different levels of staff required for a comprehensive library network.

The plan proper envisages three functional types of public libraries within the framework of the library regions. Grade 1 libraries, with holdings of one volume per inhabitant (though with a minimum of 10,000 volumes and a basic stock of reference works and bibliographies), are in future to be the smallest category. They are to be run by full-time, professionally-trained staff, be open on 5 working days for a total of at least 30 hours, be directly accessible by telephone and possess photocopying facilities. Another requirement for these libraries is that they should be linked with the central library in a system for the purposes of professional book selection and cataloguing, routine processing, reference and information service, interloans and technical services. Existing small libraries that meet these standards are to be correspondingly developed with financial aid from the future responsible authorities as well as from the Landkreise and the Länder. If this is not possible, mobile instead of small permanent libraries will take over the service.

Grade 2 libraries in the sense of the plan are systems formed by large towns or towns in conjunction with Landkreise to serve as "functional networks" in an area. They necessitate a central library, which is at the same time the main service point for the locality. Essential requirements in order to fulfil their responsibilities towards the Grade 1 libraries affiliated to them are extensive stack areas, a well-developed reference collection and technical aids, besides periodical holdings of at least 500 German-language titles. The library systems must participate directly in co-operative work within the library region, being prepared to give as well as to receive. They must employ a staff of Lektoren (cf. 4.3) who work for the system as a whole, and they must maintain a union catalogue. They must organise exchanges of publications and the central storage of older material and possess a centralised processing office. Mobile libraries would operate in the framework of a system, if necessary from several bases some distance apart. A legal agreement to provide the central services of a library system for a fairly long period must be drawn up, the funds to come mainly from the Gemeinden and the Landkreise. The Länder are expected to make grants.

Grade 3 libraries, according to the classification by function of the Bibliotheksplan, would be Staats- and Landesbibliotheken, university libraries (with corresponding responsibilities) and other major libraries in the library regions. They would co-ordinate joint activities within the region and forge links with special libraries and documentation centres, which are not themselves directly covered by the network. Moreover, in co-operation with the union catalogues they would guarantee membership of the national and international inter-lending schemes. As far as their own regions are concerned, these libraries are expected to provide centrally a bibliographical documentation service, an information service and if need be the facilities for electronic data processing. Financial support would have to be forthcoming from the Länder.

The Staatliche Büchereistellen and other regional library offices (cf. 2.53), the Arbeitsstelle für das Büchereiwesen (cf. 3.24) and the Einkaufszentrale für Öffentliche Büchereien (cf. 3.25) are named as institutions that will contribute towards the extension and growth of the public library network. The Federal Länder and the associations of local authorities are called upon to co-operate with the library bodies in the prompt implementation of the Bibliotheksplan.

Well over a year after the appearance of the Bibliotheksplan it can be said that it has not failed to make its mark; it has received official approval in principle from the Kultusminister as well as from the associations of local authorities. New considerations on library legislation in certain Länder were sparked off and influenced by the Plan. Professional discussion on the ideal structure and on matters of detail is continuing in the appropriate bodies and in the context of the Deutsche Bibliothekskonferenz (cf. 3.21). The interests and reservations especially of the academic libraries will then be considered more closely. In the not too distant future a second set of draft proposals must be reckoned with, which might indeed lay down valid conditions for future development. Such proposals will no doubt be favourably influenced by the general striving towards an efficient educational system. Other beneficial factors are the obvious sociological changes in town and country. Area development planning, administrative reforms and boundary changes will be important extraneous factors affecting them.

The realisation of regional library planning will depend critically on whether the large number of librarians needed can be obtained — by increased professional education and further training, and by supporting librarians with other staff, for example library assistants. This applies above all to the filling of senior posts.

3.2   Organisations and Institutions

3.21   Professional Associations

The Federal Republic, like the German Reich before it, has no large association embracing all branches of librarianship, such as the USA possesses in the American Library Association, Great Britain in the Library Association, and — since 1964 — even the DDR in the newly-founded Deutscher Bibliotheksverband. There were calls for a single association in the early thirties, and have been again since 1949. The associations re-founded or newly established since 1945 have thought it better, for practical reasons, not to change their structures, but to foster close contacts between one another.

An important step in this direction was taken in 1963 with the establishment of the Deutsche Bibliothekskonferenz ("German Library Conference"). This brings together, twice a year, the chairmen of the Verein Deutscher Bibliothekare, the Verein der Diplom-Bibliothekare an wissenschaftlichen Bibliotheken, the Deutscher Büchereiverband, the Verein der Bibliothekare an Öffentlichen Büchereien, the Verband der Bibliotheken des Landes Nordrhein-Westfalen and the Arbeitsgemeinschaft der Spezialbibliotheken. Questions affecting all the participants are discussed, agreed solutions sought, and special projects co-ordinated with each other or put forward jointly. The organ of the Deutsche Bibliothekskonferenz is now the "Bibliotheksdienst", a monthly published by the Deutscher Büchereiverband. The first joint — and successful — undertaking was the foundation of the Bibliothekarische Auslandsstelle ("International Relations Office for Libraries").

The oldest German association of librarians is the *Verein Deutscher Bibliothekare* (VDB) ("Association of German Academic Librarians"), an association of individuals, which was founded in 1900 — seven years after the profession of librarian was first established in Prussia. The VDB took up its old traditions again on its re-foundation in 1948. Its rules were re-formulated in 1960, though following the old rules in their fundamentals. The object of the VDB is "to foster relations between German librarians and watch over their professional interests, to assist in the exchange and extension of their professional knowledge, and to promote the work of academic libraries".

"German librarians with academic qualifications, and candidates for the administrative grade in academic libraries, may become members. There is no corporate membership." The VDB has at present about 690 members. Although it is composed of librarians, not libraries, its functions are expressly concerned both with personal professional interests and with professional activity in itself. This latter concern, which is affirmed in the 1960 rules not only in the statement of aims but also in the VDB's right to set up committees, is responsible for a large part of the association's activity.

The following 14 committees of the VDB currently exist: for alphabetical cataloguing; official publications; professional education; buildings; reader services; career matters; bibliography; doctoral dissertations; binding; manuscripts, rare books and fine bindings; incunabula; legal matters; newspapers; and union catalogues.

The intensive work to be carried out by such committees led to the conclusion that the financial resources of a librarians' association were not sufficient to meet future demands. Therefore the annual conference of the Verein Deutscher Bibliothekare decided in 1970 to set up a committee which would make recommendations for the constitution and byelaws of an institutional association of academic libraries.

The VDB has no permanent office and no library of its own. Its headquarters is located in the library whose director is currently its chairman, and changes at the time of the chairman's election — every two years, according to the rules — only remaining in the same place if the chairman is re-elected. The chairman and managing committee use their own libraries when carrying out their business for the association.

Among the activities of the VDB are its annual Bibliothekartage ("librarians' assemblies"). These are for reports to the assembled members, committee meetings at which further work is discussed, and the treatment of a few important topics by addresses and papers before the full meeting. Full reports are printed in the "Zeitschrift für Bibliothekswesen und Bibliographie". This is the organ of the VDB, although not its own publication. The association published a journal of its own only from 1947 to 1953: the "Nachrichten für wissenschaftliche Bibliotheken". It does compile and publish the "Jahrbuch der Deutschen Bibliotheken", which appears at two-yearly intervals (cf. 8.11).

Since the VDB restricted its membership to academic librarians, a new and separate association was set up for professional librarians without academic qualifications, as soon as these emerged as a distinct body. This division into two associations was re-established after 1945. The Reichsverband deutscher Bibliotheksbeamter und -angestellter, founded in 1920, was succeeded in 1948 by the *Verein der Diplom-Bibliothekare an wissenschaftlichen Bibliotheken* (VdDB) ("Association of Non-Graduate Qualified Librarians in Academic Libraries"), which was given its constitution in September 1950. Its object is defined as "to assist in the strengthening of the profession and the protection of its interests. It helps members to develop their professional knowledge practically and theoretically, and to profit from the exchange of experience". The association has about 1,300 members.

Since members of the two associations are regularly in the closest contact with each other in the course of their work, it is natural that meetings should be held jointly, and that some of the VDB's committees should be composed of members of both associations.

The present *Arbeitsgemeinschaft der Spezialbibliotheken* ("Association of Special Libraries") had its origins in the Arbeitsgemeinschaft der technischen und wirtschaftlichen Bibliotheken ("Association of Technical and Industrial Libraries"), formed for the joint solution of practical problems in the emergency conditions of the immediate post-war years. It now has about 200 members and includes libraries in all subject fields, although technology and science predominate. It holds conferences at intervals of two or three years; reports, containing the papers and discussions, are published separately. We have already referred to the periodicals list TWZ, compiled and published by the Arbeitsgemeinschaft (cf. 3.122). Among the matters with which it concerns itself, the chief are information services and the application of modern technical aids (especially data-processing equipment) to library work.

The only association to which libraries in all fields belong — in their own right or through their supporting organisation — is the *Verband der Bibliotheken des Landes Nordrhein-Westfalen* ("Association of Libraries in the Land of North Rhine-Westphalia"). This made its debut in April 1949, when it held its first general meeting and working conference. Its object is "to promote library services in North Rhine-Westphalia by

representing the common interests of the libraries, advising the departments and other bodies whose work directly or indirectly concerns
libraries, and fostering professional co-operation between libraries in the
Land". This extremely active and successful association publishes one of
the most important professional journals in the shape of its "Mitteilungsblatt". It has, in addition, instigated or itself taken on work which has
benefited libraries in the Federal Republic as a whole. This includes the
new set of cataloguing rules, the draft of the "Allgemeine Systematik für
Büchereien" ("General Classification for Public Libraries"), the creation
of the Kommunaler Leihring and the instituting of advanced training
seminars for librarians. It was, and is, supported in this work by the
activity of committees as well as the standing Arbeitsgemeinschaft der
Großstadtbüchereien ("Conference of Large Town Public Libraries") and
3 regional Arbeitsgemeinschaften of public libraries in medium-sized
towns. Today it is well able to represent effectively the interests of
libraries in North Rhine-Westphalia.

The two most important professional associations in public librarianship
in the Federal Republic are the *Deutscher Büchereiverband* (DBV) ("German Association of Public Libraries") and the *Verein der Bibliothekare
an Öffentlichen Büchereien* ("Association of Librarians in Public Libraries"). Both have devoted themselves essentially to the promotion of
municipal public library services: the Deutscher Büchereiverband primarily as a federation of municipal library authorities, and the Verein
der Bibliothekare as an organisation for qualified librarians serving in
public libraries.

The *Deutscher Büchereiverband* was founded under this name in 1949,
and owes its establishment to the decisive action of the Deutscher Städtetag. In the years that followed it assumed the title Verband Deutscher
Bibliotheken ("Association of German Libraries"), thus emphasising its
efforts to initiate a general association for all libraries. After this object
had proved to be beyond its reach, the Verband began a new phase of
development in 1957. Under its original title of Deutscher Büchereiverband, it has since aimed at the promotion of public library services and
professional skills. The increasing interest of Gemeinden and Landkreise
and other bodies in public libraries, and the constantly widening influence of the association, have caused it to grow into one of the main-
stays of public librarianship. The full, i. e. voting members of the DBV —
which since 1957 has had its headquarters in West Berlin — are Gemeinden which support public libraries with full-time staff; Landkreise which

165

support libraries directly or contribute towards library services in their area; regional associations of public libraries under these authorities; and some other bodies supporting non-profit-making libraries with full-time staff. In addition, the association has a number of associate members. Associate membership is open to all individuals and corporate bodies not eligible for full membership.

Branches of the DBV for separate Länder have been created during the course of its development but do not yet exist in every Land, although, considering the federative constitution of the country, they could be thought to have important functions. Admittedly the pattern of library services in the different Länder critically affects the composition and sphere of activity of such branches. One example is North Rhine-Westphalia, which is served by a relatively large number of public libraries in large and medium-sized towns — circumstances which favoured the formation of the Verband der Bibliotheken des Landes Nordrhein-Westfalen. By formal agreement, the public libraries belonging to this association also enjoy the rights of full members of the Deutscher Büchereiverband, and the Verband der Bibliotheken des Landes Nordrhein-Westfalen exercises the rights of a Land branch of the Deutscher Büchereiverband.

In 1970 5 sections were formed representing the public library service in: I. Towns with a population over 350,000, II. Towns with a population between 100,000 and 350,000, III. Gemeinden under 100,000 population, IV. Regional library associations and Landkreise, V. Länder.

The annual conferences of the Deutscher Büchereiverband, which in recent years have been held jointly with those of the Verein der Bibliothekare an Öffentlichen Büchereien, are of predominantly professional interest. They are, however, also intended to focus public attention on the public library situation. The Deutscher Büchereiverband also acts as publisher of a range of important works, which are distributed largely by the association's own publications department. Since these publications are produced, entirely or in part, by the Arbeitsstelle für das Büchereiwesen — which is maintained by the association — they are dealt with in that context (cf. 3.24). The organ of the DBV is the monthly "Bibliotheksdienst", also the journal "Bücherei und Bildung".

The *Verein der Bibliothekare an Öffentlichen Büchereien* ("Association of Librarians in Public Libraries"), which has its headquarters in Bremen, was also founded in 1949. Until May 1968 it bore the name *Verein Deutscher Volksbibliothekare* ("Association of German Public Librarians"), and could hark back to the traditions of a similar association which had existed since the 1920's. Full membership is open to qualified librarians in public library service, of whom the great majority are employed in libraries run by the Gemeinden, and since 1969 also to library school students. Part-time staff in charge of public libraries without professional qualifications may join as associate members. The total membership is over 3,000.

The Verein der Bibliothekare an Öffentlichen Büchereien exists primarily to represent the interests of public librarians as a profession, but it has also done work of great merit in the promotion of public library services in general. This is especially true of the first post-war decade, when the Deutscher Büchereiverband had not yet created the conditions for its subsequent effective operations. Annual conferences and training seminars organised jointly with the DBV, work on matters of professional education, and the activities of its committee on salaries and conditions of service – which is in close touch with the large trade unions – all these give some indication of current priorities in the association's work.

The publications of the Verein der Bibliothekare an Öffentlichen Büchereien are important for the profession and public libraries in general. First among these is the monthly professional journal "Bücherei und Bildung", published since 1949 jointly with the DBV. The association's own publishing house, Verlag Bücherei und Bildung, also publishes the "LZ. Leserzeitschrift", which is taken and distributed by many public libraries, and has issued separate publications. The association has recently assumed an added responsibility for the series of "Quellenschriften", published by Harrassowitz as Reihe B of the "Beiträge zum Büchereiwesen".

The Verein der Bibliothekare an Öffentlichen Büchereien has branches in all the Länder of the Federal Republic. Their opportunities for organising meetings to foster professional training and personal contacts among members are naturally determined in part by the size of the Land in question. The branches are more likely to be actively concerned with public library policy where the Land either does not possess a branch of the DBV, or where the branches of the two associations are acting in collaboration.

A considerable measure of agreement on objectives, and the desire to avoid unnecessary overlapping in the two associations' activities, have led to repeated debates about ways of co-ordinating the work of the association for library authorities and institutions and the staff organisation. There are substantial considerations opposing a complete amalgamation, because of the conflicts of interest which may easily be envisaged on certain questions, and efforts have therefore been made to achieve organised co-operation and the creation of a number of joint undertakings within the framework of a joint committee. This led in 1968 to the formation of the Arbeitsgemeinschaft Öffentliche Bücherei as a basis for common representation and for joint activities in specified areas.

Besides the large associations in the fields of academic and public librarianship and their Land branches, there are other professional organisations whose activities are more specialised. Constitutionally they are either registered societies, with a corporate status in law, or less formal bodies. They are listed in Chapter 8.

Regional associations of libraries have been formed in some Länder for the areas served by individual Staatliche Büchereistellen, usually at their instigation. The chief occasion for the Büchereistellen to exchange information and co-ordinate their activities is the *Fachkonferenz der Staatlichen Büchereistellen*. Under its auspices, representatives of the 32 Staatliche Büchereistellen meet once a year. One of the Büchereistellen assumes the central organising responsibility for a period of several years.

3.22 Bibliothekarische Auslandsstelle

The *Bibliothekarische Auslandsstelle* ("International Relations Office for Libraries") was founded in 1963 on a resolution of the Deutsche Bibliothekskonferenz. It has the form of a joint committee of those organisations in academic and public librarianship which are members of the Deutsche Bibliothekskonferenz; but it has at the same time been planned as a permanent institution, financed at present by contributions from the member organisations and a grant from the Federal Ministry of the Interior. The staff of the Auslandsstelle work in an honorary capacity as delegated representatives of the associations supporting it, thus representing different types of library. The Auslandsstelle is designed to aid the intensification and co-ordination of work with other countries. Although its members allocate the specialised fields of work among themselves, its central office acts as a first point of contact which may pass on enquiries according to the nature of each case. The Auslandsstelle is also the central office which — commissioned by the associations — works as a partner with government departments and other institutions in seeking support for the furthering of professional relations with other countries. It takes a broad view of its mandate, but sees its central task as the arranging and encouragement of study tours and working visits for foreign librarians in the Federal Republic and for German librarians in other countries. The help it can give to study tours by individuals and groups ranges from suggestions for the programme of professional visits to the organisation of the programme itself.

From the first years of its existence it has been able to arrange many study tours in the Federal Republic and other countries, in several cases with financial help from the appropriate ministries. These resulted in new professional contacts and an exchange of information and material. The arrangement of working visits, despite a number of individual successes, has proved more difficult for many reasons. On the whole, it is now understood that there are limits to an enterprise dependent entirely on unpaid work and with very limited funds to cover all its operating costs. Nevertheless — or perhaps for this very reason — there are great hopes that the recommendation of IFLA, the International Federation of Library Associations, will result in the formation of similar bodies in other countries, with which the Bibliothekarische Auslandsstelle can collaborate.

3.23 Libraries Committee and Libraries Department of the Deutsche Forschungsgemeinschaft

It has been shown in Chapter 1 what an important function central bodies, such as the Wissenschaftsrat and the Forschungsgemeinschaft, have in the decentralised structure of scholarship in the Federal Republic. There are no corresponding organisations solely for librarianship, but both of those mentioned have included academic library services among their concerns. The Wissenschaftsrat employed a specially formed committee of experts, subsequently dissolved, to prepare the second volume of its "Empfehlungen", dealing with libraries. The Forschungsgemeinschaft has a libraries committee as one of its standing advisory organs, and its central office has a separate libraries department side by side with the departments for special subject fields.

The *libraries committee* of the Deutsche Forschungsgemeinschaft is appointed by the main committee for a period of two years at a time. It consists of 8 representatives of academic libraries, 3 representatives of

institutions of higher education and the head of the Institut für Dokumentationswesen. The libraries department is headed by a qualified academic librarian and has at present a staff of 20. The libraries committee
advises the main committee on all matters to do with the promotion of
library services. It delivers reports on topics referred to it, examines the
working of present arrangements, puts up plans and suggestions for new
projects and follows trends in librarianship in Germany and elsewhere.
Preparatory work for some of the more important undertakings is done
by sub-committees: for example, for the central specialist libraries;
access to information; cataloguing of manuscripts; data processing in
libraries; co-operation between university central and institute libraries;
centralised cataloguing; and a list of 16th-century German printed
books.

The fundamental limitations on the aid given to libraries by the
Forschungsgemeinschaft have been indicated in Chapter 1. The libraries
committee deals with everything which affects libraries as instruments
of research, singly or collectively. This also covers organisational matters
not directly connected with assistance projects, such as the relationship
between university and institute libraries or the budgetary pattern of
libraries in universities and technical universities. The libraries committee has made its views known in memoranda on both these subjects.
On the other hand, it normally excludes from consideration questions of
purely internal concern to the library profession and library operations,
such as career matters and training, salaries, the legal standing of libraries, catalogues, local borrowing, buildings and equipment. On all these
subjects, any library will receive the help of the professional associations.

The members of the libraries committee and its sub-committees do their
work without payment, like all the committees of the Forschungsgemeinschaft. Despite the often considerable extra work, they feel deeply committed to these activities, to the libraries they advise, and to the world of
scholarship for the sake of which everything is done.

The work of the *libraries department* of the Forschungsgemeinschaft can
be itemised as follows:

a) It is that section of the central office in which the Forschungsgemeinschaft's assistance for libraries is elaborated. This includes everything
required for the work of the libraries committee and all its sub-committees: the preparation and minuting of meetings; the drafting of
documents and memoranda; the composing of reports; correspondence

170

with libraries; formulation of proposals; budgeting; statistics; and the representation of the Forschungsgemeinschaft at professional meetings dealing with library and information services.

b) It maintains exchange arrangements with academic libraries and institutions in other countries in support of the co-operative acquisition scheme and the central specialist libraries. This appreciably reinforces the libraries' own efforts at exchanges, since most of them have a restricted range of exchange material. For further details, cf. 8.4.

c) It acts as the Federal Republic's centre for the exchange of scholarly publications under the terms of the Unesco Convention of 1958. For further details, cf. 8.4.

d) It has funds at its disposal for the presentation of German monographs and journals to academic libraries in other countries. Requests are conveyed to the Forschungsgemeinschaft direct or through diplomatic channels, and are met as far as the available funds permit.

Varied as they are, these different activities interact widely. Now over twenty years old, the libraries department has accumulated from all of them a fund of experience which is often drawn upon by outsiders for information and advice on general and specialised library matters.

The head of the libraries department keeps libraries informed of its promotional work, at irregular intervals, through short reports in the "Zeitschrift für Bibliothekswesen und Bibliographie" and through papers presented at meetings of the professional associations.

Reports and memoranda of the libraries committee are frequently intended for internal use only. The following have been published:

Lage und Erfordernisse der westdeutschen wissenschaftlichen Bibliotheken. Bearbeiter: Peter Scheibert. Bad Godesberg 1951. (Out of print.)

Gutachten über die Lage der Institutsbibliotheken und ihr Verhältnis zu den Universitäts- und Hochschulbibliotheken. Bearbeiter: Gerhard Reincke. Bad Godesberg 1953.

Instituts- und Hochschulbibliotheken. Denkschrift der Deutschen Forschungsgemeinschaft. Bad Godesberg 1955.

Empfehlungen für die Zusammenarbeit zwischen Hochschulbibliothek und Institutsbibliotheken. Deutsche Forschungsgemeinschaft, Bibliotheksausschuß. Bonn-Bad Godesberg 1970.

The memoranda on model budgets and the co-operative acquisition scheme are printed in the symposium "Fünfzehn Jahre Bibliotheksarbeit der Deutschen Forschungsgemeinschaft 1949–1964" (cf. the list of further reading at the end of this chapter).

The work of the libraries committee has also resulted in the following publications:

Verzeichnis ausgewählter wissenschaftlicher Zeitschriften des Auslandes (VAZ). Hauptband and Registerband. Wiesbaden 1957.

Verzeichnis ausgewählter wissenschaftlicher Zeitschriften des Auslandes (VAZ). Neubearbeitung der Liste A: Grundlegend wichtige Zeitschriften. Wiesbaden 1969.

Verzeichnis laufend erscheinender Bibliographien. Hrsg. von der Deutschen Forschungsgemeinschaft. Wiesbaden 1963.

Rationalisierung in wissenschaftlichen Bibliotheken. Vorschläge und Materialien. Hrsg. von der Deutschen Forschungsgemeinschaft. Bonn u. Boppart 1970.

Automatisierung der Zeitschriftenstelle in wissenschaftlichen Bibliotheken. Ergebnisse eines Kolloquiums in Göttingen am 7. und 8. November 1968. Bad Godesberg 1970.

3.24 Arbeitsstelle für das Büchereiwesen

The Arbeitsstelle für das Büchereiwesen ("Study Centre for Public Libraries") was founded in 1958 in West Berlin as an organisation to promote professional competence in the field of public librarianship. The Deutscher Büchereiverband is responsible for the institution, which is independent as far as its professional activities are concerned and has no mandatory or supervisory function. Its financial support, however, has been undertaken jointly from the very beginning by the Bund, the Länder, the Einkaufszentrale für Öffentliche Büchereien (cf. 3.25) and the local authority public libraries. The board of trustees, which makes proposals for the work of the Arbeitsstelle and agrees estimates and long-term plans, includes representatives of these supporting bodies and an equal number of figures from the public library world, nominated by the Deutscher Büchereiverband.

The Arbeitsstelle offers its service to both individuals and institutions. Among its functions are the collection, exploitation and issue of books and other material from Germany and elsewhere which are relevant to public librarianship. It undertakes, or commissions, investigations into problems referred to it or arising from library practice, notably matters of reorganisation and technical services. Its library and the results of its investigations form the basis for information services, reports and publications. Its programme of work is co-ordinated with the activities of the Staatliche Büchereistellen, the library schools and other bodies. The constitution of the Arbeitsstelle lays particular emphasis on the responsibility of the Büchereistellen for the development of regional public library systems, and commits the Arbeitsstelle to support them in this.

The limited resources of the Arbeitsstelle in staff and equipment — and at the same time the desire to take account of regional and local experience or peculiarities when evaluating existing services or making recommendations — pointed the way to the formation of *Arbeitskreise* ("study circles"), on which libraries and interested institutions are represented, and of committees to which individuals are appointed. After the formation of the sections of the Deutscher Büchereiverband in 1970, which represent different types of public library, the number of Arbeitskreise was reduced. The following exist at present: regional library planning; youth libraries; hospital libraries; public music libraries; and indexing of journals. In addition there are the committees for information services; public library buildings; staff establishments; technical processes; and audiovisual media.

When related to its very limited financial resources, the size of the Arbeitsstelle's publishing programme is quite surprising, and moreover of undeniably high standing in matters of public library practice and policy. Individual titles include the "Handbuch der Öffentlichen Büchereien" (published every two years), the monthly information bulletin "Bibliotheksdienst", the "Beihefte zum Bibliotheksdienst", containing longer contributions, and the annual "Schnellstatistik" and "Gesamtstatistik der Öffentlichen Büchereien". Current series are the "Biobibliographien" of notable librarians, "Lehrhefte" supplying study material on aspects of public library operations, and the "Druckschriften der Arbeitsstelle für das Büchereiwesen", published by Harrassowitz as Reihe A of the "Beiträge zum Büchereiwesen". Periodical bibliographic publications are the "Fachbibliographischer Dienst: Bibliothekswesen", "Zeitschriftendienst", "Zeitschriftendienst: Musik" and "Musikbibliographischer Dienst" (cf. 6.12). The Arbeitsstelle has also published a series of selective book lists. In addition it makes available to libraries on subscription sample copies of book-lists compiled by individual libraries. Collaboration between the Arbeitsstelle and the Amerika-Gedenkbibliothek in West Berlin has produced the "AGB-Titeldienst" (cf. 4.3).

3.25 Einkaufszentrale für Öffentliche Büchereien (EKZ)

The Einkaufszentrale für Öffentliche Büchereien GmbH ("Supply Centre for Public Libraries") in Reutlingen has a special place among the central organisations for librarianship in the Federal Republic. It has the form of a commercial undertaking with the legal status of a limited-liability company, the members and owners of which are exclusively public authorities: all the Länder, about 60 towns and a few Landkreise. In its methods of business, on the other hand, the EKZ is no different from a private firm. There is no obligation to purchase, no subsidies and no tax relief, and services are provided for all customers on the same conditions.

The Einkaufszentrale was founded in 1947. The Einkaufshaus für Büchereien, founded in Leipzig in 1920, served as a model for some aspects of the work and organisation. At the centre of its services, which have been constantly expanded and improved over the years, lies the supply of books in special library bindings. The "EKZ binding" made in the EKZ's large-scale bindery for books in sheet form, is particularly important. "EKZ laminated bindings" (original bindings prepared for library use) and "EKZ paperback bindings" (paperbacks in hard covers) complete the range of books offered, which enables libraries to select from some 4,500 to 5,000 titles. All books available from stock are supplied with three catalogue cards carrying full catalogue entries and the classmark of the "Allgemeine Systematik für Büchereistellen" (cf. 4.42), a book-card with bibliographic and contents details for issue purposes, a book-card pocket and date label. Books not in the range are supplied in the EKZ laminated bindings. Special bindings and the accompanying catalogue and classification material are supplied for only a slight supplementary charge. On the other hand, the EKZ — like any other bookseller — has to abide by the publishers' pricing agreements, and accordingly gives discount of only up to 10 per cent.

The firm's range of holdings is checked by librarians. A team of subject specialists ensures that stocks appropriate to libraries' requirements are maintained. Their work relies on the extensive reviewing service provided by the journal "Bücherei und Bildung", issued by the Verein der Bibliothekare an Öffentlichen Büchereien. In return, the EKZ makes a substantial contribution to the costs of this journal, under a contractual agreement. Its own journal, "Buchanzeiger für Öffentliche Büchereien", publishes summaries of the professional reviews appearing in "Bücherei und Bildung" — about 4,000 notices of recommended books per year. The "Buchanzeiger" is supplemented by the "Hilfen für den Bestandsaufbau" ("Aids to Stock-building") which list the EKZ's stock in classified order.

The range of the stock is such that small and medium-sized public libraries can usually meet their requirements wholly or to a large extent from the EKZ. Even the public libraries of the large towns buy a not inconsiderable proportion of their books from the EKZ because of the advantages offered. The larger libraries are limited not so much by the EKZ's inadequate range of titles as by their obligation to support their local booksellers. The latter are expected to supply certain books on approval. Books in EKZ bindings can, in any case, also be ordered through the book trade. The Einkaufszentrale currently processes and sells a total of about 900,000 volumes per year, a good half of them in EKZ bindings.

Besides books, the EKZ has available the whole range of stationery, etc., needed in the different fields of library work (for example, issue records, shelf labelling, book repair, book lettering and publicity). One notable material here is the EKZ adhesive plastic (EKZ-Klebefolie) — gummed sheet supplied in rolls for libraries to cover unjacketed books. It is popular in other countries, and is exported to ten European countries.

Finally, the EKZ's comprehensive range of furniture for modern, open-access public libraries is quite significant. So far, seven different types of shelf and shelving systems have been developed under this programme, besides catalogue stands, book trolleys, lockers, and many other pieces of equipment. Chairs, tables and accessories complete the range. EKZ furniture is used in several thousand towns and Gemeinden. Organisations and manufacturers in other countries have obtained licenses for its production. About a third of the EKZ's total turnover is for furniture and stationery.

FURTHER READING

Co-operative Acquisition Schemes

Basic considerations for co-operative acquisition plans in general, with special reference to earlier and present German plans, are outlined by Fritz Redenbacher in the chapter "Erwerbung" in Band 2 of the Handbuch der Bibliothekswissenschaft.

The co-operative acquisition scheme of the Deutsche Forschungsgemeinschaft has become well known in Germany and abroad as a result of many papers, notably in the Nachrichten für wissenschaftliche Bibliotheken and the Zeitschrift für Bibliothekswesen und Bibliographie, but also, for example, in the Unesco bulletin for libraries (18, 1963, Dieter Oertel). The basis for the programme in its present form is: Memorandum über Grundgedanken und Fortführung des Sondersammelgebietsplanes. In: Fünfzehn Jahre Bibliotheksarbeit der Deutschen Forschungsgemeinschaft. Frankfurt 1966. (ZfBB, Sonderheft 4) p. 46—64.

The principles and working experience of the co-operative acquisition scheme and the Kommunaler Leihring in North Rhine-Westphalia have been dealt with in many contributions to the Mitteilungsblatt des Verbandes der Bibliotheken for that Land. A new analysis of regional book provision in North Rhine-Westphalia has been given by: Günther Pflug: Sondersammelgebiete und Kommunaler Leihring. This is a contribution to the Festschrift Wilhelm Schmitz-Veltin: Die Öffentliche Bibliothek. Auftrag und Verwirklichung. Berlin 1968, p. 147—158.

Regional Union Catalogues and Inter-Library Loans

The inter-library loan regulations of 1966 are printed in the Jahrbuch der Deutschen Bibliotheken. 42, 1967, and in: Bibliotheksrechtliche Vorschriften. Zusammengestellt von Ralph Lansky. 2. erw. Aufl. Frankfurt 1969.

The guiding principles for the Kommunaler Leihring are given in the booklet issued by the Bibliothekar-Lehrinstitut in Cologne and the Verband der Bibliotheken des Landes Nordrhein-Westfalen: Der Kommunale Leihring in Nordrhein-Westfalen. Köln 1962.

The Bavarian inter-library loan regulations are given in: Bekanntmachung über den Leihverkehr zwischen den wissenschaftlichen Bibliotheken und den öffentlichen Büchereien in Bayern, in the Amtsblatt des Bayerischen Staatsministeriums für Unterricht und Kultus. 1967, Nr. 1.

A comprehensive bibliography, listing works on union catalogues, inter-library lending and the two operations together, has been published by the heads of the Baden-Württemberg and Bavarian union catalogues, Ernst Zunker and Eberhard Semrau: Der Leihverkehr in der Bundesrepublik Deutschland. Frankfurt 1968. (ZfBB, Sonderheft 8).

This booklet is at the same time the most important source of information on inter-library lending. It contains the new regulations, with explanation and a detailed introductory essay by Heinrich Middendorf.

The standard account also remains important: Walter Koschorreck: Geschichte des "Deutschen Leihverkehrs". Wiesbaden 1958 (Beiträge zum Buch- und Bibliothekswesen. 7).

The most recent account of the Kommunaler Leihring by Günther Pflug has been mentioned under co-operative acquisition schemes.

Regional Library Planning

The two publications produced by the Deutscher Büchereiverband and its Arbeitsstelle have already been referred to in the text: Grundlagen für die bibliothekarische Regionalplanung. Wiesbaden 1966, and based on it: Bibliotheksplan. 1. Entwurf für ein umfassendes Netz öffentlicher Bibliotheken und Büchereien. Berlin 1969.

The former contains a draft scheme for development in the Landkreise. Beihefte 10 and 15 of Büchereidienst (Berlin 1965 and 1966) are devoted to the same subject: Bibliothekarische Regionalplanung (containing papers presented at a conference organised by the Arbeitsstelle in 1964) and Regionalplanung. Formen bibliothekarischer Zusammenarbeit an drei Beispielen: Bayern, Saarland, Bremen (papers for the annual conference of the Deutscher Büchereiverband in 1966).

The Bavarian library system is outlined by Gustav Hofmann in his introduction to the Handbuch der bayerischen Bibliotheken. Hrsg. Klaus Dahme. Wiesbaden 1966.

Associations and Central Institutions

Full and up-to-date information about library associations, organisations and institutions will be found in the two biennial publications: Jahrbuch der Deutschen Bibliotheken, and Handbuch der Öffentlichen Büchereien (cf. particulars in Chapter 8).

The activity of the Verein Deutscher Bibliothekare since 1950 can only be learned from its chairman's annual reports to the assembly of members, printed in the Zeitschrift für Bibliothekswesen und Bibliographie. A retrospect of its first 50 years is given in a paper by: Georg Leyh: Fünfzig Jahre Verein Deutscher Bibliothekare. In: Nachrichten für wissenschaftliche Bibliotheken, Beiheft 1 (1950), p. 1—22.

The public library organisations are dealt with in: Gustav Rottacker: Büchereigesetze und Büchereiverbände. In: Handbuch des Büchereiwesens. 2. Halbband. Wiesbaden 1965. p. 192—237.

A retrospect by Erich Wilkens is: Der Deutsche Büchereiverband 1949 bis 1964. Berlin 1964 (Büchereidienst, Beiheft 8).

The Schmitz-Veltin Festschrift (see above) contains a contribution by Werner Krieg: Der Verband der Bibliotheken des Landes Nordrhein-Westfalen. Probleme bibliothekarischer Zusammenarbeit (p. 127—146).

The aims and activity of the Bibliothekarische Auslandsstelle were first reported by its secretary, Horst Ernestus, at the IFLA conference of 1965: Libri 15 (1965), p. 373—377.

A summary of aid given to libraries by the Deutsche Forschungsgemeinschaft up to 1965, with an account of the principles and organisation of the work, reports on certain major projects, a history of the early days and a complete survey of the promotional activities, is given in: Fünfzehn Jahre Bibliotheksarbeit der Deutschen Forschungsgemeinschaft. Frankfurt 1966. (ZfBB, Sonderheft 4).

Subsequent work is reported on every year in a special chapter of: Bericht der Deutschen Forschungsgemeinschaft über ihre Tätigkeit von ... bis ... Wiesbaden.

Beiheft 16 of Büchereidienst (Berlin 1966) gives a report: Klaus-Dietrich Hoffmann: Die Arbeitsstelle für das Büchereiwesen in Berlin.

It also contains the two papers: Herbert Eisentraut and Helmut Schiller: Die Einkaufszentrale für Öffentliche Büchereien — ein Instrument des Büchereiwesens.

4   Some Aspects of Library Administration and Services

4.1   Standards, Model Budgets

In principle it is for each individual library to prepare its own budget. There are nonetheless various reasons that make the preparation of standard or model budgets for a distinct category of library seem advisable both to libraries and to the authorities. The individual library can adjust its own draft estimates by comparison with it; the sponsor receives objective criteria by which to judge financial proposals; and with the help of such standards and models it will eventually gradually be possible to level up the endowments of libraries which serve the same functions but which owing to decentralisation differ widely in their resources. Experience has taught that norms and models are only temporary. Every so often the basic principles have to be carefully reconsidered and norms and models revised.

4.11   Libraries of Universities and Colleges of University Status

The term "model budget" in the realm of academic libraries has come into common use since the Empfehlungen ("Recommendations") of the Wissenschaftsrat in 1964. Previously there were the reports of the Deutsche Forschungsgemeinschaft: "Lage und Erfordernisse der westdeutschen Bibliotheken" ("The Position and Requirements of West German Libraries"), 1951; "Gutachten über den Normaletat einer Technischen Hochschulbibliothek" ("Report on the Standard Budget of a Technical University Library"), 1957; and "Etatmodell für eine Universitätsbibliothek" ("Model Budget for a University Library"), 1958. The Wissenschaftsrat drew up one model budget for a university library and another for a technical university library. "Model" in this sense means the basic structure to be achieved by each member of this group and relates only to what might be called "normal" current requirement. The model is therefore supplemented by the "individual recommendations", in which the contemporary special functions of the particular library are considered and in which future ad hoc grants are proposed in order to compensate at least to some extent for what has not been provided in the abnormal last 25 years.

The model budgets for university libraries fall into two parts, acquisitions and establishment; the estimates for the latter give the number of different posts, but not the cost in salaries. The estimates for acquisitions are based upon the material that ought to be purchased. In this respect the basis differs from that used for public libraries; for them as for American public libraries the local population figure is used. The basis differs also from the ALA Standards for College Libraries (1959) and for Junior College Libraries (1960), according to which the college library should receive a fixed percentage of the total college budget. The number of students in a university is in Germany, quite apart from fluctuations, not a relevant criterion: library purchases, corresponding largely to the dual teaching and research function of the university, cover not only students' books but also research material — and upon that student numbers have no influence. Only for text-book collections are such numbers relevant. The policy of relating total library expenditure, for both acquisitions and staffing, to the total university budget is conceivable only in universities where the library system forms a unity; in the existing West German universities this is not the case.

Like the American standards German model budgets are based upon empirical principles. The policy of using as the starting point the literature that ought to be purchased has the advantage of being concrete and detailed and also clear to the outsider; such a policy had been adopted as long ago as 1894 in a statement about the requirements of German university libraries.

The essence of the calculations is the number of current German and foreign periodicals needed; in this respect reliance is placed upon select lists of periodicals. Expenditure on series and other works in continuation as well as on monographs is fixed in a definite ratio to the cost of periodicals; in addition there is an amount fixed for second-hand purchases and a supplement of 25 % of the total acquisitions fund for binding costs.

The estimates look like this:

Book Purchases		University Library		Technical University Library
German and foreign periodicals	3,850:	210,000 DM	2,050:	145,000 DM
Continuations and series		105,000 DM		72,000 DM
Monographs		180,000 DM		108,000 DM
Second-hand material		25,000 DM		—
Total book purchases		520,000 DM		325,000 DM
Binding		130,000 DM		80,000 DM
Grand totals		650,000 DM		405,000 DM

These figures for the model are valid for 1965. An annual increment, corresponding to increases in production and in prices, has to be added after a current examination of the book market. The annual rise has been assessed by the Wissenschaftsrat on the basis of the years 1960–1963 at 5 % for each type of increase, that is 10 % in all; consequently a university library in 1968 has to obtain 865,150 DM, a technical university library 539,055 DM. Unfortunately, this percentage rate no longer corresponds with recent trends. At the moment one has to reckon about 15 %.

With regard to technical university libraries the 1964 model is already superseded owing to the restructuring of technical universities, which in some places has started and in others has already been completed (cf. 1.22). At all events the creation of new faculties means that the library undertakes to cover a completely new field and therefore requires more funds for purchases and more staff.

An amount for the current upkeep of text-book collections (cf. 2.31) will in future be added to the model as soon as the funds for this purpose from the Volkswagen Foundation have been expended; the new figure has been set at 10 DM per student per annum.

The amounts may seem low to many observers from abroad. To put them in perspective one must make it clear that they refer only to the central libraries in universities. Institute libraries attract further considerable funds, so that the total university expenditure on libraries is substantially higher. If, taking into consideration the model budget of 650,000 DM, the total expenditure amounts to between 1.3 and 1.9 million DM, this represents a ratio of the estimates for the central library to those for the whole complex of institutes, seminar and faculty libraries of 1 : 1 or 1 : 2, which the Wissenschaftsrat considers to be acceptable. In fact, in not a few places expenditure rises to 2.6 or even over 3 million DM, which results in a ratio of 1 : 3 or 1 : 4; such proportions seem to the Wissenschaftsrat to be extreme and unhealthy.

Assessments of staffing requirements in the model budgets have been based upon the work loads and productivity of libraries with certain levels of accessions but bearing in mind the readership and the functions of a university library. The figures read as follows:

	University Library	Technical University Library
Qualified graduates (administrative grade)	14	8
Qualified non-graduates (executive grade)	36	22
Unqualified assistants (clerical grade) and administrative officers	36	21
Technical assistants (including stack attendants)	24	16
Book binders	5	4
Photographic department	4	4
Total	119	75

(The professional education and spheres of duties of the various groups of librarians are described in chapter 7).

The model estimates have not yet been fulfilled either for acquisitions or for staff, although in general the situation has somewhat improved since the appearance of the Empfehlungen.

The models apply only to conditions in the existing universities. Of course no such models could be evolved for the library system in a newly established university still at its constructional and experimental stage.

For the college of education libraries endeavours are being made to prepare a model in the course of the reorganisation of the educational library system (cf. 2.32); a report of the Arbeitsgemeinschaft pädagogischer Bibliotheken (1962) offers the first data for this model. In such matters as accommodation, growth of stock and internal routines many concrete recommendations are made, for example: a stack with a capacity of 100,000 volumes, a reading room with seats for $^{1}/_{10}$ of the student body, an open-access collection of about 7,000 volumes, a bibliographical reference section of about 2,000 volumes, and a minimum of 250 current periodicals; an audio-visual department should be established and also an open-access library consisting of multiple copies (50 and more) of text-books for school practice. The subject funds are not to depend upon the number of students but upon the needs of study and teaching; the bases for calculation must first be worked out, taking into account the corresponding investigations for other academic libraries. As for staff the minimum establishment is stated as one qualified graduate librarian in charge (in certain cases part time), together with 2 qualified non-graduates and 2 technical assistants.

For the time being the average library is still far below these suggested standards.

4.12 Academic Staats-, Landes- and Stadtbibliotheken

Instead of a model budget the Wissenschaftsrat recommends for Landes-bibliotheken, which it places in the same category as academic Stadt-bibliotheken, minimum requirements both for acquisitions and for professional personnel; the figures are intended to apply to 28 of these libraries which are subdivided into two groups. In the case of the five largest libraries the Wissenschaftsrat limits itself to specific recommendations, since it can find no basis common to all of them.

The following fixed sums are earmarked in the distribution of the book funds: 20,000 DM for collections of regional literature including literary archives, autographs, musical material, etc.; and 15,000 DM for second-hand purchases. The amounts for periodicals and series — 54,000 DM to 90,000 DM — and for monographs — 75,000 DM to 100,000 DM — are given only in the form of a sliding scale; binding costs are assessed at 25 % of the book funds, on an average about 50,000 DM. The total budget is estimated for 15 libraries at under 200,000 DM, for 13 libraries at 250,000 DM.

The following standards apply to staff:

with a budget of less than	200,000 DM	250,000 DM
qualified graduates	3	4
	(only in exceptional cases 1 or 2)	
qualified non-graduates	7	12
unqualified assistants	4	8

The Wissenschaftsrat leaves it an open question whether detailed model budgets for the Landes- and Stadtbibliotheken are possible in principle and merely not feasible at present because the concrete data are lacking. The participating libraries consider the preparation of certain standards to be desirable.

4.13 Lists of Standard Literature for Academic Libraries

Drawing up model budgets is made easier by select lists covering certain types of literature for a certain type of library, especially of current journals, which represent a constant commitment. At the same time they serve libraries as a useful guide to a basic stock, which each library will then supplement by its own selection to meet its own special responsibilities. In the public library sector a list of basic reference materials was published by the Arbeitsstelle für das Büchereiwesen in 1969. A basic list of journals for current subscription is in preparation. For academic libraries some lists of journals are available, some in preparation; they have been used in the calculations for the model budgets or are to be so used in the future.

The journals subcommittee of the libraries committee of the Forschungsgemeinschaft has undertaken this work for foreign journals since 1951.

The first result was a combined list of the so-called "A-journals" and "B-journals", published in 1957 as the "Verzeichnis ausgewählter wissenschaftlicher Zeitschriften des Auslandes (VAZ)"; the former covers foreign titles which are of fundamental importance in the individual subjects and which one should expect to find available in every major academic library, the latter comprises those specialist learned titles in all subjects for which the Forschungsgemeinschaft makes grants to the individual libraries participating in the co-operative acquisitions scheme.

Only the list of "A-journals" is a model list in the strict sense. A new revised edition appeared in 1969. It comprises approximately 2200 foreign titles in all fields of learning.

The model budgets for university libraries have laid both lists under tribute in their calculations; they assume purchase of all the A titles and in addition the purchase of a selection of the B ones — the selection varies from one library to another, but the total is about equal. The libraries in new universities are likewise guided by both lists in building up their holdings; they can go further with the B titles than the old university libraries, because they are concerned with subscriptions throughout the university.

A similar role to the list of B journals is played by the "Verzeichnis deutscher wissenschaftlicher Zeitschriften" ("List of German Learned Journals"), first compiled in 1952 by B. Sticker, who was then the publishing specialist of the Deutsche Forschungsgemeinschaft, now produced by the Deutsche Bibliothek (7th ed., 1968). Properly speaking, this is not a standard list either; on the contrary it names all current German learned journals. The term "learned" taken in a strict sense forms the criterion for inclusion. This list also has been used for the model budgets in order to determine the number of German journals to be taken by a university library.

On the other hand, as a result of a recommendation of the Wissenschaftsrat there is now being compiled, expressly as a standard list of journals, a selection of German titles in all subject fields, which is intended to serve as a guide to the Landes- and Stadtbibliotheken in their purchases. A small ad hoc working party of representatives of the participating libraries, set up by the journals subcommittee of the Forschungsgemeinschaft, made the selection, which was submitted for approval to the Arbeitsgemeinschaften of the Landes- and Stadtbibliotheken. The working party completed its task in 1969. Since the complete list — with about 820 titles and a total subscription cost of about 47,000 DM per annum — exceeds the capacity of the single library, apart from a few exceptions, it has been suggested that agreements should be reached to distribute purchases among individual libraries in such a way that within any one regional cluster at least one copy of all the journals in the list will be held.

4.14 Public Libraries

The Kommunale Gemeinschaftsstelle für Verwaltungsvereinfachung (cf. 1.56) published in 1964 a report on municipal public libraries of the Gemeinden with upwards of 10,000 inhabitants. This comprehensive document entitled "Kommunale Öffentliche Bücherei" lays down principles and measures for the organisation and cost effectiveness of these libraries. It is still the most important starting point when organisational considerations are in question or the expansion of public libraries and public library systems is being planned. For this very reason one may expect that the report will be amended on specific points from time to time in the light of new developments.

The report is significant for many reasons. It is the first time that the Kommunale Gemeinschaftsstelle (KGSt) has concerned itself so thoroughly with one of the cultural institutions of the Gemeinden. In so doing it came to the conclusion that today public libraries are to be counted as basic services of the Gemeinden. The committee preparing the report, which in accordance with the general practice of the KGSt was chaired by one of their senior consultants, comprised equal numbers of government specialists and librarians from Gemeinden of varying sizes. Close contact was maintained with the Arbeitsstelle für das Büchereiwesen and its Arbeitskreise (cf. 3.24).

The results of the work are based on profound professional library subject knowledge; on the other hand they owe their effectiveness to the participation of the government representatives and to the authority of the KGSt.

The report aims at the most efficient library service possible and considers both the present stage of development in the Federal Republic and international standards. It demands for the libraries in Gemeinden with a population of upwards of 10,000: a professional librarian in charge; a stock adequate in quality and quantity and available on open access; subject arrangement, display, and issue of stocks including information and advisory services; bibliographical tools accessible to readers; displays of periodicals; reading and study rooms or corresponding places in the circulation areas; participation in inter-library lending schemes; and adequate opening times — at least 20 to 30 hours a week, central libraries 40 to 60 hours.

As a provisional target at which to aim a stock of one book per inhabitant with a minimum of 10,000 volumes for each library and a readership of 15 % of the population is given. An average of 30 issues per annum is expected from each reader.

Such results are based upon assumptions for budgets and staffing, the figures for which are estimated from average costs. Accordingly 12 % of the stock has to be renewed each year because books deteriorate physically and become out of date in subject matter. Three per cent of the optimum holdings of the established library is regarded as an adequate figure for the annual increase in stock.

As for staffing requirements the statistics for issues and accessions are relied upon as quantitative criteria. As a basis the report quotes a figure of 30,000 volumes issued per annum per librarian. With an annual accessions rate of 15 % of the stock there would also be required for every professional librarian concerned with loans 0.2 professional staff for central duties or 1 librarian for every 7,500 volumes acquired during the year. The extra requirements in non-professional staff can be deduced from the rule that for one librarian two other employees are considered to be necessary; where there is locally strong centralisation and rationalisation, a ratio of 1 : 1 is held to be sufficient.

The report of the KGSt has led in many towns to an improved library organisation and to better personnel and financial provision; it has influenced or supplemented standards included in other documents: the "Grundlagen für die bibliothekarische Regionalplanung" ("Fundamentals for Regional Library Planning"), the "Modell eines Aufbauplanes für Landkreise" ("Model of an Expansion Plan for Landkreise"), and the "Bibliotheksplan" ("Library Plan"), all three (cf. 3.14) products of the Arbeitsstelle für das Büchereiwesen. The "Modell eines Aufbauplanes" singles out four major categories of libraries and lays down for

Category 1 (1,000—5,000 inhabitants): 2.5 volumes per inhabitant and part-time staff;

Category 2 (5,000—10,000 inhabitants): 2.0 volumes per inhabitant and 1 professional librarian;

Category 3 (10,000—20,000 inhabitants): 1.5 volumes per inhabitant and staff according to the recommendation of the KGSt;

Category 4 (20,000 and more inhabitants): 1.0 volumes per inhabitant and staff according to the recommendation of the KGSt.

A minimum size for a local library is therefore laid down as 2,500 volumes; in this connection the estimate for the size of holdings and the number of staff assume certain economies of functions at the regional level. In the model for rural libraries the book budget earmarks 10 % for the purchase of replacements of books that have deteriorated physically or become out of date in subject matter. These maintenance costs are calculated from the average price of a book, with an additional amount for processing it (including binding costs), plus a further amount for renewing library materials and library equipment.

4.2 Internal Organisation

4.21 Academic Libraries

The larger academic libraries have traditionally three main departments besides administration: accessions, cataloguing, circulation. In addition there are in certain cases special departments for manuscripts, incunabula, maps, music and for those languages like the Oriental and Slavonic ones that require specialist knowledge. The large Staatsbibliotheken have all the special departments named, whereas university libraries, Landes- and Stadtbibliotheken have only some of them. Technical installations, nowadays taking up more and more space, such as photographic, duplicating and copying services — to which also the bindery must be added — usually come under administration, but are also sometimes brought together to form a separate technical department.

The *accessions department* deals with all the ordering processes and the receipt of books; it is divided into sections concerned with purchases, exchanges, books deposited under copyright regulations, and duplicates; the section concerned with exchanges normally deals also with incoming gifts. The *cataloguing department* is responsible for the maintenance of all the catalogues in the library, the processes of cataloguing and the reproduction of entries, the preparation of recent accessions lists, and co-operative work with union catalogues. The *circulation department* comprises apart from the lending and inter-library lending services the control of the stack and the reading rooms, generally also the information service, although this has recently been granted more independence.

At the head of the departments there are academic librarians, that is, qualified graduates on the administrative grade; posts within the departments are filled according to circumstances with staff on the administrative or executive grades. Superimposed on the departmental structure is the system of subject specialisation. This is the chief task of the academic librarian in so far as he is not a specialist in charge of one of the special departments or as chief or deputy does not bear overall responsibility. Subject specialisation covers book selection, maintenance of the classified catalogue, and assistance to readers in the relevant field; in university libraries the work also includes liaison with the institutes. The allocation of subject responsibilities depends on the individual library and on the number of specialists available. Comprehensive fields, such as jurisprudence and political science, economics and sociology, medicine, usually also Germanic studies, are each generally the responsibility of one specialist; others are combined for this purpose, e. g. English with Romance languages and literatures, history with the history of art or even with Slavonic studies, Oriental studies with ethnology, philosophy with theology, etc. As far as it is at all possible, the librarian is entrusted with his own specialist subject or one of the subjects that he has studied; the understanding is that he will continue to concern himself with it. The number of accessions means that he must regularly keep abreast of the literature in the field. As a rule a subject specialist is also in charge of one of the departments or sub-departments.

The principle of the three-tier structure and of subject specialisation was confirmed in 1967 in the "Gutachten über Rationalisierungsmöglichkeiten in wissenschaftlichen Bibliotheken" ("Report on the Possibilities of Rationalising Academic Libraries"), which the consultant Hermann v. Kortzfleisch submitted to the Forschungsgemeinschaft. For academic, in the first instance university, libraries R. Kluth proposed in 1965 an organisation with academic subject departments and two central departments, one of them concerned with professional and bibliographical matters, the other containing technical installations. It is in accordance with this structure that the new University Library of Bremen is being built at the moment; by laying emphasis upon the subject element the Library is expected to be linked more closely with the University. What advantages this system offers will not be clear until after several years of experience.

Every chief is anxious that the routine work of his library should run as smoothly as possible and is ready to grasp at any innovation to this end whether in organisation or in techniques. These endeavours are supported by a co-operative investigation undertaken by librarians and the Kommunale Gemeinschaftsstelle für Verwaltungsvereinfachung (cf. 1.56); in this investigation each library process is subjected to close scrutiny in order that the best possible proposals may be made for improvement.

These endeavours have latterly received support from two investigations published by the Forschungsgemeinschaft under the title "Rationalisierung in wissenschaftlichen Bibliotheken", 1970. The one is the already-mentioned report by H. v. Kortzfleisch, which based as it is on general management principles outlines proposals for a functional organisation of library work as a whole and of individual routines in particular. The other is the outcome of an exchange of experiences under the auspices of the Kommunale Gemeinschaftsstelle (see the previous paragraph) between librarians and organisation and methods men of the public authorities. Here much light is thrown on the most important library processes, and recommendations are made for their rationalisation. Both reports are based upon the present condition of the average general academic library. They are limited to conventional measures without taking into account automatic data processing.

4.22 Public Libraries

The internal organisation of the larger public libraries is concerned on the one hand with functions inherent in the administration of *library systems* (with central libraries, permanent branches, mobile and special libraries) and on the other hand with the character of *central libraries* themselves.

a) The growth of *library systems* in large towns has caused central library administrations increasingly to take over the functions of all the libraries in the system in order to effect economies and a certain uniformity in routines and development. Central purchasing, cataloguing, classifying and processing of books ready for loan (with all relevant records) in the individual libraries, are all nowadays accepted without question. With the union catalogue and the bibliographical holdings at the main library as bases, lending for the whole system is also as a rule organised centrally. Moreover, according to how far a particular town has advanced, the preparation of subject lists and printed catalogues, together with publicity and public relations, are to a great extent concentrated. In several towns the work of the branches, the mobile libraries, and the youth libraries are each co-ordinated by a librarian at headquarters. The Hamburger Öffentliche Bücherhallen have also as part of their establishment a specialist in library building and equipment (cf. 5.2).

The report of the Kommunale Gemeinschaftsstelle für Verwaltungsvereinfachung has also suggested criteria for the centralisation and decentralisation of library functions without wishing to lay down a definite scheme in detail. Among the functions that have been centrally developed due to this report, is the Lektoratsdienst ("subject specialisation", cf. 4.3).

In some large towns such as Bremen and Munich (where such decentralisation as exists in West Berlin is not prescribed under the constitution) a regional substructure has been introduced for libraries in order to relieve the central libraries of certain functions and to achieve more manageable units with a limited economic self-sufficiency. Within such regions one of the larger libraries then assumes more or less clearly defined administrative and co-ordinating functions especially as regards acquisitions, circulation and staff.

In so far as there are in a library system subsidiary service points which spread the burden of lending but do not possess the stock and the characteristics of a fully fledged branch (e. g. professional staff), they are often administered from the branches or the main library. In some towns (Duisburg, Bielefeld) attemps have recently been made to do without a qualified librarian even in the smaller branches and to transfer professional control to a larger branch.

This is done to reduce expenditure on staff, to enable qualified librarians to perform professional duties and to achieve stricter co-ordination within the system.

The training of library assistants, which at present is being planned and pioneered by local and regional experiments (cf. 7.23), should be regarded as clearing the ground for this development.

b) In the *central libraries* because of the prevalent segregation of the academic Stadtbibliothek from the Öffentliche Bücherei and the relatively small stocks of the central libraries of the public library systems the twofold division common to many large Anglo-Saxon public libraries into "reference" and "lending" departments has not developed.

The Amerika-Gedenkbibliothek ("American Memorial Library"), opened in 1953 in West Berlin, was the first central library in a German city arranged on the principle of a "departmentalised library". Apart from a popular department for fiction and the lighter non-fiction (corresponding approximately to a large branch library), a separate children's library together with another library for young people, there are departments for the major fields of the humanities, natural sciences, technology and sociology, music and the fine arts. One feature of the departments is the linking of reading areas with open access shelves, on which the reader finds reference material side by side with lending material and periodicals. Communication with the closed stacks, the contents of which are recorded in the departmental classified catalogues, is achieved by means of pneumatic tubes and book lifts to the enquiry desks. Through the daily lending and advisory services the departmental librarians acquire specialist knowledge in the appropriate subject fields, for which they also help to select and exploit the literature. Apart from exceptional cases, issue control is maintained not in the departments but at the main service point. This departmental structure has been introduced into the main libraries of Bremen, Duisburg and Hanover.

4.3 Book Selection and Acquisitions Work in Public Libraries

The transformation and expansion of public library functions and the consequent growth of libraries and library systems not only led to new principles in book selection but also influenced routine procedures. The much greater emphasis upon non-fiction, including learned works not specifically intended for research purposes, made it essential in large public libraries that the whole of German book production should be currently examined by librarians with specialist subject knowledge. The funds available, usually still very restricted, have made careful selection obligatory.

The report of the Kommunale Gemeinschaftsstelle, "Kommunale Öffentliche Bücherei", introduced the concept of the Lektorat ("subject specialisation"); for its fullest development this required in large towns one Hauptlektor ("senior subject reader") for each of the following fields: fiction, languages and literatures, humanities, social sciences, pure sciences and technology, possibly even books for the young and music.

Such a Lektorat, the principal task of which is the central sifting and appraisal of literature as a preliminary to book selection, is today already found in one form or another in many towns. Occasionally the departmental heads in the main library act as Lektoren ("subject readers") for the whole library system.

The librarians in the branches usually participate in the appraisal of literature. In many library systems they also exercise a decisive influence upon the selection of literature for their libraries, perhaps within a fixed share of the budget or on the basis of the suggestions made by the Lektorat. In other towns the central administration (Lektorat) determines to a greater extent which titles are bought and for which libraries.

The smaller town libraries often rely upon the deliberations of the Lektoren in large towns. For libraries within the area covered by the Staatliche Büchereistellen the selected book lists issued by the latter constitute an important aid to selection. These appear from time to time either separately published or in periodicals. At the instigation of the professional conference of the Staatliche Büchereistellen there appeared in 1968 for the first time a co-operative catalogue, "Neue Bücher" ("New Books"), listing titles recommended by the Büchereistellen in the Federal Republic.

In 1970, the Conference of Large Town Public Libraries within the Verband der Bibliotheken des Landes Nordrhein-Westfalen put forward a plan for a national reviewing and cataloguing service to be sponsored by the Deutscher Büchereiverband and the Einkaufszentrale für Öffentliche Büchereien. It suggests that efficient public libraries and Staatliche Büchereistellen all over the country should accept responsibilities in certain subject areas. The whole service should be co-ordinated at Reutlingen. Later in 1970 a hearing will be held, which should then be followed by a feasibility study.

The most important bibliographical tools for assessing book production are, besides the entries in the "Wöchentliche Verzeichnisse" ("Weekly Lists") of the "Deutsche Bibliographie" ("German Bibliography") published in Frankfurt (cf. 2.11), the "Börsenblatt des deutschen Buchhandels" (cf. 1.3), with its special editions, and the wholesale catalogues of the firms Lingenbrink (Libri), Koehler-Volckmar, Wengenroth and others. Among the specialist professional aids covering more than one region is the periodical, "Bücherei und Bildung" ("Library and Education"), with about 3,000 reviews of new publications per annum submitted by over 200 reviewers (predominantly librarians). Libraries can obtain these reviews as an "express service" in the form of galley proofs about four weeks before publication. 4,000 résumés annually of reviews, most of which are published in "Bücherei und Bildung", are contained in the monthly "Buchanzeiger für Öffentliche Büchereien" of the Einkaufszentrale für Öffentliche Büchereien" (cf. 3.25). The magazine is provided with various indexes, and the supplement, "Hilfen für den Bestandsaufbau", is arranged in classified order of subject fields. Recently a current awareness service on cards has been distributed to libraries and is likely to be increased; this might form the basis for the service suggested at the Conference of Large Town Public Libraries in North Rhine-Westphalia.

Another non-regional tool is the "AGB-Titeldienst" ("AGB Cataloguing Service"), which in its annual 25 issues offers around 5,000 catalogue entries on cards of international format; distribution has been taken

over by the Deutscher Büchereiverband. The titles are selected by
librarians of the Amerika-Gedenkbibliothek from current book production and reach subscribers very quickly, serving them as notices of recent
noteworthy publications and also as basic aids to cataloguing.

The final decision on purchase is often not taken until the books themselves have been examined. The possibility of this is offered by many
well-developed town bookshops, which are increasingly expected to
supply books on approval in the first instance. The Einkaufszentrale für
Öffentliche Büchereien displays books for inspection in its headquarters
in Reutlingen, but also maintains display and sale rooms in most of the
Staatliche Büchereistellen of the Länder.

4.4 Catalogues and Cataloguing

4.41 Academic Libraries

Immediately on the resumption of work after the War great efforts were
made to revise or completely reconstruct library catalogues, which owing
to bomb-damage very seldom corresponded to holdings.

As a rule the academic libraries in the Federal Republic maintain the
following catalogues:

1. an alphabetical author catalogue, in which works by known and
anonymous authors are indexed in one sequence (there are sometimes
two copies of this catalogue, one for use by the public and one for use
by the library staff);

2. one, or more, subjects catalogues either in "systematic", i. e. classified,
order or as a Schlagwortkatalog ("alphabetical subject catalogue") or
even divided into various catalogues each devoted to one class.

The principle is that the whole stock of the library is covered by entries
in the catalogues and that the catalogues are accessible to readers. When
a library maintains two subject catalogues side by side, one a classified
catalogue and the other a Schlagwortkatalog, certain categories of works
(e. g. theses and fiction) are often omitted from the latter on grounds of
expediency.

It only remains to mention the shelf register, which, since the arrangement of the classified catalogue was separated from that of the books on
the shelves, serves now only as an inventory, an aid to assigning call

numbers and a tool for stocktaking. It is therefore intended only for internal use, and the entries are severely abridged; for reasons of economy it is nowadays frequently combined with the accessions register.

The large dictionary catalogue, common in the USA, which enters in one sequence every work under its author, subject and title, is not found in Germany.

Among the comparatively few aids in our general academic libraries that have universally been maintained according to the same rules is the *alphabetical catalogue*. Since 1960 or thereabouts this sentence has needed qualification. The normative code, the "Preußische Instruktionen" ("Prussian Instructions") (Instruktionen für die alphabetischen Kataloge der preußischen Bibliotheken, Berlin 1899, 2nd. ed. 1909), is at the moment being transformed. Consequently the cataloguers of the new foundations have adopted the already accepted changes in the earlier rules and the union lists of periodicals follow the new filing principles, whereas the existing libraries ordinarily cannot but continue to follow the old rules.

The fact that some points in the "Instruktionen" called for reform had long been known to German librarians. After 1945 the Verband der Bibliotheken des Landes Nordrhein-Westfalen ventured upon the revision and set up a cataloguing committee. This project received decisive encouragement from the movement initiated by IFLA towards an international agreement on cataloguing practice. After basic preliminary work on the part of German cataloguing experts the representative of the Federal Republic at the International Conference on the Principles of Alphabetical Cataloguing in Paris in September 1961 was able to assent to two important points which overthrew principles behind the "Instruktionen". The first was the filing of titles according to their natural word order instead of the grammatical and logical word order, which had until then been the rule. The second was the introduction of corporate authorship as an element in the form of the entry just as decisive as the author and, in the case of an anonymous work, the first significant noun had hitherto been. In addition there were a few less important changes in the form of compound names.

Both changes have been adopted since 1966 by the Deutsche Bibliothek for the arrangement of the "Deutsche Bibliographie". What work may be involved in revising a catalogue for an existing older library is carefully investigated before a commitment is made. From January 1965 to May

1966 two small study groups in the University Libraries of Mainz and Saarbrücken, financed by the Forschungsgemeinschaft, made some experiments, the results of which were not sufficient to persuade a library to accept the dislocation of its filing system. The other expedient, that of "freezing" the old catalogues on some appointed day and making a fresh start with new rules, would not be altogether satisfactory.

At the moment all the larger libraries are striving hard to rationalise and expedite cataloguing procedures. If one could assume that the new rules would enable this goal to be reached more quickly than the old ones, that would be a reason for existing libraries to adopt them as soon as possible. The rules can be the driving force for new university libraries because they, following the example of Bochum, intend to avail themselves of electronic data processing in their cataloguing.

One essential aid to rationalisation, the central reproduction of entries by one library, had been established through the Prussian State Library and was gradually developing from its early beginnings in 1898. Recent accessions of foreign literature were covered by a co-operative venture of German academic libraries with its headquarters in the State Library in Berlin; German recent accessions were covered by the Deutsche Bücherei in Leipzig, the compilers of the "Nationalbibliographie". Both libraries prepared printed cards, which could be ordered by all libraries. A corresponding service for academic libraries today in the Federal Republic does not exist. Entries for recent German publications began to be available from the Deutsche Bibliothek in Frankfurt from 1951 onwards, but ceased after a number of years because the DB could not produce them sufficiently promptly for libraries to feel the benefit of relief and speed. Of course it is possible to incorporate in one's own catalogue material from the single-sided weekly printed edition of the "Deutsche Bibliographie (wöchentliches Verzeichnis)". Following the production of this bibliography with the aid of a computer a new approach towards a catalogue card service as well as the provision of entries on magnetic tape are under consideration.

In contrast with the fundamental uniformity of the alphabetical catalogue in academic libraries there is a far-reaching diversity in *subject catalogues*. This is typical of the German situation. There existed and still exist subject catalogues in the form either of a classified catalogue or of a Schlagwortkatalog, in many libraries even both together; there existed and still exist differently constructed systems, but no uniform model. The vehement debate between 1920 and 1940 about questions of principle, such as the introduction of the Decimal Classification, a decision for or against the then rather modern Schlagwortkatalog, has not been revived; the proposed standard system, for which a committee on subject cataloguing was set up by the VDB in 1933, has owing to the War not materialised, and it has been only recently that voices have again been raised in favour of such a system.

Of course it is merely the form that varies; libraries agree over the function and purpose of the subject catalogue. The system of arrangement of the most important component of the library, its bookstock, is no longer an end in itself and does not exist merely for the sake of the library staff. The old-fashioned subject catalogue as the preserve of the academic librarian, kept in his room, accessible to the reader only with professional assistance, belongs to the past. So does the use of the subject catalogue as the shelf register — though there have been recent revivals of this practice.

Undoubtedly the subject catalogue is a means of making holdings accessible to the reader. The divorce of the arrangement in the catalogue from that on the shelves resulted from a famous paper by Georg Leyh in 1912, "Das Dogma von der systematischen Aufstellung" ("The Dogma of Classified Arrangement"). The change, which took place at first in isolated cases and eventually owing to post-War reconstruction in all university libraries, gave librarians a free hand in reshaping their subject catalogues. A feature of the reconstruction period has been the concept of a new scheme of subject cataloguing founded solely on the point of view and experience of the individual library, without attempting to find on co-operative grounds a basis suitable for all. And so it happened that — as W. Gebhard proved from a survey in 1959 — out of 15 libraries that had started a classified catalogue since 1945 10 had a home-made system. Not until the new university libraries were founded did the principles change again: classified arrangement has been introduced, and a co-operative attempt is being made within this circle to arrive at a model subject classification.

From the period before 1945 two classification schemes, apart from the Decimal Classification, have survived, the "Eppelsheimer Method" and the "Gülich System". The spheres of influence of the DC and the Gülich System are primarily special libraries, that of the Eppelsheimer Method general libraries. There are however exceptions: 6 university libraries base their classified catalogue wholly or for certain subjects upon DC, 10 special libraries besides 9 general libraries rely on Eppelsheimer.

The form of arrangement which H. W. Eppelsheimer had devised for the Stadtbibliothek Mainz and brought to public notice at a librarians' conference in 1929 puts a method into the hand of the cataloguer without laying down a system. The freedom to determine the underlying system of subject fields themselves, the flexibility of the method, a certain approximation to the Schlagwortkatalog had already between 1929 and 1939 but especially during the period of reconstruction since 1945 won a number of adherents. One principle in particular has proved highly valuable in cataloguing practice, that of providing "Schlüssel" ("standard subdivisions") — a "general", supplemented if necessary by a "geographical" and a "literature", table of subdivisions — in order to bring the recurring formal aspects of any subject into a fixed order and thereby facilitate the use of simpler notation.

The system which W. Gülich evolved from 1924 onwards in the Library of the Institut für Weltwirtschaft at Kiel out of the material there (works on world economic relations in the broad sense) has been conceptually and technically extremely well devised. It has the external form of the Schlagwortkatalog, although through the subdividing of major topics many of them appear almost as if they were in classified order. The five different sections of the catalogue, covering subjects, corporations, regions, persons and titles, constitute when taken together the great reference tool which answers the enquirer's questions about the material in stock. The Kiel catalogue served as a model for the establishment of the Library of the Bundestag and has furthermore been used by some institute libraries as a basis for the building up not only of the catalogues but also of the collections themselves. The fact that the Kiel Library supplied to subscribers complete or partial sets of its catalogue cards with classification numbers makes it easier to adopt the system (cf. 2.41 and 6.13).

On the initiative and with the strong financial support of the Forschungsgemeinschaft the *cataloguing of manuscripts* has made great progress during the last 10 years. In this connection two spheres of interest need distinguishing. The "Katalogisierung der orientalischen Handschriften in Deutschland" ("Cataloguing of Oriental Manuscripts in Germany"), begun in 1958 and covering also holdings in East Germany, is an undertaking in classified order, centrally edited by W. Voigt (of the Staatsbibliothek Preußischer Kulturbesitz), uniformly arranged by language regions, compiled by university teachers and librarians, and with a uniform plan for publishing the individual volumes. So far 29 volumes are available, from the Steiner publishing house of Wiesbaden; others are in preparation.

The cataloguing of both medieval and modern Western manuscripts and literary remains began on a fairly large scale in 1961 after a few pioneering local attempts. The project covers, in accordance with German tradition, the manuscript holdings of specific libraries. The compilers are financed predominantly from the funds of the Forschungsgemeinschaft, but partly also from the libraries themselves. Only the catalogues of medieval and modern codices have been printed, but not in uniform format and not tied to one particular publisher. Deliberately no attempt has been made to produce a full-scale corpus; during the German Reich the attempt was twice made and twice interrupted by a war. Nevertheless uniform methods of compilation are ensured by printed instructions, by the permanent oversight of the results by the consultants of the Forschungsgemeinschaft, and by study conferences at which the compilers and the consultants meet to discuss problems of cataloguing principles and practice. By the end of 1969 30 volumes had appeared or were in the press.

Altogether the Forschungsgemeinschaft is now contributing to both undertakings more than 1 million DM per annum.

4.42 Public Libraries

Public libraries have available the same *main catalogues* as those already treated in more detail under academic libraries: alphabetical author catalogues and classified catalogues in card form are keys to the whole stock of individual libraries. As union catalogues in library systems they also supply locations in branches or other dependent libraries. Unlike the classified catalogue the Schlagwortkatalog is more rarely seen except that fairly frequently a Schlagwortregister ("subject index") refers to the classes and sub-classes in the classified catalogue.

The shelf register as a tool for stocktaking is found likewise in public libraries. The particular desire in a public library to help the reader, often without any academic education, to find his way round has given rise to *special types of indexes to stock*: e. g. title catalogues for fiction and children's literature, biographical catalogues, and subject guides that classify belles lettres from the standpoint of genre and content.

Many public libraries add to the bibliographical data keywords or even carefully formulated "subtitles" as aids to the reader. The same details are then often repeated on the book card kept in the book for issue purposes.

The catalogue and book cards supplied with the books from the Einkaufszentrale für Öffentliche Büchereien are also provided with such subtitles. The publishers of "Bücherei und Bildung" offer with their "subtitle service" about 1,800 subtitles per annum on catalogue cards of international format, a service which is likely to be discontinued in the near future.

Apart from the card catalogues for readers and library staff, public libraries and Staatliche Büchereistellen compile *printed or duplicated partial and select lists,* available to the public at cost price or even gratis. Many such lists arise from the collaboration of several libraries or Büchereistellen; frequently catalogues, issued by one library, are taken over by others. The Arbeitsstelle für das Büchereiwesen acts as a clearinghouse. It collects all booklists published by libraries and Büchereistellen and regularly sends specimens to subscribers to its catalogue exchange scheme. The lists range from leaflets to large bound catalogues. They appear separately or in series. Many are outstanding in form and content.

Cataloguing in public libraries follows the "Preußische Instruktionen" or the "Berliner Anweisungen" ("Berlin Instructions"). The latter, evolved in the early thirties as a simplified form especially for the then contemporary "Volksbüchereien", are based — unlike the Prussian code — on the filing of entries according to the natural word order. Both codes are locally often slightly modified. The Einkaufszentrale für Öffentliche Büchereien chose the Berlin one for its sets of cards.

The international agreement on cataloguing rules, long awaited and now achieved, caused some public libraries to look for a link between the Prussian code and filing according to the natural word order. The cataloguing service of the Amerika-Gedenkbibliothek supplies entries in this form.

Such a development is a move towards the uniform presentation and arrangement of entries, which is of obvious significance for library users as well as for library co-operation, e.g. the preparation of printed catalogues and booklists not confined to one locality or the further extension of centralised cataloguing and processing services.

An "Allgemeine Systematik für Büchereien" (ASB) ("General Classification for Public Libraries") could not be developed until after the War.

The time was ripe because almost everywhere the change from closed to open access had been completed, a change that imposed other demands on the display and classification of holdings. The preliminary work on the new scheme however stretched out over a rather long period; many libraries therefore arrived at their own solutions; others went their own ways because they believed the ASB to be inadequate. So there are now as before a host of different schemes, even though the ASB has been adopted in very many libraries, above all within the sphere of activity of the Staatliche Büchereistellen. One substantial contribution to its popularity is the fact that the Einkaufszentrale für Öffentliche Büchereien decided to provide its cataloguing material with the ASB numbers. Also the reviews in the periodical "Bücherei und Bildung" and in the EKZ's "Buchanzeiger für Öffentliche Büchereien" give ASB numbers.

The ASB divides subjects into 22 main classes (A–Y), which are in turn subdivided to a greater or lesser extent. For notation the ASB adopts a combination of letters and figures.

A new version of the ASB is at present being prepared by a committee of the Verband der Bibliotheken des Landes Nordrhein-Westfalen, which was also responsible for the first version. A "Systematik für Kinder- und Jugendbüchereien" ("Classification for Children's and Youth Libraries"), derived from the ASB, was compiled by an Arbeitskreis of the Arbeitsstelle für das Büchereiwesen in 1964.

The committee on classification of the Arbeitsgemeinschaft für Musikbüchereien of the German section of the AIBM has compiled a "Systematik der Musikliteratur und der Musikalien für Öffentliche Musikbüchereien" (cf. 2.83).

Recently renewed discussions have taken place, not least with the potentialities and requirements of electronic data processing in mind, to achieve a standard classification scheme for libraries of all types in the Federal Republic. At present it is not possible to pronounce on the success of such endeavours.

4.5 Problems Affecting Reader Service in Academic Libraries

For all types of libraries in the Federal Republic the principle holds good that the whole of a library's holdings should both be entered in the catalogues and also be at the disposal of adult readers without restriction. In academic libraries — and to some extent in large public libraries — in order to protect the physical substance of that part of the stock that needs to be preserved and not treated as expendable, certain restrictive measures are required, e. g. insistence upon use in the library only or for bona fide scholarly purposes only.

Two special reader service problems, singled out for discussion in the present section, affect academic libraries in the main.

Open or Closed Access

Public libraries have decided in favour of open access. In central libraries in large towns the stocks are indeed growing at such a rate that the question of splitting the stock into an open-access and a reserve collection is now arising. The difficulty increases also owing to the specialisation in literature, the acquisition of extensive runs of periodicals and the collecting functions of the libraries. Since there are no new buildings for libraries of this size and developments are in a state of flux, there is no compulsory standard governing the extent of large open-access libraries. Present plans provide for up to 300,000 volumes in open-access areas. Normally in the larger academic libraries of the Federal Republic (more in general than in special libraries) there is at present a closed stack with the bulk of the material available for loan. In this stack the older stock is shelved in classified order in conformity with the subject catalogue, the more recent stock simply in accession number order ("numerus currens"), either within broad subject classes or in one sequence throughout. At the same time there is a reference collection on open shelves of selected literature usually housed in a large general reading room, a periodicals room and also, according to the type of library, special reading rooms for manuscripts, incunabula, music, maps, and in large libraries even for Oriental and East European material. Moreover the bibliographical tools are so shelved that they can be personally consulted by the reader on the spot. He can borrow any book not shelved in the reference section and as a rule take it home; only distinct categories of particularly valuable or unique books come under the regulation that they must be consulted only in the reading rooms. Access to the stacks was formerly granted to privileged readers, e. g. in the university libraries to members of the teaching staff. With the change-over from the classified to the numerus-currens arrangement this has generally ceased, since interest in browsing palls when there is no collocation of subjects.

The retreat from the classified arrangement, which most of the larger general academic libraries have gradually accepted, has affected the library service more deeply than was thought at the outset. In the period of reconstruction after 1945 the libraries saw themselves compelled to adopt the administratively more rational arrangement when faced with the constant shortage of staff and space. It was only gradually seen that in so doing they had sacrificed much of their appeal, which had rested upon the direct contact between readers and books. Special and institute libraries have for this reason been preferred in that the readers have access to the books at any time. Therefore today the central university libraries in particular are breaking down the strict segregation of the inaccessible mass of stack material from the limited selection of reference material and instituting larger open-access sections.

The following are some of the measures to this end:

a) establishment of text-book collections in university libraries (cf. 2.31);

b) extension of the reading areas by "departmental" reading rooms, either near the large general reading room or instead of it with correspondingly substantial reference collections;

c) establishment of "departmental" open-access stacks each physically connected with a "departmental" reading room;

d) extension of the "departmental" reading room stock by displaying and at certain intervals renewing, alongside the reference collection properly so called, a section of "current" open-access loanable books on the relevant subject field;

e) and finally there is even, though only in some of the new university libraries, the classified arrangement of the whole stock in reference collections, sectional libraries and stacks with free access to all members of the university.

All these measures have been conceived in connection with plans for new buildings and have been introduced in new buildings (cf. 5.1). They show that the academic library of today is anxious to make the reader feel at home in the library and familiar with its resources, so that he can as far as practicable help himself.

Issue Procedure

In public libraries only one form of issue is known, the so-called "Sofortausleihe" ("immediate issue of books") even when it is a question of large central libraries with part of the stock on closed shelves. The same applies to most special libraries. This means that the reader can take away a book that he wants directly after completing the issue formalities. In the general academic libraries this happens only with the open-access collections. In the case of stack material, the sharp increase in library use in the 20th century has made the "reservation service" the rule, since this is the most reasonable procedure from the administrative point of view; under this method the reader places his issue slip in the appropriate box and fetches the book some hours later or on the following day (if all goes well). The procedure was the subject of frequent complaints from scholars. As one means of improving their service many libraries have therefore arranged for their staff to provide a Sofortausleihe, at least for those readers who desire it; in this case a wait of 10 to 20 minutes is thought to be tolerable. Certain conditions of staffing and accommodation must admittedly be fulfilled beforehand. In order to achieve success as quickly as possible after recognising the necessity, the Forschungs-gemeinschaft made initial grants to a number of university libraries for two or three years for appointing the extra establishment required; the expenditure has later been transferred to the normal funds. Favourable accommodation cicumstances could not usually be achieved except when new buildings were envisaged. In many instances with a new building the installation for such a service has been made permanent and stan-dard, which is what the Wissenschaftsrat also recommends.

4.6 Readers' Advisory and Information Services

It has always been one of the accepted duties of the librarian to give the reader every conceivable help in finding his way round the library. In German public libraries part of the essence of professional service (deriv-ing from its educational tradition) has been and still is today at least a willingness to advise the reader in his choice of reading. Special attention is paid to catalogues and select lists. Advisory functions in the American and British sense of "reference and information services" have never-theless not been generally developed except in special libraries. Sup-plying information as the other side of retrieving information is among the activities peculiarly appropriate to this type of institution.

4.61 Academic Libraries

The general academic libraries present a varied picture as far as advisory services are concerned. They are thoroughly aware of the task as such, especially after the emphasis given to it in the Empfehlungen of the Wissenschaftsrat. The way in which it is carried out varies according to the individual circumstances of each library. There are no prescribed regulations. In the larger libraries there is a tendency to concentrate the advisory services, which were formerly dispersed over the various departments.

Making the advisory services into a separate department — which is what has today been partly attempted and partly achieved — needs good staff and a sufficient number of them, an extensive bibliographical collection and working places easily accessible to the public. In the model budgets the Wissenschaftsrat proposed 4 non-graduate qualified librarians for a university library, 2 for a technical university library; the latter figure was attacked by the librarians concerned as too low. The Forschungsgemeinschaft assisted a number of university libraries to achieve this establishment by means of short-term grants.

It is general practice to entrust the major part of dealing with enquiries, primarily requests about the location of books and bibliographical queries, but also much else, to non-graduate qualified librarians, who are especially suited to this work. For subject information in scholarly fields the enquirer is referred to the specialist academic librarians; in many libraries a subject specialist has responsibility for the advisory service besides his other duties, or he may be engaged full time on answering enquiries. Information is given by word of mouth, over the telephone or in correspondence. In so doing one principle prevails: helping the enquirer to such an extent that he can then help himself. The librarian cannot and must not do all his work for him. Assembling the literature on a specific theme is part of the work of the scholar. Students in particular, who are expected to acquire the techniques of scholarly research, are therefore supplied only with references, by which they can get their bearings, but not with detailed assistance in exploiting the literature. This limitation in principle distinguishes the information service in general academic libraries from that in special ones.

Since the provision of the necessary bibliographical tools in many libraries had lagged behind that of other more urgent acquisitions, the Wissenschaftsrat in its individual recommendations for all the libraries under discussion (except for special libraries) proposed special funds for the building up of bibliographical material. How far problems of space affect this has again been shown in new library buildings, where there has been an immediate increase in demand for the services offered.

A bibliographical information agency for the Federal Republic, after the pattern of the former Auskunftsbüro der deutschen Bibliotheken at the Preußische Staatsbibliothek, does not at present exist. Whether, as the Wissenschaftsrat recommends, one of the regional union catalogues can undertake this function, is still being examined. As central agencies with restricted terms of reference the following should be mentioned: for bibliographical information on German literature since 9 May 1945 the Deutsche Bibliothek in Frankfurt; for all information in technology, agriculture and economics the appropriate central specialist libraries; for medicine the Deutsches Institut für medizinische Dokumentation und Information; and for details of locations within the regions the seven regional union catalogues.

4.62 Public Libraries

Public libraries have not until recent years and even then only hesitatingly accepted information services as a function to which particular attention should be paid along with advisory services. The time is still far off when the public library either for librarians or for private citizens serves as Everyman's information centre. Bibliographical information is the kind most likely to be expected from the public libraries, at all events within the limits imposed upon many places by the scanty provision of bibliographical resources. In imparting factual information of all kinds the difficulties lie not only in the lack of reference works, for which there is in the Federal Republic still nowhere nearly as good a publishers' market as there is, say, in the USA and Britain — not least owing to the existence in those countries of libraries actively involved in information service. It is rather due to a vicious circle in that on the one hand factual information to any notable extent is offered only by a few libraries and not yet particularly propagated as a public service and that on the other hand such a service still hardly figures in the educational curriculum of librarians.

Notwithstanding, there is ground for optimism in judging the future growth of information services. In professional debate and in the appeals addressed to the public by bodies representing the profession this library function is now often urged. In the report of the Kommunale Gemeinschaftsstelle für Verwaltungsvereinfachung on the "Kommunale Öffentliche Bücherei" the information service is treated side by side with the advisory service. The Arbeitsstelle für das Büchereiwesen has appointed a special committee to deal with these matters. As a first result of its activities a basic list of reference works was published in 1969 which suggests titles to form the minimal collections for central libraries in towns of 10,000 population as well as for branches in library systems. Above all however in certain public libraries there are solid foundations for such an information service. In the central libraries of Bremen, Duisburg and Hanover special information departments have been created and manned by their own staff. In this people were following the model of the Amerika-Gedenkbibliothek, which since its foundation in 1953 as the first "public" library had provided an information service as a matter of course and maintained it with great success. In the general information department of this West Berlin central library bibliographical and factual information is supplied besides the general answers about the whereabouts of books; specialist queries are referred to the appropriate departments in the library.

As an unusual regional solution the Bücherkundliche Arbeits- und Auskunftsstelle für Erwachsenenbildung ("Bibliographical Study and Information Centre for Adult Education") in Schleswig-Holstein deserves to be mentioned. It was set up in 1952 at the instigation of the Kultusministerium in agreement with the Landesverband der Volkshochschulen ("Land Association of Evening Institutes") and the Büchereizentrale Rendsburg. As a link between the evening institutes and the public libraries and as a clearing-house for them it supplies bibliographical and factual information in response mainly to written enquiries. The Arbeits- und Auskunftsstelle prepares its own booklists on current topics and arranges loans of requested titles from public libraries or even from the University Library at Kiel.

4.7 Technology in Libraries

By technology is understood here the application of technical tools and apparatus to rationalise the library service. A distinction should be made between the two main categories of aids: the conventional one includes technical office equipment, photographic and duplicating machines and conveyor systems; the other, electronic data processing installations, with which experiments have been made only during the last few years.

4.71 Academic Libraries

In the larger academic libraries, even in old buildings, there are now-adays well-equipped photographic work-rooms; duplicating apparatus for the reproduction of catalogue cards; microfilm cameras, enlargers and readers; and each of the university libraries has at its disposal one or more xerox machines, some for self-service copying by readers. In the new buildings transport installations — conveyor belts, paternoster book-lifts, pneumatic tubes, two-way communications in the stacks by means of lights and intercom installations — facilitate rapid communication be-tween stack and issue desk.

The major technological question of today however is the application to libraries of *data processing*. Since about 1964 various plans have materialised as concrete experiments. Both new and old foundations are participating. Some projects, supported by the Forschungsgemeinschaft, serve as models. Their results are expected to benefit the other libraries eventually.

The attempts to use data processing for large-scale "housekeeping" tasks and thereby to profit in speed and precision affect almost all aspects of library routine. Some of the current projects are past the trial stage, for others it is still uncertain how far they would lead to rationalisation. Specific projects worth mentioning are: accessioning of monographs (Bochum UB) and periodicals (Göttingen SUB); general cataloguing (Bochum UB, Konstanz UB, Regensburg UB, Bremen UB, Ulm UB); cata-loguing of a large periodical stock (Göttingen SUB); compilation of a union catalogue of several special libraries (museum libraries in Cologne); recording of issues and dispatch of overdues (Berlin TUB, Bochum UB — an on-line system is being prepared for Aachen THB); and the same combined with a system for transmitting book requests to the stacks (Jülich KFA and in preparation for Münster UB). (Situated at Jülich is the Kernforschungsanlage ("Nuclear Research Establishment"), a research library and a documentation centre). Hamburg SUB works with "con-ventional" machine punched cards. The object of all the projects, at all events in the new foundations, is complete automation; Bochum would seem likely to achieve this before the others.

A special position is held by the "Deutsche Bibliographie", which since 1 January 1966 has been compiled with the assistance of a computer (cf. 2.11).

Those libraries attached to institutions in the field of information science which are geared to automation are to some extent likewise affected.

So far it has not been considered necessary for libraries to have their own computers. Libraries in universities use the one belonging to their university. In Bochum the library shares a computer with the administration. The new University of Regensburg has received a grant from the Volkswagen Foundation for a computer, which is at first to be placed exclusively at the disposal of the library.

Up to now the individual libraries have largely had to rely on themselves in technical matters. Although they naturally exchange experiences so as to learn from one another, there is no central body where they can obtain reliable and objective advice about modern equipment and methods. Even assimilating the required technical knowledge is left to the librarians themselves. Programming courses, which the Deutsche Rechenzentrum ("German Computing Centre") in Darmstadt and the Zentralstelle für maschinelle Dokumentation ("Centre for Mechanisation in Documentation") in Frankfurt have arranged for information scientists and librarians (hitherto however not regularly), have contributed to the spread of technical knowledge. Studies in American libraries, which are incomparably more advanced in the application of electronics, and discussions with American colleagues, such as those held with five academic librarians who made a study tour financed by the Forschungsgemeinschaft in April and May 1965, must be looked upon as a particularly effective form of apprenticeship.

It is the Forschungsgemeinschaft that since 1963 has done its best and not without success to plan and co-ordinate joint projects and new developments. These include, for instance, the rationalisation of interlibrary lending by the universally accepted practice of supplying photocopies of individual periodical articles almost gratis and by the scheduled service of book vans within certain regions (cf. 3.13), but above all the applications of electronic data processing.

The leading specialists in this field regularly meet as members of a subcommittee set up by the libraries committee of the Forschungsgemeinschaft to advise on new projects and technical developments. It was first of all in this group that the plan for a headquarters for library technology was recognised as essential and its development fostered.

As recently as 1969 such an institution, called the Arbeitsstelle für Bibliothekstechnik ("Study Centre for Library Technology") and initially financed by the Forschungsgemeinschaft, was established in Berlin at the Staatsbibliothek Preußischer Kulturbesitz. In a division of labour between it and the Arbeitsstelle für das Büchereiwesen, also housed in Berlin, it is in the first instance to concentrate its research upon the application of electronic data installations, chiefly to issue procedures and the maintenance of catalogues.

4.72 Public Libraries

A number of technical aids are to be found also in public libraries. Of particular relevance to the needs of these libraries are the new procedures for mechanising issue systems. It is worth recording that numerous libraries have gone over to "photocharging" or "thermocharging", and also that in some libraries it has been possible to evolve individual systems of this kind and improved ones too, e.g. in Bielefeld, Hamburg and Lübeck.

Under closer consideration now are the possibilities of new means of communication for lending and information services. For instance, the Cologne Public Library has installed an automatic telephone answering service, allowing the branch libraries and the public at any time to telephone their requests and communications to headquarters, where they are recorded on tape. Some libraries are investigating the possibilities of installing teleprinters.

The Büchereizentrale in Rendsburg for the production of a regional union catalogue makes use of punched cards suitable for sorting to meet various requirements. The individual cards have in addition side perforations, which enable one to construct a simple set of "clipped" entries in any desired order and at varying distances apart. These entries are reproduced photomechanically on small offset masters.

On the other hand the Büchereizentrale in Flensburg has recently been producing the entries for its union catalogue and the regularly cumulated supplements by means of a tape typewriter. Control is achieved by feeding in data (punched cards) which are suitable for sorting. Small offset is used for the rest of the process as at Rendsburg.

As for *electronic data processing*, public libraries for long hesitated about committing themselves to it. It was not so much that they were less progressive, but they are by their size and nature scarcely able to hire their own computers and exploit them adequately. The problem is further aggravated by the multiplicity of library units in individual library systems which would need incorporating in the network of automation. Only Duisburg Public Library has been experimenting with data processing since 1966 and has had part of its routine processes computerised. For this it avails itself of the computer belonging to the municipality.

In Duisburg the target is the best possible application of the computer to the library service, that is, for circulation, cataloguing, and acquisitions, including the control of accounts. A start has been made with the registering of readers, the issue procedures (charging and discharging as well as statistics), the despatch of overdue notices and the recording of fines.

The new issue processes were introduced at the beginning of 1966, first of all in the central library. As investigations proved that the processes were carried out more economically, more simply and more speedily, since then all the 20 branches have been incorporated into the system.

For a long time the Library, the organisation department of the City administration and the computer specialists have been working towards transferring cataloguing processes to the computer. It is planned to produce the library catalogue with the help of electronics at the earliest possible moment. Preliminary work is far advanced. The crux lies in programming, since in current library work very large amounts of data have to be first collected, then prepared, punched and checked.

Questions arising from the automation of acquisitions and book-keeping are as yet unanswered. It seems however certain that an electronic cataloguing system gains in cost effectiveness when the acquisitions process is linked with the cataloguing, in that data available when a book is ordered have already been recorded in the store of the computer and only need completing later.

Long-distance transmission of data still seems to be premature today. When such a system is developed new and remarkable possibilities for library efficiency are expected to emerge; the Duisburg Public Library counts on being linked within a few years to the City network of data transmission.

The good results already achieved at Duisburg as in other libraries at home and abroad, and the fact that more and more government offices are installing computers of constantly improved types give grounds for expecting that within the next few years automation will be increasingly available also to public libraries in the Federal Republic.

As a central specialist body the Arbeitsstelle für das Büchereiwesen in Berlin takes a special interest in technology in libraries. It supplies information, prepares reports, and draws attention in its publications to new developments.

FURTHER READING

Standards, Model Budgets

A connected account, containing both the main deliberations and the actual proposed standards of the Forschungsgemeinschaft and the Wissenschaftsrat, is given in the paper by Wilhelm Grunwald: Etatmodelle für wissenschaftliche Bibliotheken. In: Fünfzehn Jahre Bibliotheksarbeit der Deutschen Forschungsgemeinschaft 1949—1964 (Zeitschrift für Bibliothekswesen und Bibliographie, Sonderheft 4), p. 78—93.

For standards and matters of internal organisation, including the public library Lektorat, reference has already been made in the text to the report of the Kommunale Gemeinschaftsstelle für Verwaltungsvereinfachung, Kommunale Öffentliche Bücherei, Köln 1964, a reprint of which is obtainable from the Deutscher Büchereiverband in Berlin. Standards are also found in the documents produced by the Deutscher Büchereiverband and its Arbeitsstelle für das Büchereiwesen, published under the titles: Grundlagen für die bibliothekarische Regionalplanung. Wiesbaden 1966, and: Bibliotheksplan. Berlin 1969.

For standards concerning special types of libraries such as mobile libraries, school libraries and hospital libraries readers should refer to the respective sections in chapter 2.

International Organisation — Book Selection and Acquisitions Work — Cataloguing — Reader Service

Anyone wishing to gain a deeper insight into the administration of West Germany academic libraries than it has been possible to give within the scope of our introduction will find full information in the explanatory text-book by Hermann Fuchs: Bibliotheksverwaltung. 2. Aufl. Wiesbaden 1968.

Alongside this work on the practice of librarianship there is the following work on the theory: Rolf Kluth: Grundriß der Bibliothekslehre. Wiesbaden 1970. This takes as its starting point the common concept of a library, without distinguishing between the academic and the public sector, and treats the thus re-interpreted theory of librarianship as part of the science of communication.

The German background and fundamental considerations affecting the various spheres of activity in academic libraries are provided by the three chapters in Band 2 of the Handbuch der Bibliothekswissenschaft: acquisitions (Fritz Redenbacher); cataloguing (Heinrich Roloff); and reader service (Wilhelm Martin Luther).

Special problems relating to the organisation of academic libraries are treated by the 2 studies mentioned in the text: Rolf Kluth: Bibliotheksstruktur und Baustruktur. ZfBB 12 (1965), p. 3—33; and Rationalisierung in wissenschaftlichen Bibliotheken. Vorschläge und Materialien. Hrsg. von der Deutschen Forschungsgemeinschaft. Bonn u. Boppard 1970.

Hansjörg Süberkrüb has discussed the report of the Kommunale Gemeinschaftsstelle für Verwaltungsvereinfachung, purchasing policies and problems of exploiting stock in public libraries in a series of lectures under the title: Die Öffentliche Bücherei. Aufgaben/Politik/Zukunft. Berlin 1967. (Bibliotheksdienst, Beiheft 19).

On the problem of the Lektorat, to which space was devoted also in the professional periodical, Bücherei und Bildung, Johannes Schultheis wrote a paper, Das Lektorat. In: Festschrift Wilhelm Schmitz-Veltin. Die Öffentliche Bibliothek. Auftrag und Verwirklichung. Berlin 1968, p. 85—90. A survey of the present situation which has met with some criticism was carried out by Bertold Manch: Lektoratsarbeit in Öffentlichen Bibliotheken. Berlin 1969. (Bibliotheksdienst, Beiheft 42). In this context reference may be made to the chapters in the Handbuch des Büchereiwesens (2. Halbband. Wiesbaden 1965): Jürgen Busch, Büchereiverwaltung (p. 1—129) and Ludwin Langenfeld, Buchauswahl und Bestandserschließung (p. 130—191).

As a step towards revising the rules on alphabetical cataloguing contained in the "Preußische Instruktionen" the appropriate committee of the Verein Deutscher Bibliothekare has published: Regeln für die alphabetische Katalogisierung. Teilentwurf. Frankfurt 1965. (ZfBB, Sonderheft 2); followed by two mimeographed publications in 1969 under the same title, pending the final report.

Among the articles published also in this periodical during recent years on subject cataloguing we cite only such as discuss the contemporary situation and certain problems in academic libraries: Walter Gebhart: Die Sachkatalogisierung als Aufgabe des wissenschaftlichen Bibliothekars. 6 (1959), p. 222—241; Erich Zimmermann: Einige Grundfragen der Sachkatalogisierung. 7 (1960), p. 315—332; Artur Brall: Der gegenwärtige Stand der Sachkatalogisierung nach der Methode Eppelsheimer. 14 (1967), p. 316—330; and Ulrich Fellmann: Die Sachkatalogisierung nach der Dezimalklassifikation. 14 (1967), p. 330—338.

Sonderheft 1 of the ZfBB is devoted to theoretical and practical questions affecting the cataloguing of manuscripts: Zur Katalogisierung mittelalterlicher und neuer Handschriften. Frankfurt 1963. The principles of the project for cataloguing manuscripts, supported by the Forschungsgemeinschaft, are contained in a contribution by Gustav Hofmann to the already often cited volume, Fünfzehn Jahre Bibliotheksarbeit der Deutschen Forschungsgemeinschaft (p. 153—161).

The Allgemeine Systematik für Büchereien, the Systematik der Musikliteratur and the Systematik für Kinder- und Jugendbüchereien were issued in 1956, 1963 and 1964 respectively by the publishers of Bücherei und Bildung in Reutlingen. In addition certain libraries have published their classification schedules in volume form, inter alia the Amerika-Gedenkbibliothek in Berlin, the Bielefeld Public Library and the Hamburger Öffentliche Bücherhallen.

In Beiheft 13 of Bibliotheksdienst Karl-Heinz Pröve made a survey of Zentralkatalogisierung für Öffentliche Büchereien, in which in particular experience with the AGB-Titeldienst was considered.

For discussions of the principle of both open access and classified arrangement, especially in new buildings and newly established university libraries, see: Hermann Tiemann: Neue Lesesaalaufgaben in den wissenschaftlichen Universalbibliotheken. ZfBB 3 (1956), p. 171—186; Clemens Köttelwesch: Zum Neubau der Stadt- und Universitätsbibliothek Frankfurt a. M. In: Buch und Welt. Wiesbaden 1965. p. 125—136; Joachim Stoltzenburg: Bibliothekssystem und systematische Aufstellung. ZfBB 14 (1967), p. 298—315.

Reference and Information Services

The provision of information as an important function even of general academic libraries, and one which urgently needs strengthening, is the theme of a lecture by Johannes Fock: Die Auskunftserteilung als bibliothekarische Aufgabe. ZfBB 9 (1962), p. 322—341.

The present state of information services in libraries, the necessity for them and the problems involved are treated by Horst Ernestus: Auf dem Wege zum Auskunftsdienst (Festschrift Wilhelm Schmitz-Veltin. p. 91—108).

Technology in Libraries

The application of electronic data processing to specific library processes has been the subject of a number of articles in recent years in professional periodicals. We here draw attention to very few of them. First, two recording the present state of affairs in West German libraries:

Günther Pflug: Automatisierungsbestrebungen im deutschen Dokumentations- und Bibliothekswesen. Mitteilungsblatt, Verband der Bibliotheken des Landes Nordrhein-Westfalen 16 (1966), p. 75—103.

Walter Lingenberg: Computereinsatz in Bibliotheken der Bundesrepublik Deutschland. ZfBB 16 (1969), p. 1—13.

Secondly, several special questions based on the experience of the libraries concerned:

Die automatische Buchausleihe. Erfahrungen an der Universitätsbibliothek

Bochum. Mit Beiträgen von C. Bossmeyer, B. Adams, H. Heim und G. Pflug. Bochum 1967.

Elektronische Datenverarbeitung in der Universitätsbibliothek Bochum. Ergebnisse — Erfahrungen — Pläne. Hrsg. von Günther Pflug und Bernhard Adams. Bochum 1968.

Automatisierung der Zeitschriftenstelle in wissenschaftlichen Bibliotheken. Ergebnisse eines Kolloquiums in Göttingen am 7. und 8. November 1968. Deutsche Forschungsgemeinschaft 1970.

Kurt Köster: Der Einsatz von Computern bei der Herstellung von Nationalbibliographien, dargestellt am Beispiel der Deutschen Bibliographie. Nachr. f. Dokumentation, Beiheft 17 (1968), p. 146—165.

Paul Niewalda und Gertraud Preuss: Die Elektronik im Dienste der Katalogisierung der UB Regensburg. ZfBB 16 (1969), p. 86—118.

Joachim Stoltzenburg und Günther Rabe: Das Konstanzer Schema zur Erfassung bibliothekarischer Daten. ZfBB 16 (1969), p. 119—153.

Experiences with issue systems involving photocharging apparatus and transaction cards as well as the reproduction of catalogue entries were described by various authors in Beiheft 6 of the Büchereidienst under the title: Rationalisierungstechnik für Öffentliche Büchereien.

In 1965 there were reproduced in Beiheft 11 of the Büchereidienst the results of a comparative investigation involving four machines, partly developed in the Federal Republic: Mikrofilm- und Thermo-Verbuchungsverfahren.

The year 1967 saw the book by Ingeborg Sassenberg: Ausleihverbuchung. Darstellung und Vergleich traditioneller und moderner Verfahren. Wiesbaden 1967.

Also worth noting is the paper by Helmut Prinz: Die Bücherei und die Datenverarbeitung, which draws on the experiments made by the Duisburg Public Library (Festschrift Wilhelm Schmitz-Veltin. p. 109—126).

5 Library Building

The following account simply provides a brief survey of recent developments in library building and highlights modern trends. References for further reading will be found at the end of the chapter.

5.1 Academic Libraries

After a phase between 1875 and 1914, when many new buildings were erected, there came a period of inactivity lasting until 1939. The severe destruction and damage caused by the bombing of 1939–1945 left scarcely a single building unscathed. A period of great activity in the building of academic libraries began about 1951/52. By 1940 at the latest most of these libraries would in the normal course of events have had to be altered, expanded and modernised. The destruction through bombing made this absolutely imperative.

The years of improvisation in half-destroyed buildings, which were temporarily repaired, or in buildings never intended for libraries but pressed into service for that purpose, began drawing to an end from 1951 onwards. Of the university libraries today only five still have no new buildings: two that remained completely undamaged (Erlangen and Heidelberg); and three that had suffered damage severe in part but not beyond repair (Freiburg, Göttingen and Münster). They have meantime made do with a complete overhaul, alterations and extensions within their existing walls. Even for them new buildings, or at least new extensions, are planned.

Only for the last few years with the establishment in 1962 of the Kommission für Baufragen ("Buildings Committee") of the Verein Deutscher Bibliothekare has there been the nucleus of a central advisory agency concerned with the building of academic libraries; even so, this is for the time being not an institution with a permanent headquarters and its own office but merely a body of voluntary members. Through its collection of sketches and plans and an extensive survey, which it is undertaking jointly with the department Entwerfen VI ("Project VI") of the Faculty of Architecture of the Berlin Technical University, a reference collection

14 Bamberg:
Staatsbibliothek in
the Neue Residenz,
modern converted
interior

15 Rendsburg: Büchereizentrale Rendsburg, Überlandbücherei 3,000 (a special mobile Library holding 3,000 vols.)

16 Bochum:
Universitätsbibliothek
der Ruhr-Universität
Bochum, automated
charging procedure

of new library building plans is gradually being built up which will in the future serve as a source of information. The Committee is even now being called upon to advise on new plans. One early result of practical assistance was the setting up of building seminars, some of which extended over several days, when new university libraries were planned in the presence of the architects responsible.

Most of the new buildings now completed were planned as individual projects, before the Committee was established, by collaboration between librarians — as a rule the chief and one member of the academic library staff — the architect and the building authorities and with the agreement of the financial sponsors. It was left to the members of this small group to decide how much advice they would seek and from what source. In practice they always availed themselves of the experience gained from buildings already erected; they obtained that information from enquiries and above all from study tours at home and in neighbouring countries, and in a number of cases as far away as the USA.

The 20th-century library building has been conceived and realised in the USA. Flexibility as a building principle, the intermingling of reader and book space as a normative structural principle, these supersede what has determined library building since the mid-19th century, the clear division into three immovable units: stacks, public rooms, administration.

In practical contact with American libraries and their planners and in theoretical discussions of the papers outlining their projects, new building concepts have developed in the Federal Republic during the last 15 years. Although these cannot yet be reduced to a common denominator, some common trends can be clearly discerned. The three-fold division, generally maintained as a basis, is no longer a rigid dogma. The boundaries between books and readers, between circulation and administration are giving way, areas of contact are being formed. This is seen in the "subject departmentalisation" of the large general reading room (cf. 4.5), either into several self-contained reading rooms or into one reading area flexibly constructed so that it can be divided into departments. It is also seen directly in the dominant place afforded to the complex of catalogues, bibliographical reference books and the enquiry desk. Only the stack usually remains as a separate block. The most significant types of stack are: the tower (Berlin FUB, Frankfurt DB, Giessen UB, Hamburg SUB, Karlsruhe UB, Saarbrücken UB); a superstructure filling the centre of the building, covering a wide surface area but not rising upwards as a tower (Marburg UB); and the underground store (Bonn UB, Hanover TIB/

TUB, Stuttgart UB, Kiel UB). It is only in the new university libraries, which are departing from the arrangement of books by accessions numbers and are adopting a structural principle different from the customary one, that new solutions in this direction may be expected. Modern technical installations ensure smooth communication between stack and issue desk and between stack and reading room for issue slips (pneumatic tubes), for books (conveyor belts with delivery baskets, paternosters and lifts) and for communicating with stack attendants by means of light-signals and intercom installations, so that readers' requests are immediately satisfied (cf. 4.5).

Boundaries between books and readers are giving way in two places. One is the open-access area or open-access shelves as a half-way house between stack and reading room. The other is the reading room itself, already mentioned in chapter 4. The efforts of the librarian to allow the reader direct access to a major part of the stock pose new problems for the architect. The solution takes various forms. We single out only a few examples that are particularly characteristic of the deployment of space.

On the first and second floors of the Universitätsbibliothek Stuttgart there is within the large reading-room area a flexible open-access library containing 20,000 volumes of heavily-used monographs published in the last 30 years and in addition a periodicals reference library containing about 30,000 volumes with the last ten years of all titles; should demand increase, further stack floors can be added.

The Stadt- und Universitätsbibliothek in Frankfurt has built up reference collections comprising literature of permanent value and of relevance to the appropriate subject field (source material, critical editions and monographs) and physically connected to the reading room reserved for that subject. These collections may be used only by suitably qualified readers (research workers, and students preparing for doctorates or for the entrance examination to an academic career); individual study rooms for such readers are provided nearby. It is structurally possible to make the open-access area, at present enclosed by a glass partition, available to all readers.

In an extension to its reading-room area, consisting of three stack floors, the Bayerische Staatsbibliothek in Munich has added a stock of about 500,000 volumes; related or heavily-used subjects are juxtaposed to make them more quickly available to readers. The structure is such that these sections of the stack could be thrown open to readers.

The reading room itself has completely changed its traditional appearance. Instead of the large room, with shelves along the walls and long rows of tables with seats in some cases along both sides, modern buildings have rooms with a less formal arrangement. There are tables for two or individual tables, shelves often running at right angles into the room and breaking it up into sections, and the rooms are sometimes grouped around an inner courtyard. Particular attention has everywhere been paid to the functional design of chairs and lighting, attractive colours and sound-absorbent floor-covering. There are many carrels (some equipped with typewriters or dictaphones), although not as yet inside the closed book stacks, as in the USA. The total number of work places available is much greater than it used to be; in the university libraries there are today on an average 600–800 seats, and it should be remembered that there are many additional ones in the institute libraries. Reference collections in reading rooms are more comprehensive than before, since the accommodation has increased. The principle that such material should be confined to the library is firmly adhered to.

One interesting innovation is provided for in the new building of the Staats- und Universitätsbibliothek Hamburg. In a reading-room block housing 7 subject fields there is apart from the proper reference collection an open-access one of heavily-used current literature in the relevant subjects (sources and texts, but also much discussed and quoted monographs); books from this collection may be borrowed for home reading.

The administrative offices are generally planned so that each of the processes from the receipt of the book via accessioning, assigning call numbers, cataloguing and binding, to the final shelving may run in a continuous flow. The principle formerly determining the order of the rooms, that the paths of readers and administrators should not cross, is no longer strictly observed. Besides, it cannot be observed in places where there is only one copy of the alphabetical catalogue, which both parties must use.

Building construction according to the modular system makes for a certain flexibility within the individual groups of rooms, although the stack usually remains excluded from such considerations. The exterior presents the most varied forms of a 20th-century building, with a clearly defined structure, large surface areas, often glass walls; the proportions of height and breadth are affected by the surroundings and are planned either to contrast or to blend with them. Architects with a high reputation have been engaged to plan library buildings.

As for sites, all the university libraries have succeeded in obtaining one in the immediate neighbourhood of the main university buildings. In the case of the large Staats-, Landes- and Stadtbibliotheken, provided they were not new foundations, they were as far as possible left free to rebuild on the sites of their old buildings, which had been destroyed.

One problem equally difficult for architects and librarians arose where an old building was still well preserved, or was even badly damaged but had to be rebuilt for reasons of town-planning, yet was no longer adequate. Examples are offered by the Universitätsbibliothek Tübingen and the Bayerische Staatsbibliothek in Munich, in which modern extensions have been added to the original buildings. By means of alterations and a complete internal reorganisation the Herzog-August-Bibliothek in Wolfenbüttel has created a library that meets modern requirements while it preserves an old building intact.

5.2 Public Libraries

The devastation caused by the War, but still more the ensuing change and growth of the public library service, made it essential to erect new buildings for existing and emergent libraries or to house these libraries in new premises. The economic recovery of the Federal Republic since the fifties enabled the Gemeinden to realise many such plans. Some Länder made limited grants available, which benefited in the first instance the smaller Gemeinden. The Federal government supported for a time as part of the Bundesjugendplan ("Federal Youth Plan") the foundation of model libraries for children and young people. In all parts of the Republic new library buildings appeared. However different in size and conception, they increased the attraction of public libraries.

There were different approaches in planning these buildings, for there was new ground to break; sometimes librarians and architects had different ideas, because the local situation might impose a limitation or permit a fortunate solution; nevertheless some outstanding universal features do emerge. Whenever possible the new libraries are outward looking, they give the passer-by a chance to look in, they invite him to enter and to linger. Much value is placed upon light, pleasantly constructed rooms. All new public libraries are open-access ones, which enable readers to choose books direct from the shelves. Reading areas with study tables and chairs or even comfortable armchairs tempt people to study and read in the library. One also comes across separate reading rooms for adults and for children as well as periodical and newspaper rooms, although the large reading rooms that were formerly found everywhere have recently been giving way to reading and study areas. Many of the larger libraries have at their disposal special rooms for groups and extension activities.

Suppliers of library furniture nowadays find a good market in the Federal Republic as in other countries. Consequently, a number of firms, among which the Einkaufszentrale für Öffentliche Büchereien holds pride of place, produce complete lists of furniture ranging from shelving, catalogue cabinets, book trolleys, issue desks and lockers for briefcases to troughs for picture-books and suitable stools for children's libraries. Such sources of supply exercised a great influence upon the functional and attractive furnishing of many libraries.

On closer inspection it may seem strange that the libraries run purely by the Gemeinden do not have buildings of the size found in North American, British or Scandinavian cities. Again the explanation lies in the historical coexistence of the academic Stadtbibliothek and the Öffentliche Bücherei. In some towns, however, where the two are combined, the necessary funds or even an adequate understanding for forward-looking planning did not exist.

The Amerika-Gedenkbibliothek, opened in 1953 and constructed on an American pattern, is the central City Library of West Berlin and is preeminent among city libraries. The building — presented by the United States — was built for a stock of about half a million volumes, of which a good 100,000 are on open shelves in the separate departments.

The main libraries in the twelve West Berlin districts are significantly smaller. However, the many new buildings for main libraries and branches, which are the result of overall planning, help to make a visit to the city extremely worth while for any one interested in library building.

The City of Duisburg, which in 1966 converted a warehouse in the City centre into a highly functional, modern library, in which space is found for 250,000 volumes on open shelves, thus possesses what is at present the largest central library in any German city. Moreover, the visitor finds in Duisburg a number of fine new branch libraries. Smaller, though likewise departmentalised, are the central buildings of the Stadtbibliothek of Hanover and the Stadtbibliothek of Bremen. With a building extension the Stadtbibliothek of Hanover is soon likely to become the largest municipal central library in the Federal Republic. Hanover like Bremen can boast also of many splendid branches.

Apart from West Berlin the most extensive building programme has been carried out in recent years by the Hamburger Öffentliche Bücherhallen. The large-scale building operations, which solved the problems of many libraries in the City's suburbs, make the lack of a central library in this, the largest German public library system, particularly noticeable. Besides Hamburg other cities, e. g. Cologne, Frankfurt, and Munich have not yet got beyond the planning stage for building suitable central libraries. Even the central libraries in Düsseldorf and Essen, erected since the War and at the first held in high esteem, proved within a few years to be too small. An unusual solution to the problem of co-ordinating independent libraries was found by the Dortmunder Haus der Bibliotheken ("Dortmund Library Building"), which houses the Stadt- und Landesbibliothek, the headquarters of the Stadtbücherei and the Westfälisch-Niederrheinisches Institut für Zeitungsforschung ("Westphalian and Lower-Rhine Institute for Research into Newspapers").

Among the smaller cities with populations between 100,000 and 400,000 inhabitants the following, inter alia, have obtained new central libraries: Brunswick, Bremerhaven, Darmstadt, Krefeld, Ludwigshafen, Mannheim, Mönchen-Gladbach, Offenbach, Remscheid, Wanne-Eickel and Wilhelmshaven. In 1967 the Stadtbücherei of Heidelberg opened a new building planned on a generous scale and with a built-in flexibility; the modern architecture was also impressive. In 1969 the new building of the central library at Mülheim a. d. Ruhr was completed.

Among the towns of between 50,000 and 100,000 inhabitants Flensburg should be mentioned; with its new central library, the Bücherei Nordertor des Deutschen Grenzvereins ("Northern Gate Library of the German Frontier Union"), and the central library of the Danish minority population, it possesses three remarkable library buildings. Other noteworthy buildings are at Hamm, with its central library opened in 1966, Rüsselsheim and Hof.

In some towns modern, functional central libraries have been set up in an appropriate style in existing or restored historical buildings, e. g. in Freiburg, Heilbronn, Koblenz, Lübeck, Münster, Rendsburg, Reutlingen, Ulm and Würzburg. An outstanding achievement of this kind is the new central library of Stuttgart in the restored Wilhelmspalais.

Again in other Gemeinden emphasis was placed upon combining central or branch libraries with other cultural or social institutions. So the new headquarters of the Stadtbücherei of Wolfsburg arose within the cultural centre created by Alvar Aalto. Two branches of the Hanover City Libraries are housed in Freizeitheime ("Leisure Hostels"). A similar example is offered by the Hamburg-Haus in the Eimsbüttel district of Hamburg. In Hesse the public library is often an integral part of the Bürgerhäuser ("town houses") in small Gemeinden. It is not rare to find the library in the immediate neighbourhood of the Volkshochschule ("evening institute") or under the same roof as it, for instance in the Bildungswerk ("Educational Enterprise") of the town of Marl and in Ludwigsburg, where a modern multipurpose building caters for the Stadtbücherei, the Volkshochschule and the Haus der Jugend ("Young People's Centre"). The links with schools have been discussed elsewhere.

Apart from the new buildings in the large and medium-sized cities and towns all the Länder in the Republic have seen in recent years excellent buildings in the smaller Gemeinden. This is largely thanks to the initiative and expert counsel of the Staatliche Büchereistellen, from whom further details can be obtained. In Schleswig-Holstein a resident architect is employed at the Büchereizentrale Rendsburg in the Verein Büchereiwesen in Holstein ("Association for the Public Library Service in Holstein"); he advises the Gemeinden in detail about the building, rebuilding and furnishing of libraries. In the Hamburger Öffentliche Bücherhallen the work of a specialist in library building has developed over the years; he draws up the numerous plans in collaboration with the architects and supervises operations with them.

Estimates of the optimum minimum size of branches in municipal library systems change with the increasing demands made upon public libraries. Nowadays people are unwilling to erect permanent branches, unless there is a catchment area consisting of a permanent community of at least 10,000 inhabitants housed round a shopping centre; a stock of over 10,000 volumes would then be required. In rural districts Gemeinden of fewer than 2,000 inhabitants are increasingly considered to be the domain of mobile libraries. In the case of the smallest permanent libraries one thinks in terms of a stock of 2,500 volumes; the link with a full library system is then essential (cf. 3.14).

In the towns as well as in the sphere of the Staatliche Büchereistellen efforts are being made to extend systematically the provision of public libraries according to principles in which such estimates of size are a decisive factor. In some towns — among them West Berlin, Hamburg and

Duisburg — the extension of the library system has been based upon building plans officially approved by the town councils. Where such plans do not exist the libraries are anxious to strengthen the existing network of permanent and mobile libraries and in co-operation with town planning to guarantee a prompt and far-sighted provision of libraries for any new housing developments.

Universally accepted, detailed standards for accommodation in public libraries did not exist until recently. As a rule of thumb the report of the Kommunale Gemeinschaftsstelle für Verwaltungsvereinfachung mentions a figure of 30 square metres for every 1,000 volumes. Taking into consideration the "Richtlinien für den Raumbedarf" ("Principles for Assessing Accommodation Requirements"), issued by the educational authorities in Hamburg in 1960, other local, regional and foreign standards such as those drawn up in the building programme of Werner Mevissen — in his work, "Büchereibau/Public Library Building" — a committee of the Arbeitsstelle für das Büchereiwesen prepared and published in 1968 standard figures for calculating the areas required by public libraries.

These calculations of space, which are contained in an abridged form also in the documentation for the "Bibliotheksplan" (cf. 3.14), are based on the figures laid down in the report of the Kommunale Gemeinschaftsstelle für Verwaltungsvereinfachung (cf. 4.14). For libraries holding between 15,000 and 100,000 volumes detailed standards of requirements have been evolved and fully explained. The bases for the calculations are classified according to areas of service: issue counter and cloakroom, book selection and acquisitions, shelving and circulation areas, reading places, catalogue area, stack, administrative offices and other rooms. The requirements laid down under these heads are clearly tabulated. Further sections contain exhaustive calculations for music libraries and mobile library headquarters as well as detailed figures for shelving.

The Arbeitsstelle für das Büchereiwesen keeps a close watch on library building, to which a permanent working party devotes its time. In the archives of the Arbeitsstelle dealing with the subject all kinds of data are collected and used in publications and for enquiries.

Apart perhaps from the question of relative size it can be said that in the Federal Republic since the War and above all in recent years library buildings have been erected well able to withstand international comparison. German librarians made a very attentive study of buildings and plans in other countries. Today many buildings and internal furnishings are likely to interest even visitors from abroad.

FURTHER READING

The present state of the building of academic libraries is portrayed in a compilation edited by Gerhard Liebers. It comprises about 45 separate reports from the libraries themselves of their new buildings or adaptations, with ground-plans, tables and illustrations, and singles out trends that have influenced the individual buildings: Bibliotheksneubauten in der Bundesrepublik Deutschland 1945—1968. Herausgegeben von Gerhard Liebers. Frankfurt 1968 (Zeitschrift für Bibliothekswesen und Bibliographie, Sonderheft 9).

Chapter 12 of Band 2 of the Handbuch der Bibliothekswissenschaft, entitled Das Haus und seine Einrichtung, by Georg Leyh, shows the gradual growth of the functionally designed building of an academic library in the 19th century; but features of the present-day modern German library are scarcely discernible. These come to light in the section written by Gerhard Liebers on the period 1930—1960 in non-German-speaking countries, where the strong influence of the USA on the origin of new ideas and forms of building is evident. A supplement to the account in the "Handbuch" for the period 1930—1960, covering developments throughout Europe and at the same time serving as a practical guide to the layout and technical installations of a library, is offered by the monograph published in 1962: Rainald Stromeyer: Europäische Bibliotheksbauten seit 1930. Wiesbaden 1962 (Beiträge zum Buch- und Bibliothekswesen. 9), with a comprehensive bibliography. Individual descriptions are given here as examples of specific problems, with the addition of numerous ground-plans and cross-sections.

The recognition that in building academic libraries American experiences can profitably be turned to good account led also to the dissertation of the architect engaged in the new building for the Bibliothek der Technischen Hochschule Stuttgart: Klaus-Jürgen Zabel: Der Wandel im Bibliotheksbau unserer Zeit. Diss. TH. Stuttgart, 1959.

Theoretical articles as well as numerous descriptions of individual libraries are to be found in the professional literature and in building periodicals.

Werner Mevissen drew on foreign as well as German experiences in his internationally acclaimed book, Büchereibau — Public Library Building. Essen 1959. He arrived at requirements for building programmes which are quoted as standard by architects as well as librarians. The 1st edition of the work is out of print, the 2nd edition is in preparation. He is also the author of the chapter on public library building in the 1. Halbband of the Handbuch des Büchereiwesens.

Standards and figures developed by the Arbeitsstelle für das Büchereiwesen for calculating the required space for public library buildings were published in: Flächenbedarf Öffentlicher Büchereien. Berlin 1968. (Bibliotheksdienst, Beiheft 37.)

A detailed introduction to the essentials of an aesthetically and likewise professionally satisfying layout of the circulation rooms in modern open-access public libraries is given in the work by Gertrud Seydelmann: Inneneinrichtung Öffentlicher Büchereien. Berlin 1967. (Bibliotheksdienst, Beiheft 27.)

Under the title, Bücherei und Fertigbau, the architects, Manfred Krug and Bernhard van der Minde, and the librarian, Emil Pelikan, have offered proposals and plans for 3 basic types of small libraries (5,000 volumes, 10,000 volumes, single and double storeys). The work was published by the Arbeitsgemeinschaft der Staatlichen Büchereistellen in Nordrhein-Westfalen and appeared in 1968 as a special issue of the journal, Gemeindebücherei in Nordrhein-Westfalen.

Noteworthy public library buildings of the Federal Republic are recorded — up to 1959 — in the first edition of Mevissen's book, Büchereibau — Public Library Building. Other and more recent accounts of individual buildings will be found especially in the professional journal, Bücherei und Bildung.

6   Bibliography and Information Science

During the last twenty years bibliography and information science in
the Federal Republic have developed into a large special field of their
own; any account of them can be accurate only if it includes the German
situation within the international one. Nevertheless both are closely
connected with library science so that they must not be left out of our
survey. We here limit ourselves to discussing the main characteristics of
their current development in so far as they affect libraries. It seems unnecessary to go into the keen and long drawn-out controversy about the
main difference between the tasks of the librarian and the information
scientist; both partners through their work have in practice long been
brought together and therefore learned how their tasks starting from a
common background are different and yet closely related.

6.1   Bibliography and Information Science in Libraries

6.11   General Academic Libraries and Professional Library Bodies

We said in chapter 4 that one of the most important responsibilities of
general academic libraries is to offer bibliographical and documentation
services by maintaining collections of reference material accessible to the
reader and by providing an information service.

However, general libraries are themselves actively engaged in compiling
current bibliographies. We are thinking of bibliographies, the preparation of which comes within the proper sphere of a library or a library
body, not the numerous bibliographical studies made by individual
librarians.

We list the following bibliographical enterprises which are of general
significance:

a) The current bibliography of new publications in German, the "Deutsche Bibliographie" with its various subsections, the half-yearly and the
five-yearly cumulations as well as the four supplementary special lists,
is published by the Deutsche Bibliothek in Frankfurt, the central agency
for the collection and bibliographical exploitation of such literature. In

addition to the three series A, B and C (cf. 2.11) there are the lists of periodicals and official publications spanning a fairly long period of time and the select lists, "Das Deutsche Buch" (currently from 1950 onwards) and "Verzeichnis deutscher wissenschaftlicher Zeitschriften" (taken over by the Deutsche Bibliothek from the 6. Aufl. 1965 onwards).

b) Regional bibliographies, covering the literature on a Land, a smaller region or even a town, come within the purview of the Landesbibliotheken and the academic Stadtbibliotheken (cf. 2.2). Some are published; others are compiled in the form of card-index catalogues and are available to readers in the relevant libraries. Examples are: Westfälische Bibliographie ("Westphalian Bibliography"), Stadt- und Landesbibliothek Dortmund; Bibliographie zur schleswig-holsteinischen Geschichte und Landeskunde ("Bibliography of Schleswig-Holstein History and Topography") (5 annual volumes), Landesbibliothek Kiel; Saarländische Bibliographie ("Bibliography of the Saarland"), University Library of Saarbrücken; Nachweis von Berlin-Literatur ("Guide to Literature on Berlin"), Senatsbibliothek Berlin; Sonderkatalog mit Monacensienliteratur ("Special Catalogue of Literature on Munich"), Stadtbibliothek München.

c) Articles in selected major journals in the field of English, Germanic and Romance studies have been catalogued since 1962 by the University Libraries of Frankfurt and Marburg, with financial support from the Forschungsgemeinschaft, in order primarily to offer university students of these "Massenfächer" ("popular subjects") an easily usable tool for their guidance. Since 1969 the entries prepared on cards according to a uniform layout and classified according to standard rules have been sent to subscribing libraries and institutes, where this catalogue of periodical articles is freely available to readers. Continuation of the project, expanding it to cover more subjects, will be provided for in the near future.

d) A similar project for theology was launched in 1960 by the libraries section of the Arbeitsgemeinschaft für das Archiv- und Bibliothekswesen in der evangelischen Kirche (cf. 2.61). Under this, about 160 theological journals from Germany and elsewhere are indexed, the entries reproduced in card form and distributed to — at present — 90 subscribers.

e) Since 1966 sets of catalogue cards for "Fortschrittsberichte" ("Progress Reports") have been circulated, so far free of charge, to a circle of 60—70 libraries; the Staatsbibliothek Preußischer Kulturbesitz (Berlin) with the assistance of specialists in other libraries supplies the entries in the field of the humanities and social sciences, the Technische Informationsbibliothek (Hanover), those in science and technology (excluding biology and chemistry). Both enterprises were got under way by the Forschungsgemeinschaft, which gives the libraries concerned financial assistance.

Since by "Fortschrittsbericht" is understood not only a critical assessment of the present state of research in a distinct subject field, but also comprehensive bibliographical summaries of the "year's work" type, cooperation has begun with the preparation of "Bibliographische Berichte" ("Bibliographical Reports").

f) The half-yearly publication, "Bibliographische Berichte", arising out of a supplement to the "Zeitschrift für Bibliothekswesen und Bibliographie", under the auspices of the Bibliographisches Kuratorium (cf. 6.21), and compiled by its Secretary, E. Zimmermann (in 1970 taken over by the Staatsbibliothek Preußischer Kulturbesitz), is a critical select list of important German and foreign bibliographies in all subject fields, regardless of whether they are published separately, as articles or as contributions to a symposium.

g) A list of current bibliographies and information services, compiled by the Forschungsgemeinschaft, was published by the Steiner Verlag, Wiesbaden, in 1963.

Finally it may be sufficient simply to refer to the compiling of special bibliographies, which are willingly and frequently undertaken by libraries on special occasions (e. g. university jubilees, birthdays or anniversaries of leading librarians or of personalities having particular relevance to a library).

6.12 Public Libraries

Public librarians for a long time confined themselves to making their own bookstocks accessible to their readers on the spot by card catalogues and printed lists. Recently they have seen themselves faced with new tasks in the supply and exploitation of literature owing to the enlarged and increasingly specialist circle of readers. The substantial extra pressure on inter-library lending, the attention paid to special collection fields, the extension of periodical holdings, the increased use of the new photocopying processes and the growing reference service, all underline the significance of bibliographical aids. In addition interest in information retrieval has been awakened, and librarians are seeking to cooperate with individual documentation agencies and central bodies.

Efforts towards a more intensive exploitation of literature in the sense of information retrieval are to be observed not only in individual libraries; they are seen also in co-operative library enterprises such as the "Zeitschriftendienst" ("Periodicals Service") and the "Zeitschriftendienst: Musik" ("Periodicals Service: Music"). Compiled in public libraries and issued by the Deutscher Büchereiverband and its Arbeitsstelle für das Büchereiwesen, both publications are restricted to abstracting a limited number of periodicals. Just because of this however these periodical services can be more readily available and more closely tailored to the needs and financial resources of medium-sized public libraries. Other, more specialised, undertakings are at present under consideration.

The "Musikbibliographischer Dienst" ("Bibliographical Service: Music") appears six times a year and is prepared by 12 public music libraries. The purpose is to provide information as quickly as possible on new musical scores of a serious nature issued by German and foreign publishers. Catalogued according to the Full Code and classified by the "Systematik für Musikliteratur und Musikalien für Öffentliche Musikbüchereien" (cf. 2.83), the "Musikbibliographischer Dienst" is available in parts (the 6th part being also the yearly cumulation) or as complete catalogue entries on cards.

One reference tool important for all libraries is the "Fachbibliographischer Dienst: Bibliothekswesen" ("Special Bibliographical Service: Library Science"), issued by the Arbeitsstelle für das Büchereiwesen since 1965. It contains entries for monographs and articles in collections and periodicals with so far as possible references to reviews of the works cited. It indexes also unpublished studies prepared for examinations at the library schools in the Federal Republic and the unpublished final dissertations submitted at these institutions. The subject coverage includes the whole field of library science and a selection of material on the book trade. The geographical coverage is essentially that of German-speaking countries; but professional literature of other countries is also taken into account. The selection and collation of titles are in the hands of German and foreign librarians. The "Fachbibliographischer Dienst: Bibliothekswesen" appears about every two months; the single parts are cumulated into annual volumes.

6.13 Special Libraries

The real sphere of bibliographical and documentary activity in librarianship is the special libraries.

The *central specialist libraries* are involved in various ways with documentation and information activities. The Technische Informationsbibliothek in Hanover (cf. 2.41) has set up its own active documentation and information service for material in its special fields of Eastern languages, primarily Russian, but also Japanese and Chinese. Since a reorganisation in 1969 the Library has been sending out to subscribers two kinds of information lists, a "Schnell-Informationsdienst" ("current awareness service") and a "Sonder-Informationsdienst" ("special information service"), both in classified form. The former makes use of existing documentation services by copying indexes or short abstracts in German or English of about 500 journals. With the second list the Library itself plays an active part by exploiting publications such as series, collections, and conference reports, which are missed by the average abstract journals. The titles are translated, and short abstracts are added. Orders from subscribers based on the lists are dealt with by return of post, since all the material is in stock at the Library. In preparing the lists data-processing equipment is to be used in future. Part of the same project is the card-index of translations from the Russian, which are notified to the Library by other West German sources or commissioned by the Library itself. Lists of references to this material are issued every two months.

The Zentralbibliothek der Wirtschaftswissenschaften in Kiel (cf. 2.41) possesses in its large catalogue, divided into five sections, a fine tool for information retrieval, thanks to the classification with its many well-chosen subdivisions and instructive guide-cards and to the fact that articles from Festschriften, collections, congress reports and journals are all included. The catalogue has always been heavily used by scholars on the spot and through a card service covering at least part of the field has assisted similar libraries and institutes outside Kiel; through the publishing house of Hall the whole catalogue in printed form will in future be accessible and of good service to a wider public. Since its expansion into a central specialist library the Zentralbibliothek has run a regular information service based on its catalogue. Reference enquiries are answered by sending copies of the 20 most recent entries on the topic in question.

The Zentralbibliothek der Landbauwissenschaft in Bonn is to co-operate

closely with the documentation of the agricultural sciences, which is at
present at the organisational stage (cf. 2.41). The same applies to the
Medizinische Zentralbibliothek in Cologne and the Deutsches Institut
für medizinische Dokumentation und Information, which are both still
being established (cf. 2.41).

The fact that for *special libraries* in the narrower sense documentation
and information retrieval rank as essential and characteristic functions
has already been stated in chapter 2. Various stages of documentation
and information activity are to be distinguished. It is normal to provide
a classified catalogue, well subdivided by subjects and including even
non-separately published material; this serves as a reference tool to
members of the institute, organisation, etc. Compiling recent accessions
lists and bibliographical guides, with and without annotations, likewise
for internal consumption, is also often part of the service. The next
stage is making the material prepared in this way available to outside
persons, institutes and libraries. This is achieved for example by lists of
references circulated to a specific circle of subscribers or by currently
published printed bibliographies and eventually even by providing
individual information in response to direct enquiries based on the collation of literature on a definite research topic. Examples of these various
stages are found among libraries of research institutes, public authorities,
parliaments and to a great extent (cf. 2.42) among those in industry. In
most instances the functions of librarians, bibliographers and information
scientists merge into one another. In many institutions the library and
the documentation centre are separate but interlocking services; in many
places all the work devolves upon the library, elsewhere the library is
only the basis for the activities of the documentation service. The best
guide is offered by the "Verzeichnis von Schrifttumsauskunftsstellen"
("List of Information Centres") (6. ergänzte und erweiterte Aufl. 1968).
This supplies details for each centre concerning any guides to literature
produced and the kind of service provided (unrestricted, to members
only, etc.).

For a few of the very many special libraries we explain the varying forms
of activity in the fields of bibliography, documentation and information
retrieval.

The Bibliothek des Max-Planck-Instituts für ausländisches und internationales Privatrecht ("Library of the Max Planck Institute for Foreign
and International Civil Law") in Hamburg is like all the libraries of this,
the largest research organisation in the Federal Republic, intended as a

research tool for its own academic members; but as the most comprehensive special library in its field it is also open to visitors and is ready to make its resources available to a wider specialist public. Apart from issuing a wide-ranging number of reports the Library has developed a regular documentation and information service not confined to the activities of the Institute. The bibliography, "Deutsches Schrifttum über ausländisches und internationales Privatrecht" ("German Literature on Foreign and International Civil Law"), published intermittently in the Institute's journal, is another way in which the Library keeps the professional world informed.

The Bibliothek des Deutschen Literaturarchivs im Schiller-Nationalmuseum ("Library of the Archives of German Literature in the Schiller National Museum") at Marbach was originally an annexe to the Archives Department, the main role of which lay in collecting the literary remains and manuscripts of German writers and in publishing scholarly editions. Since 1959 by currently indexing papers in journals, collections, Festschriften and anthologies as well as by retrospectively indexing journals from the years 1880–1958, the Library has been building up a comprehensive, well-classified catalogue, which today acts as a reference tool in information retrieval. Enquiries are answered by sending a copy of the catalogue entries for the topic in question.

Each of the highest Federal courts possesses, partly connected with, partly separated from the library, its own reference and information office, with an administrative-grade officer in charge; the office houses legal material, decisions of its own and related courts, commentaries and critical observations on such decisions, together with relevant literature, articles from periodicals and collections, official publications, and so forth. This reference material is an indispensable aid to judges. The Bundesgerichtshof ("Federal Supreme Court") and the Bundesverfassungsgericht ("Federal Constitutional Court") recently agreed that the work performed by their senior librarians in selecting literature, in exploiting journals and in classifying should be made available to the whole legal profession through the publication of the "Karlsruher Juristische Bibliographie. Systematischer Titelnachweis neuer Bücher und Aufsätze in monatlicher Folge" ("Karlsruher Bibliography of Jurisprudence. Classified Monthly Catalogue of New Books and Periodicals"); this has been published from 1965 onwards.

The Research Division of the Bundestag has delegated the collection and exploitation of all the material necessary and important for the work of the Bundestag and the problem of making this material readily available to 6 sections: Library, Archives, Legislative Documentation, Press Cuttings, Legal Documentation, and Specialised Documentation. Combined, these offer a speedy reference and information service, with each section complementing the others, for the members of the Bundestag, the political parties, the research services and all other persons connected with the Bundestag. The outside world is served by the select list (published from 1952 onwards) of periodical articles and the series of bibliographies (begun in 1963) in certain major subject fields.

The Verein Deutscher Ingenieure ("Association of German Engineers") (VDI) in Düsseldorf maintains a library and documentation centre, subdivided into eight specialist documentation offices. It currently issues index volumes, lists of references and bibliographies, and supplies information on a wide scale about literature on all relevant fields to university and research institutes and to research and development offices in the industry.

Similar services in their own fields are rendered by the following bodies — to name only a few of many: the Bergbau-Bücherei ("Mining Library") in Essen, which issues the twice-monthly "Hinweise auf neuere Zeitschriftenaufsätze" ("References to Recent Periodical Articles"); the Fachbücherei und Dokumentationsstelle des Vereins Deutscher Gießereifachleute ("Research Library and Documentation Centre of the Association of German Foundrymen") in Düsseldorf, with the "Gießerei-Literaturschau" ("Literature Survey on Foundry-Work") in the periodical, "Gießerei" ("Foundry-Work"); the Bibliothek des Vereins Deutscher Eisenhüttenleute ("Library of the Association of German Iron-Workers") in Düsseldorf, with the "Zeitschriften- und Bücherschau" ("Survey of Books and Periodicals") in the periodical, "Stahl und Eisen" ("Steel and Iron"); the VDE-Bücherei des Verbandes Deutscher Elektrotechniker ("Library of the Association of German Electrical Engineers") in Frankfurt, with the "VDE-Schnellberichte" ("VDE Express Reports"), titles of publications in electrical engineering and its basic sciences.

All these places readily supply information to the general public.

6.2 Supra-Regional and Central Bodies

6.21 Bibliography

In the Federal Republic preparing and publishing bibliographies depends on individual initiative, whether personal or institutional, that is, academic, industrial and technical organisations, editors of learned journals, often also learned publishing houses. There is no central office charged with direction or co-ordination.

The *Deutsches Bibliographisches Kuratorium* ("German Bibliographical Board") functions as an advisory body. Founded at the end of 1951 on the initiative of Unesco with representatives of organisations involved or interested in bibliographical projects, it was reconstituted in February 1965 as a committee of the German Unesco Commission. The members of the Kuratorium represent associations of libraries, information centres, the book trade, two large libraries, the German Unesco Commission and the Forschungsgemeinschaft. A small headquarters is situated in the Hessische Landes- und Hochschulbibliothek of Darmstadt. It has a card-index of bibliographies, which is used for information purposes. The Kuratorium prepares an annual report for Unesco on advances in bibliography in Germany (both West and East) and also publishes the "Bibliographische Berichte" (cf. 6.11 f). Through its meetings the Kuratorium offers participants a forum for discussing matters of principle or methodology within the bibliographical sphere. Through the medium of informed surveys it propounds its views on new bibliographical enterprises; to bring these into being, to foster them, let alone to complete and publish them, does not fall within its terms of reference.

The *Deutsche Forschungsgemeinschaft* has a special section concerned with encouraging bibliographical work in those cases where it receives an application for assistance with the compilation or printing. Before deciding about such applications the advisers investigate the bibliographical situation in the fields in question both in Germany and abroad. Since a positive decision is made only when there is a gap in research and since recommendations are also made that older existing bibliographies should be consolidated, there is here a natural process of selection; new possibilities of overlapping and duplicating are avoided and old ones are gradually removed.

The *Institut für Dokumentationswesen* ("Institute for Documentation")

(see 6.221) is also called upon to support bibliographical projects. This
however happens only in special cases, if for instance bibliographies are
to be completed by a comprehensive index volume; in every case agreement with the Forschungsgemeinschaft is required.

6.22 Documentation

The wide field of documentation and information services in the Federal
Republic is at the moment in a state of flux. Ventures in documentation
as in bibliography have arisen in isolation without the influence of the
state and without any organisation to provide direction or support. A
beginning was made, in part far back in the 19th century, with the major
abstracting journals, "Chemisches Zentralblatt", "Physikalische Berichte",
"Zentralblatt für Mathematik", the medical "Zentralblätter" of the Sprin-
ger Verlag, and the two great "Handbücher" of organic and inorganic
chemistry (Beilstein and Gmelin respectively). All of these are still in progress except for the "Chemisches Zentralblatt", which was replaced in 1969
by the "Chemischer Informationsdienst", published in the Federal Republic,
as a current awareness service. Between the Wars, but especially since
1945, documentation centres of all kinds have grown up, scattered throughout the Federal Republic, wherever there were individual needs, often
with no cognisance of one another and with no co-ordination. Into this
heterogeneous and chaotic state of affairs certain elements of order have
gradually been introduced. In the mid fifties a start was made through the
ceaseless efforts of certain persons concerned with the Deutsche Gesellschaft für Dokumentation ("German Society for Documentation"); it is
thanks to them that the importance of documentation for research,
industry and government is now recognised by the state and its support
accepted as a state responsibility. These efforts did not result in
systematic planning until the foundation in 1961 of the Institut für
Dokumentationswesen (see 6.221).
In the first place the new arrangements affect certain fairly large and
particularly important specialist fields. The services offered by documentation centres and special libraries in a field are grouped round a central
co-ordinating office and brought together into a united co-operative
system. This means that the form that co-operation takes is adapted to
the current situation. In all cases a uniform method for accessioning,
indexing and classifying is aimed at in advance, and the material is

divided in a specified way among the participating institutions. One procedure often adopted ensures that material is checked and abstracted by the individual institutions, while headquarters is responsible for editing and distributing. Moreover it is the function of headquarters to follow developments abroad and to foster contacts with international bodies concerned with information retrieval. We give the following examples:

for *nuclear research*: Zentralstelle für Atomkernenergiedokumentation ("Central Agency for the Documentation of Nuclear Research") at the Kernforschungsanlage in Karlsruhe (formerly at the Gmelin-Institut, Frankfurt);

for *space research*, space flights and space technology: the Leitstelle für Weltraumdokumentation ("Co-ordinating Office for Space Documentation") in Munich has since 1963 been housed at the Zentralstelle für Luftfahrtdokumentation und -information ("Central Agency for the Documentation of Aeronautics");

for *agricultural sciences*: the headquarters in the Bundesministerium für Ernährung, Landwirtschaft und Forsten ("Federal Ministry for Food, Agriculture and Forestry") in Bonn in connection with the Zentralbibliothek für Landbauwissenschaft ("Central Library for Agricultural Sciences") also in Bonn;

for *educational theory*: 7 institutions, co-ordinated with the Pädagogisches Zentrum ("Pedagogical Centre") in Berlin, are linked to form a "documentation circle";

for *political science*: the co-ordinating office for political documentation is the Otto-Suhr-Institut at the Free University of Berlin.

for *industrial relations*: Informationsstelle für gewerbliche Wirtschaft beim Rationalisierungskuratorium der Deutschen Wirtschaft ("Information Agency for Industrial Economy of the Board for Rationalising the German Economy") in Frankfurt co-ordinates 12 German institutions concerned with industrial relations as well as corresponding centres in England, France and Italy; through it the mutual exchange of material is being organised;

for *geographical research* on the major areas of Latin America, Asia, the Far East and Africa the corresponding four Institutes of the Übersee-Institut ("Overseas Institute") in Hamburg form the co-ordinating body and are united into one system.

6.221 Institut für Dokumentationswesen ("Institute for Documentation")

The Institut für Dokumentationswesen, established in 1961 under the auspices of the Max-Planck-Gesellschaft, is financed half by the Bundesministerium für Bildung und Wissenschaft ("Federal Ministry for Education and Research") and half by the Ländergemeinschaft ("Länder Community"). The Institut co-ordinates and promotes documentation and information work in the Federal Republic within the context of international co-operation. The first results of co-ordination (see 6.22) were preceded by a survey of the documentation services available. Promotion takes the form of advising on the preparation and execution of specific documentation projects in science, industry and administration, of submitting informed reports and recommendations and of providing financial aid. These projects cover primarily research into the bases and methods of documentation, such as terminology, classification, and the techniques of information retrieval with special reference to automation, but also training for information science and co-operation with international projects. For specific individual projects initial and temporary grants are made. One essential function of the Institut is the maintenance of contacts abroad. A special reprographic department set up in October 1967 serves the advisory and developmental aspects of documentation as well as the training and further education of information scientists.

6.222 Zentralstelle für maschinelle Dokumentation ("Centre for Mechanisation in Documentation")

In 1964 the Zentralstelle für maschinelle Dokumentation was established in Frankfurt in close collaboration with the Institut für Dokumentationswesen. The Zentralstelle is a service organisation, the function of which is to enable documentation and information services to carry out the mechanical part of their work, to advise them on the organisational and methodological aspects of producing machine-readable data, to process for use in Germany computer programmes from other countries; e.g. the national bibliography of the Union of South Africa, and in general to serve research and development in the field of automated documentation. The Zentralstelle has held several programming and introductory courses for information scientists and librarians.

6.223 Deutsche Gesellschaft für Dokumentation ("German Society for Documentation") (DGD)

The Deutsche Gesellschaft für Dokumentation, founded in 1941 a few years after the first World Congress on Documentation (1937), was revived in December 1948. According to its charter it has as its object, "to promote research and organisation in the fields of theoretical and practical documentation and information science and to foster links with the national and international institutions that are working in the same fields". Membership may be personal or corporate. The Gesellschaft, which has its own office in Frankfurt, has published the "Nachrichten für Dokumentation" ("Documentation News") since 1950. For important specialist matters expert committees and working parties have been formed. The activities of the Gesellschaft, the lectures at its conferences and the papers of its members — we single out Erich Pietsch, former head of the Gmelin-Institut für anorganische Chemie — have aroused public interest in documentation, obtained financial aid from the Federal Government, and finally led to the establishment of the Institut für Dokumentationswesen, a body that has decisively influenced the development of the subject in the Republic. The Gesellschaft and the Institut are closely linked. Both have strong and active connections with other countries. Jointly and together with the Verein Deutscher Dokumentare ("Association of German Information Scientists"), which was founded in 1961 to represent professional interests, they have concerned themselves with training for information science.

6.224 Deutscher Normenausschuß ("German Standards Committee") (DNA)

The Deutscher Normenausschuß is closely linked with library and information science through its Fachnormenausschuß Bibliotheks- und Dokumentationswesen, formed in 1927 and revived in 1948, and the committees on terminology and classification. The committee for classification is responsible for everything relating to the Universal Decimal Classification, in particular with the continuance and expansion of the German Decimal Classification. The concise edition of this classification, financed by the Institut für Dokumentationswesen and issued by the classification committee in 1965, is the result of the work of its members, H. Schuchmann and K. Fill. The original text is the German version, of which translations have appeared in other languages.

The special committee for librarianship, books and periodicals has revised a number of DIN-Normen ("German Industrial Standards"). The committee participates in the recommendations of the International Standards Organisation (ISO), which are concerned with the presentation of abstracts, indexes to periodicals, title-pages and the transliteration of Cyrillic (DIN), Arabic, Hebrew and Greek (ISO) scripts into Roman.

The representation of Germany on the two large international bodies, the ISO and the Fédération Internationale de Documentation (FID) is undertaken by the DNA.

6.3 Lehrinstitut für Dokumentation ("Teaching Institute for Documentation")

With the increased number of documentation centres has come an increased need to employ staff who not only are experts in the relevant subject fields but who also understand something of the widely differing aspects of information science. Since 1953 the Deutsche Gesellschaft für Dokumentation has held courses, short ones at first, but later ones extending over a fairly long period of time; these were intended primarily for those already engaged in information science who wished to give their work a firm foundation. In 1967 there arose as a result of these courses the Lehrinstitut für Dokumentation in Frankfurt, established at first as part of the Deutsche Gesellschaft für Dokumentation and financed by the Institut für Dokumentationswesen. It has a full-time head, two full-time lecturers and a quite large number of part-time ones.

The foundations for a future regular, rationally recognised career structure for the information scientist and his employment as a government officer or as an employee are being laid by the Lehrinstitut. For the time being the DGD is assuming responsibility for professional education. It drew up in 1969 education and examination regulations for the "wissenschaftlicher" and for the "diplomierter Dokumentar", that is, the "academic (graduate)" and the "professionally qualified (non-graduate) information scientist" respectively; there are also proposals for "Dokumentationsassistenten" ("information assistants") and for "Dokumentationsgehilfe" ("ancillary staff"). In these respects the hierarchy exactly corresponds to that of the library profession (cf. chap. 7). The requirements for admission, length of training, division into practical and theoretical periods are also parallel. One difference is that theoretical instruction takes up a number of weeks within a year, as things stood in 1970 eleven weeks (312 periods) for graduates. For Dokumentationsassistenten a special theoretical and practical course is provided for in the 12th, 18th and 24th months of training at the Institut für Dokumentationswesen or at the Lehrinstitut. At all three stages the practical part of the course is spent in recognised employment in the field of information service; theoretical instruction is provided by the Lehrinstitut.

The syllabus comprises for academics 16, for non-academics 14, subjectfields, which in both cases include: the fundamentals and history of documentation work and library science, questions of methodology, terminology, classification, information retrieval as well as an introduction to the practical work of acquiring and exploiting documents, the use of punched cards, automation, the particular functions of special libraries, the setting up of documentation centres, reproduction techniques, legal and administrative matters. In the teaching of the academics emphasis is laid upon questions of theory and method and upon making research available to readers.

The courses finish with an oral and written examination.

FURTHER READING

The most important source of information for modern ventures in the whole sphere of bibliography and documentation is the periodical, Nachrichten für Dokumentation. Reference should also be made to the conference reports — Bericht über die ... Tagung — of the Arbeitsgemeinschaft der Spezialbibliotheken, as well as the professional library periodicals.

Some details may be found in the Handbuch der Bibliothekswissenschaft, Bd 2, in the chapters on Benutzung, section Auskunftserteilung, and Spezialbibliotheken, section Dokumentation.

The enterprises named in 6.11 c and d have been discussed, in summary fashion, by Werner Krieg: Die Verbesserung der Literaturerschließung in den Universalbibliotheken. In: Fünfzehn Jahre Bibliotheksarbeit der Deutschen Forschungsgemeinschaft. Frankfurt 1966. p. 142–152.

A report on the work of the Institut für Dokumentationswesen is made by its Director, Martin Cremer, in the Jahrbuch der Max-Planck-Gesellschaft and in the Mitteilungen aus der Max-Planck-Gesellschaft; brief information appears in the Nachrichten für Dokumentation.

The organisation and activities of the Zentralstelle für maschinelle Dokumen-

tation are described in Die ZMD in Frankfurt am Main. Hrsg. von Klaus
Schneider. Berlin, Köln, Frankfurt 1969.

The measures adopted by the Bund to support documentation and information work are assembled in Bundesbericht Forschung I, 1965, II, 1967 and III,
1969. The underlying principles are discussed by Heinz Lechmann: Dokumentation und Information als Anliegen der Bundesrepublik Deutschland.
Frankfurt 1964.

As a result of discussions the Gemeinschaftsausschuß der Technik submits
proposals for the establishment of a comprehensive information network in
the Federal Republic under the title Information und Dokumentation in
Wissenschaft und Technik. Gemeinschaftsausschuß der Technik (GDT). Düsseldorf 1969 (GDT Schriften. 1).

On the profession and training of information scientists see:

blätter zur berufskunde. Bielefeld:

bd 2/XC 20 dokumentationsassistent. 1969

bd 2/XC 30 diplomierter dokumentar. 1969

bd 3/XC 01 wissenschaftlicher dokumentar. 1969

Deutsche Gesellschaft für Dokumentation, Institut für Dokumentation. Jahreslehrgang zur Ausbildung wissenschaftlicher Dokumentare — Jahreslehrgang
zur Ausbildung diplomierter Dokumentare. Last issues for 1970.

7 Librarianship as a Career

The library profession, as it appears today in the Federal Republic, has gradually evolved in the present century a detailed hierarchical structure. Yet in academic as well as in public libraries the situation is fluid. The first stage, der höhere Dienst ("the administrative grade"), for the librarian with a degree or similar qualification, was created in Prussia in 1893; at that time this was intended for the librarian pure and simple who was appointed for all kinds of duties whether in academic or public libraries. With further differentiation within the profession this higher grade was restricted to the service in academic libraries. In the public sector the possibilities of a separate higher grade are being discussed. The second stage, der gehobene Dienst ("the executive grade"), for the non-graduate qualified librarian who has undergone professional training, a grade first legally established in Prussia in 1909, was again originally intended to be uniform for all kinds of library. The setting up of a distinct service for public libraries, which was seen in the examination regulations of October 1930, in accordance with which there were two examination boards and separate certificates, was continued in 1940 by the Reich training and examination regulations for non-graduate qualified librarians in academic libraries, and completed after 1945 by separate regulations for the academic and public library sectors in the individual Länder. The third stage, der mittlere Dienst ("the clerical grade"), was not begun until 1964 and has been introduced initially only in a few Länder and then only in academic libraries; a corresponding development for public libraries is under way.

This strong trend towards splitting the profession and professional education into two distinct categories runs counter to an endeavour not to commit non-graduate librarians too narrowly during their training, especially since they constitute by far the greatest proportion of the profession. Some months of their practical work are reserved for the other types of librarianship; the possibility of change during or after the conclusion of the course is kept open. This separation has been introduced for practical reasons. The situation is in a state of flux, and it could very well be that the segregation will disappear altogether: for example, a common course of instruction is already being envisaged at Hamburg.

What is common to all the groups named is the two-fold possibility of

appointment as an employee or as a government officer. The establishments of most academic libraries contain both classes, though in very
different proportions in the individual Länder. In public libraries civil
service status was for a long time reserved essentially for staff in senior
posts; however, in the last few years a number of mainly large towns
have promoted library staff to this status on a generous scale. Working
conditions for employees are regulated by a contract, those of officers
are based upon a public-law agreement concerning "service and loyalty";
this is usually for life and includes an obligatory welfare provision on
the part of the employer. Although in duties, salaries, pensions and protection against unlawful dismissal the differences between employees and
officers have increasingly diminished, the tradition, prestige and security
associated with civil service status are for the most part still considered
as desirable as ever. The fact that people of the same basic education
doing similar work in the same organisation are on a different legal
footing entails many disadvantages both for those concerned and for
their seniors.

Alongside the professionally qualified staff on the three grades described,
there are in all types of library workers on a library technicians grade;
their functions will not be discussed except in the case of the ancillary
staff in public libraries.

7.1 The Academic Library Service

7.11 Administrative Grade

In academic libraries the staff structure of administrative, executive and
clerical grades corresponds to the extent to which the profession itself
has become hierarchical with the increasing differentiation of duties.

Professional library education for the administrative grade in academic
libraries begins as a rule after the completion of a university course leading to a doctor's degree and a civil service examination. At present the
traditional insistence upon the two examinations is supported in principle by the VDB and also by most of the Länder. Hesse and Baden-
Württemberg require only *one* leaving examination and thereby conform to a recommendation of the Wissenschaftsrat.

The university course for the librarian does not in any way differ from that for the teacher, doctor, judge, clergyman or engineer. Any academic subject and any combination of subjects is possible. Besides the specialists in the humanities, who are generally more strongly orientated towards librarianship, there is today a demand for graduates in pure and applied sciences, engineering and medicine. "Library science" may, in the sense in which it is taught at all in universities today come within the field of studies, but only in the sense of an auxiliary historical discipline and in no case as a compulsory subject for future librarians. A modern interpretation of library science, in conformity with the new developments in information and communication science, as well as in advanced data processing, all of them influencing the librarian's work, is now under discussion. Thus the situation may already be changing in the near future.

Admission requirements, courses of instruction and examinations are laid down in the training and examination regulations of the Länder. Since 1945 Bavaria (1955 and 1967), Baden-Württemberg, Hesse, and Rhineland Palatinate (all 1968) have issued new regulations. Other Länder, for example Hamburg, are preparing new ones. Meanwhile they rely upon the earlier regulations of 1938 (Deutsches Reich) and 1928 (Prussia), which are closely linked and from which the conditions no longer applicable today have been removed. Koordinierungsrichtlinien ("Co-ordinating Principles") for the careers of the administrative and executive grades in academic libraries were drawn up in 1965 at the Kultusministerkonferenz ("Conference of Ministers of Culture and Education").

When admitted to a course of instruction the candidate is normally designated a Bibliotheksreferendar (a "trainee") and receives a maintenance grant lasting throughout his course. An upper age limit, varying between 30 and 35, is laid down for admission.

The course lasts either two or two and a half years. In the first practical year the Referendar becomes familiar by personal experience with all the routines of an academic library. Approved training grounds for this purpose are all the university libraries, the three great libraries of Marburg/Berlin, Munich and the Deutsche Bibliothek in Frankfurt, together with the larger Staats- and Landesbibliotheken. For the second year, when theoretical instruction begins while practical work continues (but in another library), there are four training institutions: the library schools in Frankfurt, Cologne, Munich and the Staats- und Universitätsbibliothek Hamburg.

Theoretical instruction, given partly in lectures, partly in discussion classes or as exercises, comprises (according to the Koordinierungsricht-linien, which more or less correspond with the individual syllabuses): bibliology (history of writing and palaeography, the printed book, book illustration, binding, bookselling and publishing); library history; the organisation and institutions of learning; bibliography; library organisa-tion (acquisitions, cataloguing, information science, circulation, buildings, technical departments); law and administration.

Special emphasis is laid upon bibliology and, what is of major importance for later practice, the subjects of library administration and bibliography; recently library history has fallen more into the background, at least in some schools. Moreover, the Referendar is expected to extend his know-ledge of languages. In Cologne an introduction to Russian is offered.

The course is completed by an oral and written assessment, based partly on examinations, partly on work done in the students' own time. The assessment is conducted by a State examinations board. Having passed the examination the candidate is entitled to be called Bibliotheksassessor ("probationer"). He has however still no automatic claim to a civil ser-vice post, but must apply for one himself. Not infrequently he returns to the library where he received his training.

The Bibliotheksassessor, if he gains civil service status, enters upon a definite career with fixed stages of promotion from Bibliotheksrat (a grade roughly equivalent to an assistant librarian) to Direktor ("chief librarian"). Even with employee status his advancement is ensured. As a rule general academic libraries appoint to their academic staff only people who have completed the prescribed training. Exceptions are made occasionally for natural scientists, medical men or engineers, who then become familiar with library processes during their work. Special libraries are not uniform in this respect. An increasingly large number, especially those of the larger State research institutes, of parliaments and government, prefer properly trained librarians. Libraries in industry and independent institutions do not feel bound by the regulations. Library work and information science are one and the same thing to them. The courses for information scientists (cf. 6.3), which also cover library functions, often serve as a useful preparation for the profession; such courses supplement specialist study, which is in any case still the essential prerequisite.

The field of activity of the academic librarian is many-sided. As a subject specialist or as a member of the staff or the head of a specialist department he remains in touch with his specialism, must keep abreast of current literature and increase his skill in judging whether or not a work is worth acquiring for his library. As the head of the large departments of acquisitions, cataloguing, circulation, as the librarian in charge of a union catalogue, still more as the chief librarian, he has to master organisational and administrative tasks which often go beyond the sphere of his own library into that of co-operation between academic libraries. Heads of university libraries frequently combine their office with a teaching post, a lectureship, in isolated cases even a professorial chair, a possibility open to other academic librarians as well.

Published works on library topics, bibliographical papers, publications on questions in his own research field are among the projects expected of an academic librarian. In some Länder those engaged in such projects are granted reduced hours of duty.

The academic library profession combines administrative and scholarly functions. Which predominates depends upon the individual's field of work. In all the discussions on the scholarly nature of the profession, about which there have been in recent years lively differences of opinion, there is nevertheless agreement in principle. Faced with the excessive burden of administrative tasks, inevitable in the early post-War period, the Wissenschaftsrat recommends redressing the balance between these and scholarly activity.

7.12 Executive Grade

After 1945 most of the Länder as well as the Bund issued training and examination regulations governing the admission of candidates to the executive grade in academic libraries. The Koordinierungsrichtlinien of the Kultusministerkonferenz drawn up in 1965 reinforce the endeavours of the education committee of the VDB towards unification. Agreement exists on the most important matters. Differences occur over the length of the course of training, which varies between 2, $2^{1}/_{2}$ and 3 years, over the age limit, which is normally about 30, and over the method of allocating practical and theoretical instruction. The general fundamental requirement is the Reifeprüfung (cf. 1.211) as a condition of entry, although provision is made for exceptional cases: Hesse alone accepts as sufficient the successful completion of 10 years at a Realschule or a Gymnasium. However, like the others, the Hessian regulations demand evidence of acquaintance with three foreign languages, including Latin (Kleines Latinum). In Bavaria and Hesse admission is made dependent upon a special test of their own, in Baden-Württemberg upon a two-week practical course in an approved library with an accompanying discussion class.

At the present time there are plans afoot to reorganise professional education on the lines of a university course with emphasis upon theoretical instruction and a brief practical period. This still leaves open the question whether the course is to be completed as hitherto in special training institutions, which have the character of a professional college, or within the framework of existing professional colleges or even universities.

The present procedure for entry and the training resemble that for the administrative grade: the award of a maintenance grant lasting throughout the course, the division of the curriculum into a practical and a theoretical section, and the completion of the practical period in institutions approved for that purpose. As before, such institutions are mainly general academic libraries (university libraries or Staats-, Landes- and Stadtbibliotheken) with special libraries as well and, in some cases, those of parliaments and government. Like the total length of training, the time allotted to each section of the course varies; frequently the division between practice and theory is half and half. As a rule the practical part comes at the beginning. North Rhine-Westphalia however introduces a four-month "induction semester" at its School in Cologne. Practical preparatory training is for the most part gained at one library. There the newcomer becomes familiar in a specified period with the organisation of an academic library and is thoroughly grounded especially in those duties which form his future sphere of work. Moreover in order to broaden his knowledge of the various possibilities of librarianship he has, according to most training regulations, to spend a certain time in a public or even a special library. Theoretical instruction is usually provided in one of the library schools named below. Baden-Württemberg transfers the second, theoretical, year to a library. In accordance with the Koordinierungs- richtlinien the syllabus comprises the following subjects: bibliology, library organisation, the theory and practice of cataloguing, information science, bibliography, history of learning, library history, literary history, the book trade, civics, law and administration, and supplementary courses in foreign languages. Special emphasis is laid upon subjects of practical relevance, namely library organisation and cataloguing, as well as the history of learning and bibliography, as matters which are at first very strange to the newcomer but with which he must be able to cope in his later career. Visits to other libraries and information centres, study tours at home and even in nearby foreign countries stimulate a positive outlook.

The course is completed by an oral and written assessment with examinations, in some schools combined with work done in the students' own time. After passing the examination the candidate is a Diplom-Bibliothekar für den gehobenen Dienst an wissenschaftlichen Bibliotheken ("qualified librarian on the executive grade in academic libraries") or (as a government officer) Bibliotheksinspektor zur Anstellung ("unestablished library inspector"). The further stages in his career extend from Bibliotheksinspektor to Bibliotheksoberamtsrat. In special cases even promotion to the administrative grade is possible. In the Federal salary scales for employees the initial pay and first increment were revised a few years ago; but promotion prospects lag behind those of officers to an unsatisfactory degree.

Although the qualified librarian, whose profession was created in 1906, was thought of as an "assistant" to the academic librarian, whom he was expected to relieve of routine work, he has meanwhile become a colleague with an independent sphere of activity and special responsibility. A major part of practical librarianship in acquisitions and cataloguing, in enquiries and reader services, is carried out by him. In the institute, special and government libraries the qualified librarian provides the only professional manpower. It is in fact these posts that are preferred by many young recruits.

In order to familiarise librarians of some years' experience with modern developments in library science a few Länder (North Rhine-Westphalia and Baden-Württemberg) have introduced refresher courses lasting several days, and these have enjoyed considerable favour.

7.13 Clerical Grade

The clerical grade in academic libraries, with this designation and as a definite career, had not been introduced in the Federal Republic until recently and so far only in Bavaria (1964), Baden-Württemberg (1966) and, it is expected, in Lower Saxony soon. In practice without special training and without civil service status, there has for a long time been in every sizeable library a clerical grade in the form of unqualified as-

sistants; they come from school or commercial college or from other
employment and are trained in the library for specific tasks. They co-
operate closely with staff on the executive grade; under their supervision
and guidance in acquisitions, in cataloguing literature in German, at the
issue desk and in the reading room they relieve them of routine work.
The trend is towards delegation of further responsibilities to this
group.

Applicants are accepted who are at least 15 or 16 and not more than 30
years old or who may already be employed as library staff. Training lasts
1 ¹/₂ or 2 years. It includes practical and theoretical instruction. As regards
practical instruction, which takes place in an approved library, Bavaria
and Baden-Württemberg agree basically: the newcomer is to learn the
jobs for which he is needed later. For the theoretical syllabus a full year
is provided in Munich, in Baden-Württemberg only 3 weeks. The subjects
in both cases are library organisation, fundamentals of cataloguing,
introduction to bibliography, fundamentals of budgeting, bookkeeping
and accountancy, the law concerning government officers and employees,
and civics. The course finishes with a short oral examination and some
written test-papers. A member of the executive grade is on the examining
board.

General principles for the training of the clerical grade can still not be
deduced from these regulations, which differ radically in character. The
Bavarian ones are conceived as analogous to those for the administrative
and executive grades; those of Baden-Württemberg leave more scope to
the training libraries in that they lay the main emphasis upon practical
work. The possibility of making the clerical grade another step of the
library profession is under discussion. It still cannot be clearly seen
whether all the Länder will agree to establishing a special career structure.
The Wissenschaftsrat, which pronounces in favour of a clerical grade as
the preliminary step to the executive grade, leaves open the question of a
separate career structure.

The three grades, administrative, executive and clerical, are not completely divorced from each other. For especially gifted and diligent staff
promotion to the next grade is possible. For the time being such people
are exceptions. In the great salary reform of the Federal Republic such
a "dovetailing of careers" is legally provided for.

7.2 The Public Library Service

7.21 Executive Grade

In contrast to the courses of training for academic libraries there are for the public ones at present only courses for the executive grade; these lead to a diploma. In order to ensure a certain uniformity, and on the assumption that the examinations conducted by individual library schools should be recognised throughout the Federal Republic, outline agreements on training were issued by the Ständige Konferenz der Kultusminister; from time to time the training was to be adapted to fit new developments. So at present the method of training for the public library service is still partly determined by the outline agreement of 1963; meanwhile changes in ideas and practices supplied the impetus for the preparation of a new agreement, which was concluded in January 1968 and which is now being implemented.

Admission to courses is determined by officers or committees working with the library schools under state regulations. In general the schools, like the universities, require the Abitur. Only in exceptional cases is the leaving certificate of a Realschule or an equivalent qualification accepted. In addition, however, such candidates are expected to have completed their training in some profession relevant to librarianship. Moreover, according to the outline agreement they are to be at least 21 years old and must usually take a supplementary examination. As rare exceptions the Library School of North Rhine-Westphalia allows full-time staff who have served in professional positions for years without qualifying to take an external examination.

Since the candidates must not be older than 30, the average student age is considerably lower than in many library schools outside Germany.

The uniform three-year course is divided into theoretical semesters with lectures, exercises and study groups at the schools and into practical ones in the training libraries to which the students are assigned by the schools — in North Germany by the joint admissions office of Bremen, Hamburg, Lower Saxony and Schleswig-Holstein. The sequence and duration of parts of the syllabus were until recently fixed differently for individual schools. In most cases they are now following the 1968 outline agreement of the Kultusminister, which requires that out of a theoretical course of 6 semesters at least 4 months' practical instruction should be gained in the holidays between semesters. A student with a university education may be excused up to two semesters of the course. Practical instruction takes place at libraries, where in accordance with modern library regulations trainees are supervised by qualified librarians. Most Länder urge that part of the theoretical training should take place at one of the Staatliche Büchereistellen, where the students are introduced to the special problems of librarianship in country districts and small towns. At present the course normally also includes a practical orientation period in an academic library.

In future a reduction in the length of the practical period will allow students to gain only an impression of library routines and of the librarian's sphere of activity; thorough training in individual library routines will have to be postponed until later.

The theoretical course treats not only library science in the wide sense but also and in particular bibliology and bibliography, the study of literature, history of learning, law and administration, and library history. The differences between this training and that for the parallel grade in academic libraries lie today principally in the emphases and extensions of the syllabus in the various subjects. Lectures and practical exercises are supplemented by visits and study tours.

The final assessment is made by an examinations board under the chairmanship of a representative of the Kultusministerium; the board includes members of the teaching staff of the library school and practising librarians. The assessment consists of a written part (test-papers and also work done in the students' own time) and an oral part, which covers the theoretical sections of the syllabus. Attainment in the practical work is taken into account in the report. Anyone failing the examination may resit it once. Nevertheless, in practice the number of failures is not very large. This is no doubt primarily due to the relatively high entrance requirements.

The expenses of training on the one hand and financial support of students on the other are not fixed uniformly. Such questions figure in discussions on the reform of training; relevant factors are the status of the library schools and the extent to which the training regulations conform to the law concerning civil servants. At present students preparing for the public library service do not as a rule possess the status of Beamten auf Widerruf ("unestablished civil servants"), which guarantees for most students preparing for the executive grade in academic libraries a not inconsiderable maintenance grant throughout their course. During their practical course they receive from the authorities of the training libraries a probationer's allowance of varying amounts; for the period of theoretical training they receive from the state a grant which also varies according to circumstances. If appropriate, the student's fees, which are levied at many schools, may also be waived.

Qualified public librarians are eligible for employee or civil-service appointments on the executive grade in the public library service of the Bund, the Länder and the Gemeinden including senior professional posts in individual public libraries or library systems or in the Staatliche Büchereistellen.

Most public librarians have employee status. Their classification into specific salary groups is determined according to the tasks they perform. The Bundes-Angestellten-Tarif ("Federal Employees' Salary Scales") in recent years defined in detail a whole series of executive grade library tasks, partly based on bookstock and annual loans statistics. This has resulted in a stricter differentiation of staffing and in improved promotion prospects. However, the somewhat rigid definitions were bound occasionally to prove a hindrance to an appropriate classification, so that additions and corrections are being pressed for. Apart from the initial grade for new entrants the professional library qualification is required for executive grade posts; the standing of librarians is thereby granted a certain protection.

A number of librarians trained for the public sector take posts in denominational or works libraries. Not infrequently they also find their way into various kinds of academic libraries, just as those trained for the academic sector later move in the opposite direction.

By no means do these librarians always take the prescribed supplementary examination for the executive grade of the other sector. The great shortage of staff facilitates the transfer from one type of library to another, as does the partial assimilation of tasks and routines due to modern developments.

Both the public library associations have expressed to the Kultusminister of the Länder their concern that the uniformity of curricula in the various sectors of the library profession should be preserved in order that comparable examinations should be mutually recognised.

The authorisation in the Ministers' outline agreement for supplementary examinations in special fields has been taken advantage of by the Library School at Stuttgart. Special examinations for youth librarians and similar ones for music librarians have been introduced; these are open to diplomates of other library schools. In music the entrance requirements are above all a special knowledge of music theory and practice, together with practical experience in those music libraries recognised for this purpose. For most students preparation for these special papers runs parallel to that for the general diploma examination.

7.22   Administrative Grade

The lively discussion about content, form and extent of the courses for the public library service led in recent years to divergent plans for reform in the individual Länder. If these disconnected plans were to come to fruition, they would endanger the unity of training hitherto safeguarded in essential points by the agreement of the Kultusminister. In this situation the Verein Deutscher Volksbibliothekare (now Verein der Bibliothekare an Öffentlichen Büchereien) and the Deutscher Büchereiverband presented to the Ministers' Conference in Spring 1967 joint proposals for a new outline agreement. Besides making the theoretical training for qualified librarians more thorough, something that is now stipulated by the 1968 outline agreement, the associations proposed a systematic training for the administrative grade in public libraries on the normal basis of a completed university education.

In support of this there are good reasons, for with the intensive post-War development there have arisen even in the public library system more and more functions and posts on an administrative level: senior posts in large city systems, the chiefships of the larger town libraries and individual Staatliche Büchereistellen, and teaching posts at library schools. At present such posts are held either by non-graduate qualified librarians who have proved themselves to be exceptional by long years of experience, by librarians who before or after taking their diploma have completed an academic education or even by graduates who had trained for the administrative grade in academic libraries. For various reasons this situation cannot be satisfactory. For one thing, the course for qualified librarians in public libraries, which is admittedly shortened for graduates to two years but is otherwise the same as for non-graduates, does not meet the specialist and high demands of the senior positions. Secondly, for graduates there is only a limited appeal in the public sector, since there is no distinct training linked with their university courses and leading to a definite career on the administrative grade.

Again, graduates who have been specially prepared for this grade in academic libraries do not always find it easy to find their feet in the routine organisation of public libraries.

The decision whether or not a distinct training for the administrative grade in public libraries is to be established has not yet been made. What is certain is that even then non-graduate qualified librarians will not be debarred from access to appointments on the administrative grade.

7.23 Library Assistants

Concurrent with the deliberations about a course for the administrative grade in public libraries are the attempts to find ways of freeing the qualified librarian of a number of duties and to create the profession of "library assistant" for definite tasks hitherto almost everywhere reserved for librarians; the new post would be comparable with the clerical grade in academic libraries. The title of the post still needs final approval.

The initiative comes from the professional side. In proposals of the Deutscher Büchereiverband and the Verein der Bibliothekare an Öffentlichen Büchereien to the Ständige Konferenz der Kultusminister the sphere of work of the library assistants is described as formal library tasks and responsible work in the administration of the smaller libraries in suburban or regional library systems. The entrance requirement for training is to be the leaving certificate of the Realschule or its equivalent. A scheme, prepared in North Rhine-Westphalia, suggested a two-year, predominantly practical course with a theoretical part of at least two months and at least 200 hours, to be completed by a written and oral examination at the local Verwaltungs- und Sparkassenschule ("school of public administration"), which is to take over this part of the course. More recently a committee of the Deutscher Büchereiverband has been set up to consider in detail the education and the range of duties to be performed by such library assistants.

Professional discussion in depth, draft syllabuses and initial experimental courses, as also the resultant organisational consequences within individual library systems, reveal both the uncertainties and also the possibilities of the new development. In the last analysis the employment and the career image of the assistant will be decisively determined by the future development of the profession as a whole.

7.24 Ancillary Staff

Besides qualified librarians there are at present in public libraries very many ancillary staff — apart from the workmen, who in binderies, as drivers of mobile libraries, as stack attendants in the larger libraries, as printers or duplicators are entrusted with technical and mechanical duties. Ancillary staff undertake numerous tasks in the central administration of the library and in counter work except of course for the readers' advisory service. Of such staff no special previous education is expected. They are initiated into their duties while working or, alternatively, are systematically trained for the various jobs open to them. In some towns and at some Staatliche Büchereistellen they have the opportunity of completing this instruction with a formal examination. However, there is as yet no general organised training and grading of such staff as a basis for a distinct career. The present tendency is simply toward the in-service training of ancillary staff.

The report of the Kommunale Gemeinschaftsstelle für Verwaltungsvereinfachung lays down detailed criteria for the demarcation of professional duties and recommends the ratio of 1 : 2 of librarians to other staff, or in the case of strong centralisation and rationalisation one of 1 : 1.

As far as the whole public library service is concerned, the above-mentioned proposals by the two public library associations to the Kultusministerkonferenz envisage the possibility of promotion to the next grade.

7.25 Further Education

Another demand of the associations is for the systematic further education of all public library staff. Of recent years significant progress has been made in this field with the advanced seminars for qualified librarians sponsored jointly over a period of two years each by the Verband der Bibliotheken des Landes Nordrhein-Westfalen and the Cologne Library School. The Deutscher Büchereiverband and the Verein der Bibliothekare an Öffentlichen Büchereien thereupon organised in a somewhat modified form seminars for participants from all over the Federal Republic.

Those taking part in these advanced seminars are carefully selected, and their active co-operation is expected. Mere attendance therefore constitutes a certain qualification, even if at the end only a certificate to that effect is given.

The success of these seminars leads one to expect that, with certain changes made in the light of experience, they will become a permanent feature.

In the overwhelming majority of public libraries in the smaller Gemeinden there are neither professional librarians nor even full-time staff. The instruction and further education of part-time or honorary staff is an important responsibility of the Staatliche Büchereistellen.

7.3 Library Schools

In the Federal Republic including West Berlin there are nine state or state-recognised library schools: Berlin, Bonn, Cologne, Frankfurt/Main, Göttingen, Hamburg, Hanover, Munich and Stuttgart. The responsible authorities are the Länder of Berlin, North Rhine-Westphalia, Hamburg, Lower Saxony, Bavaria, Baden-Württemberg, the City of Frankfurt, the Roman Catholic Borromäusverein and the Protestant Church in Germany. The regional power of the individual library schools is subject to a certain, even if not strict, control by the agreements between the Länder. Both the denominational library schools prepare staff not only for work in libraries run by the churches but also for work in other libraries, and the admission of applicants is not restricted to members of their respective communions.

The present status of the library schools is not unambiguous, but they are best compared with specialist institutions of higher education (cf. 1.221). The titles of the individual schools differ: Bibliotheksschule ("library school"), Bibliothekarschule ("librarians' school"), Bibliothekarakademie ("librarians' academy"), Bibliothekar-Lehrinstitut ("librarians' training institution"). The future status of the schools will depend on the outcome of professional discussions on education and on the reconciliation of partially divergent ideas. Whether the schools themselves will achieve university status, whether perhaps they will be affiliated to existing universities or comparable institutions, will also depend on any general reform of higher education. An increased emphasis upon theoretical training and the extension of it to six semesters would at all events result in an expansion of the schools, in an improvement in status and in closer links with universities, all of which should make additional study facilities accessible to students.

The present schools differ in the opportunities that they offer for training for the various types and branches of librarianship (cf. the table below).

Just as the curricula of the schools vary, so do their capacities. At the moment the number of students, including those gaining practical experience at a training library, lies between 300 and 400 at Hamburg and at Cologne, between 200 and 300 at Stuttgart, between 100 and 200 at Munich, and so far below 100 at the other schools.

For 1969 the schools in the Federal Republic reported 65 students as having completed the examination for the administrative grade and 271 for the executive grade in academic libraries, and 298 for the executive grade in the public sector.

Compared with library schools outside Germany the number of full-time teaching staff is extraordinarily low, and the staff-student ratio is in consequence unfavourable. In these circumstances the schools rely to a considerable extent upon part-time lecturers, which is possible because the schools are situated in major library centres. According to the outline agreement of the Kultusministerkonferenz the full-time teaching staff are expected to have completed their professional training and a university examination, and to have had at least two years' professional library experience. In fact, the full-time teaching staff, who normally hold administrative-grade appointments, are predominantly graduates.

The supply of a sufficient number of suitable lecturers is a sine qua non if any of the attempts at reform are to be realised.

Library Schools

Place	Title of school Responsible authority	Training for[1]	Full-time teaching staff[2]
Berlin	Berliner Bibliothekarakademie Land Berlin	GWB, ÖB	4
Bonn	Staatlich anerkanntes Bibliothekar-Lehrinstitut Bonn Borromäusverein	GWB, ÖB	1
Cologne	Bibliothekar-Lehrinstitut des Landes Nordrhein-Westfalen Land Nordrhein-Westfalen	HWB, GWB, ÖB	11

Frankfurt a. M.	Bibliotheksschule Stadt Frankfurt am Main	HWB, GWB	2
Göttingen	Evangelisches Bibliothekar-Lehrinstitut Evangelische Kirche in Deutschland	GWB, ÖB	2
Hamburg	Bibliothekarschule der Freien und Hansestadt Hamburg Freie und Hansestadt Hamburg	GWB, ÖB	10
Hanover	Niedersächsische Bibliotheksschule Land Niedersachsen	GWB	2
Munich	Bibliotheksschule der Bayerischen Staatsbibliothek Freistaat Bayern	HWB, GWB, MWB	2
Stuttgart	Süddeutsches Bibliothekar- Lehrinstitut Land Baden-Württemberg	ÖB	12

[1] Training for HWB — Höherer Dienst an wissenschaftlichen Bibliotheken ("Administrative grade in academic libraries")

GWB — Gehobener Dienst an wissenschaftlichen Bibliotheken ("Executive grade in academic libraries")

MWB — Mittlerer Dienst an wissenschaftlichen Bibliotheken ("Clerical grade in academic libraries")

ÖB — Dienst an öffentlichen Büchereien ("Public library service")

[2] Full-time teaching staff including full-time heads of schools.

FURTHER READING

The profession and professional education have chapters devoted to them in the two major manuals of librarianship. The "classical" exposition for academic librarians is by Georg Leyh: Der Bibliothekar und sein Beruf. In: Handbuch der Bibliothekswissenschaft. Bd 2. 2. Aufl. Wiesbaden 1961. p. 1—112. In the Handbuch des Büchereiwesens the corresponding chapter on public librarians appears in the 1. Halbband.

Those wishing to keep abreast of new developments are referred to the professional library journals, in which numerous contributions bear witness to the significance of the theme.

An incentive towards a radical reassessment of professional education for the administrative and executive grades in the light of modern requirements, especially the essential acquaintance with information theory and technique, is afforded by the paper by Wilhelm Grunwald: Der Bibliothekar und seine Ausbildung. ZfBB 16 (1969), p. 154—169. A symposium at the Bibliothekarstag in 1969 gave an opportunity for the various reactions to Grunwald's proposals to find expression. Cf. Joachim Stoltzenburg: Der Bibliothekar und seine Ausbildung. ZfBB 16 (1969), p. 381—392.

A lively international discussion arose from the paper by Joachim Wieder: Berufssorgen des wissenschaftlichen Bibliothekars, Libri 9 (1959), p. 132—165.

On the types of libraries and the training for a career in them detailed information is given in the Blätter zur Berufskunde. Hrsg. von der Bundesanstalt für Arbeitsvermittlung und Arbeitslosenversicherung. Bielefeld:

Bd 3/X B 01   Bibliothekar (höherer Dienst an wissenschaftlichen Bibliotheken). 3. Aufl. 1968.

Bd 2/X B 02   Diplom-Bibliothekar (gehobener Dienst an wissenschaftlichen Bibliotheken). Veränderter Neudruck 1968.

Bd 2/X B 31   Diplom-Bibliothekar für den Dienst an öffentlichen Büchereien (Volksbibliothekar). 5. Aufl. 1969.

The official text of all the admission, training and examination regulations currently in force for the academic library service is printed in Bibliotheksrechtliche Vorschriften. Zusammengestellt von Ralph Lansky. 2. erw. Aufl. Frankfurt 1969. Supplements are to follow.

A corresponding compilation for the public sector exists at present only for North Rhine-Westphalia in the Denkschrift zur Neuordnung des Dienstes an öffentlichen Büchereien im Lande Nordrhein-Westfalen. Köln 1966.

The separate regulations of the Länder on education for librarianship are reprinted in the professional press.

A comprehensive report on the advanced seminar for public librarians, sponsored jointly by the Deutscher Büchereiverband and the Verein Deutscher Volksbibliothekare (Verein der Bibliothekare an Öffentlichen Büchereien), is provided by Helga Rethfeldt: 1. Fortbildungsseminar des DBV und des VDV 1966/1967. Berlin 1967 (Bibliotheksdienst, Beiheft 28).

More detailed data on the library schools in the Federal Republic are available in the Jahrbuch der Deutschen Bibliotheken and the Handbuch der Öffentlichen Büchereien.

8   Practical Information

Everything we have said in previous chapters is intended as a first introduction to German libraries in general, to the separate branches of library activity, and to questions we have felt especially important. In this final chapter we set out primarily to inform our foreign colleagues how to obtain further details and whom to approach in seeking contacts with librarians and library services in the Federal Republic.

8.1 Professional Literature and Library Organisations

8.11 Professional Literature

What follows has been compiled as a brief guide and not as a bibliography proper. It gives some of the basic reference works and journals, and also some of the organisations and publishing houses whose output is worth watching.

Publishing and Publishers

The major part of the professional literature is published by the library associations and central institutions (cf. 3.2, 2.6, 2.8). Staatliche Büchereistellen of the Länder are also active in this field. Their varied publications are intended as working aids for the libraries in their area of activity, but have in some cases a more general significance (cf. 2.53). Of the library schools, only the largest — the Bibliothekar-Lehrinstitut des Landes Nordrhein-Westfalen in Cologne — has yet produced any publications. Of the union catalogues, those in Berlin and Hamburg have issued local library directories.

Since 1945 a number of academic libraries have resumed the useful practice of publishing regular annual reports, or summarised reports covering several years, in duplicated or printed form: the university libraries at Brunswick, Erlangen, Kiel, Mainz and Tübingen, the Staatsbibliotheken at Hamburg (SUB), Bremen (since 1965), and the Staatsbibliothek Preußischer Kulturbesitz.

Notable among the few cities which produce fairly comprehensive reports on the state of their libraries are West Berlin, with its printed
annual report "Berlins Öffentliche Büchereien", and Hamburg, with the
reports of the Öffentliche Bücherhallen (1949–59, 1960–63).

Hanover's public libraries have published a report on their development
in the period 1956–1965. Some larger libraries produce annual reports in
mimeographed form, e. g. Hanover, Munich and the Amerika-Gedenkbibliothek in West Berlin. Other descriptions of public library work at
local and regional level have appeared as a result of professional meetings, including "Büchereien in Schleswig-Holstein" (Büchereizentrale
Flensburg, 1963), "Texte, Bilder, Zahlen" (Stadtbücherei Bielefeld, 1965),
"Büchereien in Dänemark und Schleswig-Holstein. Eine Ausstellung im
Jahre 1966", "Stadtbücherei Duisburg. Versuch einer modernen Öffentlichen Bücherei" (1968), "Zwischen Bücherei und Bibliothek. Die Volksbüchereien der Freien Hansestadt Bremen 1969".

Many libraries have booklets as a guide to their arrangement and
services. The numerous printed book-lists put out by public libraries and
Staatliche Büchereistellen have already been mentioned.

Certain of the organisations named have to a great extent themselves
taken on the printing and marketing of their own publications. This
applies above all to the publications of the Deutscher Büchereiverband
and its Arbeitsstelle für das Büchereiwesen in Berlin, and to the Verein
der Bibliothekare an Öffentlichen Büchereien with its Reutlingen publishing house Bücherei und Bildung.

Among the general publishers who have included professional literature
in their lists, Harrassowitz at Wiesbaden deserves pride of place as the
publisher of the two major manuals ("Handbuch der Bibliothekswissenschaft", "Handbuch des Büchereiwesens"), the "Jahrbuch der Deutschen
Bibliotheken", the annual "Bibliothek und Wissenschaft", the "Beiträge
zum Buch- und Bibliothekswesen" and the "Beiträge zum Büchereiwesen".
Principal among the others are Vittorio Klostermann at Frankfurt, with
the "Zeitschrift für Bibliothekswesen und Bibliographie" and its supplements, and the Greven-Verlag at Cologne, from which appear, among
other things, the "Arbeiten aus dem Bibliothekar-Lehrinstitut des Landes
Nordrhein-Westfalen".

Bibliographies

The literature on librarianship which appears in the Federal Republic is listed and reviewed in international and certain foreign bibliographies and professional journals, as well as in German ones. The "Fachbibliographischer Dienst: Bibliothekswesen", published by the Arbeitsstelle für das Büchereiwesen since 1965 (cf. 6.12), has aimed at a complete coverage. It is obtainable through the Deutscher Büchereiverband.

A selection of the professional literature in German published before 1965, with over 4000 references, can be found in the "Bibliographie zum Bibliotheks- und Büchereiwesen" by Jürgen Busch, edited after his death by Ursula von Dietze (Wiesbaden, 1966). It is linked with the "Fachbibliographischer Dienst: Bibliothekswesen" by reciprocal references in the catch-word index.

A comprehensive and important bibliography, listing separately-published documents as well as periodical articles in the field of legislation and regulations concerning libraries of all types, is: Ralph Lansky: "Bibliographie zum Bibliotheksrecht". Frankfurt 1970.

Manuals

Each of the two main types of library is the subject of a basic standard work which has been or is being published by Harrassowitz.

The "Handbuch der Bibliothekswissenschaft", edited in its first edition by Fritz Milkau and Georg Leyh (Bd 1—3, 1931—1942), is available in a second edition, revised and brought up to date. Its editor is Georg Leyh; the individual chapters have been in part modified and in part rewritten by librarians specialising in the relevant fields. It comprises:

Bd 1 (writing and the book), 1952.

Bd 2 (library administration), 1961.

Bd 3, Teil 1—2 (history of libraries), 1955, 1957.

The first volume deals with the history of writing, palaeography, book illumination, printing and book illustration, binding, the book trade and bibliography; the second with acquisitions, cataloguing, reader services, shelving, statistics, buildings, training and the profession, and separate sections on special libraries and music libraries; the third with the development of libraries from their beginnings to the present day: from the start of the modern era, detailed chapters are devoted to the separate countries of Central and Western Europe and to the United States. The Handbuch is, as its title states, a manual of library science and not a guide specifically to the German library world. Nevertheless, this latter occupies a relatively large amount of space, so that the Handbuch must still also be regarded as the most detailed account of German academic librarianship.

After the Second World War a parallel work appeared, the "Handbuch des Büchereiwesens", edited by Johannes Langfeldt. The second half-volume was the first to be completed, in 1965, with chapters on public library administration, book selection and exploitation of stock, public library legislation and organisations, public libraries in urban and rural areas, Catholic and Protestant libraries, different types of special public libraries, public libraries in East Germany, in other German-speaking countries, and German libraries abroad. The first half-volume has had allocated to it the chapters on public library history, sociological and psychological foundations of public library work, training and the profession, and public library buildings. The chapters, written by different authors, deal with German history and tradition in each field of public library work, besides the present situation.

Basic publications in particular areas of librarianship have been noted in the preceding chapters.

Yearbooks (Directories)

A mass of information can be found in two publications, both appearing at two-yearly intervals.

The "Jahrbuch der Deutschen Bibliotheken", compiled by the Verein Deutscher Bibliothekare, has been published by Harrassowitz since 1902. The first volume published after the last war, after a seven-year interval, was volume 34, 1950. The yearbook contains, in concise form, the essential data on academic libraries and their staff, union catalogues, library schools, the Deutsche Forschungsgemeinschaft, the Verein Deutscher Bibliothekare with its committees and working-parties, professional associations, detailed statistics, brief biographies of academic librarians and a bibliography of library directories.

The "Handbuch der Öffentlichen Büchereien" is compiled by the Deutscher Büchereiverband e. V. in conjunction with the Verein der Bibliothekare an Öffentlichen Büchereien, and compiled by the Arbeitsstelle für das Büchereiwesen. It gives particulars — often in great detail, including staffing information — of important institutions in the field of public librarianship: the responsible offices of the Kultusministerien in the Länder, the Staatliche Büchereistellen, library schools, municipal public libraries with full-time staff and in Gemeinden with over 10,000 in-

habitants, music libraries, mobile libraries, Landkreis libraries, addresses
of central offices and organisations, and a list of members of the Verein
der Bibliothekare an Öffentlichen Büchereien. It is distributed by the
Deutscher Büchereiverband.
The following directories for special libraries have been published:
"Verzeichnis der Spezialbibliotheken". Aachen, 1965.
"Verzeichnis von Schrifttums-Auskunftsstellen". 6. Aufl., Berlin, 1968.
"Verzeichnis der Parlaments- und Behördenbibliotheken". Bonn, 1964.

Statistics

Statistics on libraries in the Federal Republic are compiled and published
by various agencies. Certain minor overlappings have been unavoidable
here, while in a few areas statistics are not available or very inadequate.
Annual reports of individual libraries contain important data for statistics on academic libraries. A general survey of each year is given by
the statistics published in the "Jahrbuch der Deutschen Bibliotheken".
These fall into two parts: "increase in stock" and "circulation". Increase
in stock is broken down by subject and mode of acquisition showing
expenditure as well as number of titles. Statistics of circulation
distinguish local issues, inter-library loans and photographic services.
Annual budgets for book purchase and staff establishments are given in
the first section of the yearbook among the details of individual
libraries. Since 1969 the ZfBB has published annually in its second issue
a statistical table containing the previous year's figures for acquisitions
(basic grant and special funds), circulation (local and inter-library loans)
and personnel, as well as figures for the current year's budget and personnel. The table covers university libraries, the Staatsbibliotheken,
Landesbibliotheken and academic Stadtbibliotheken and a selection of
special libraries.
For local authority public libraries, the Deutscher Büchereiverband and
its Arbeitsstelle für das Büchereiwesen produce — by mid-February of
each year — the "Schnellstatistik kommunaler Öffentlicher Bibliotheken
und Büchereien". These statistics cover all local authority public libraries
with full-time professional staff. They contain figures, as at 31st December
of the previous year, for the number of inhabitants, size of bookstock,
number of loans for the year just ended; for the current calendar year
(which in the Federal Republic is identical with the financial year), inter

alia, information on budgets and establishments. The Schnellstatistik also contains data on average book prices and expenditure by the Länder on public libraries.

The "Gesamtstatistik der kommunalen Öffentlichen Büchereien der Bundesrepublik", arranged by region and now published annually, is also edited and produced by the Arbeitsstelle für das Büchereiwesen of the Deutscher Büchereiverband. The statistical information is provided by the Staatliche Büchereistellen. Within each of the Länder, figures are given separately for the Stadt- and Landkreise of each Regierungsbezirk. The Gesamtstatistik shows the number of Gemeinden maintaining public libraries and their inhabitants, the number of libraries and volumes, issues and expenditure, as well as the most important proportional figures arising from these. Figures for the whole Federal Republic are derived from a survey of Länder. Every three years the regional statistics are supplemented by statistics classified by size of locality.

The Schnellstatistik and Gesamtstatistik are obtainable from the Deutscher Büchereiverband.

The article "Büchereien" which appears every two or three years in the "Statistisches Jahrbuch Deutscher Gemeinden", issued by the Deutscher Städtetag (Waisenhaus-Buchdruckerei und Verlag, Braunschweig), is intended as a survey of libraries of all kinds in Gemeinden of more than 20,000 inhabitants and towns outside Kreis jurisdiction. The first two of its five tables give data on the public libraries maintained by the Gemeinden themselves. The statistics supplement in some respects the Schnellstatistik and Gesamtstatistik of the Arbeitsstelle für das Büchereiwesen. Table 3 gives figures for those academic libraries in the Gemeinden which contain over 5,000 volumes. A further table, which has the least claim to completeness, covers works libraries, small special libraries, school libraries, and denominational libraries. The final table contains statistics for libraries established by foreign cultural agencies in the Gemeinden.

For the denominational public libraries the Arbeitsgemeinschaft der kirchlichen Büchereiverbände Deutschlands produced for the first time in 1965 the combined "Statistik der kirchlichen öffentlichen Büchereien in der Bundesrepublik". This covers Protestant and Roman Catholic libraries and is divided into sets of regional statistics (arranged by Regierungsbezirke and Länder), geographical statistics (places being arranged by relative size), statistics showing Landeskirchen or dioceses and statistics showing the Stadtkreise and Landkreise. This publication has so far appeared at intervals of three years.

Additional statistics are produced from time to time, as independent publications or in professional journals and other organs, by the relevant offices.

Professional Journals

Journals in librarianship appearing in the Federal Republic are addressed predominantly to different types of library and their staffs.

The journal for academic librarianship, and the official organ of the Verein Deutscher Bibliothekare and the Verein der Diplom-Bibliothekare an wissenschaftlichen Bibliotheken, is the "Zeitschrift für Bibliothekswesen und Bibliographie", published by Vittorio Klostermann at Frankfurt. Its first volume (1954) supplanted the first, modest post-war information bulletin, the "Nachrichten für wissenschaftliche Bibliotheken" (1948–1953). Besides major articles on theoretical and practical topics, it publishes shorter articles on current questions, news items on individual libraries, book reviews and a list of new German and foreign publications on books and librarianship. Special issues are devoted to particular subjects.

The professional journal for information science, which is indispensable for librarians too, is the "Nachrichten für Dokumentation", issued by the Deutsche Gesellschaft für Dokumentation since 1950, in which questions of classification, terminology and mechanised procedures are given prominence. It also reports on the activities of the Institut für Dokumentationswesen.

A regular publication, though not a journal in the true sense of the word, is "Bibliothek und Wissenschaft", an annual produced by librarians in Heidelberg published by Harrassowitz, with substantial articles.

The professional journal of local authority libraries is "Buch und Bibliothek", until 1970 "Bücherei und Bildung", issued monthly by the Verein der Bibliothekare an Öffentlichen Büchereien. Part A of this journal contains articles and notes, reports and reviews on the theory and practice of public librarianship and the state of public libraries, and also, occasionally, on questions of literature and adult education. Part B contains reviews by librarians of books in all subjects.

"Bibliotheksdienst" — formerly "Büchereidienst" — is issued monthly by the Deutscher Büchereiverband. The brief reports and notices in its news section give fairly up-to-date information on developments in public librarianship. They also extend to events in the field of academic librarianship. Since 1969 the "Bibliotheksdienst" has also been the official organ of the Deutsche Bibliothekskonferenz and the Bibliothekarische Auslandsstelle. The news section is supplemented by topical articles, notices of new professional literature and a calendar of events. Supplements to "Bibliotheksdienst" appear irregularly and contain more substantial articles of professional interest. (Distribution: Deutscher Büchereiverband).

A leading place among the local journals in librarianship is held by the "Mitteilungsblatt" of the Verband der Bibliotheken des Landes Nordrhein-Westfalen. It is addressed to all types of library. Its emphasis, naturally, is on developments in North Rhine-Westphalia, but there are many articles which are of wider interest. The journal appears approximately quarterly and is obtainable — usually by exchange — from the Verband der Bibliotheken.

Other professional journals are issued by Staatliche Büchereistellen for the public library field of individual Länder. Thus there appears, for Bavaria "Die Neue Bücherei", for Lower Saxony "mb: Mitteilungsblatt des öffentlichen Büchereiwesens in Niedersachsen", for North Rhine-Westphalia "Biblio" and for the Rhineland Palatinate "Die Bücherei". They contain chiefly reports and announcements, articles on public library practice, and book reviews.

Matters to do with denominational academic libraries are treated in publications of the two Arbeitsgemeinschaften concerned: the "Mitteilungsblatt der Arbeitsgemeinschaft katholisch-theologischer Bibliotheken", published since 1953, and the "Veröffentlichungen der Arbeitsgemeinschaft für das Archiv- und Bibliothekswesen in der evangelischen Kirche", published since 1962 by the Arbeitsgemeinschaft, and its "Mitteilungen" since 1969, by Degener Verlag (Neustadt a. d. Aisch).

Information and professional articles on the work of denominational public libraries are contained in the "Mitteilungen aus der Zentrale des Borromäusvereins Bonn" — 2—5 issues annually — with its supplements "Werkhefte zur Büchereiarbeit", which appear as an irregular series. The Arbeitsstelle der katholischen Büchereiarbeit in Deutschland issues "informationen" irregularly in three series (A — Aktueller Informationsdienst, M — Materialdienst, I — Interner Informationsdienst für die katholische Büchereiarbeit). The "Mitteilungsblatt für die katholischen Volksbüchereien des St. Michaelsbundes", devoted to Bavaria, comes out four times a year, and the "Jahresberichte" of the St. Michaelsbund every two years. The information bulletins, "Unsere Sammlung" (Aachen, Cologne, Essen and Limburg) and "Informationen" (Münster), are devoted to individual dioceses.

For Protestant library work, the reviewing journal "Der Evangelische Buchberater" also contains announcements and professional news. (Issued by the Deutscher Verband Evangelischer Büchereien e. V. — Zentralstelle für Buch- und Büchereiarbeit in der Evangelischen Kirche in Deutschland, Göttingen). An information service is run from the same office.

The organ of the Arbeitsgemeinschaft Werkbüchereien für das Bundesgebiet und Berlin e. V. is "Werkbüchereiarbeit", currently appearing twice a year. The journal "Dokumentation, Fachbibliothek, Werkbücherei" (Nordwest Verlag, Hannover), attempts to include coverage of public librarianship.

The Arbeitsstelle für Bibliothekstechnik in Berlin issues intermittently "Informationen" mainly concerned with developments in automatic data processing.

8.12 Organisations

In the search for information the right reference is not always to be found in the professional literature. The enquirer may wish to approach a particular agency about some special question, while uncertain which of the numerous organisations mentioned in the previous chapters is the appropriate one. In the survey which follows we summarise various areas, for each of which individual organisations are given as sources of advice or of further contacts. We should note here that very few of them possess their own, properly-staffed information service. Addresses are given only for organisations with a permanent headquarters, and the names of prominent persons only where the post is their primary one. For the rest, the reader is referred to the entries in the latest two-yearly edition of the "Jahrbuch der Deutschen Bibliotheken" and the "Handbuch der Öffentlichen Büchereien".

For general questions on academic librarianship, especially subjects for which standing committees exist (such as cataloguing; circulation, including national and international inter-library loans; union catalogues; library buildings; MSS and incunabula; binding; government publications and newspapers), but also for statistics and matters of budgeting: Verein Deutscher Bibliothekare.

Information on the *academic library system*, co-operative undertakings, particularly the co-operative acquisition scheme, central specialist libraries, the exchange of scholarly material, new technical and organisational developments:

Deutsche Forschungsgemeinschaft, Bibliotheksreferat
5300 Bonn-Bad Godesberg, Kennedyallee 40.
Head: Dr. Dieter Oertel.

On questions of *library technology*, especially automatic data processing for libraries, apply to

Arbeitsstelle für Bibliothekstechnik
bei der Staatsbibliothek Preußischer Kulturbesitz
1000 Berlin 30, Reichpietschufer 72/76
Head: Dr. Walter Lingenberg.

Questions concerning the group of *special libraries* will be answered by the

Arbeitsgemeinschaft der Spezialbibliotheken e. V.,
with which is amalgamated the
Arbeitsgemeinschaft der Kunstbibliotheken.

The following *Arbeitsgemeinschaften*, sponsored by the Verein Deutscher Bibliothekare, will give information on questions referring to the type of library concerned:

Arbeitsgemeinschaft der Hochschulbibliotheken
Arbeitsgemeinschaft der Landesbibliotheken
Arbeitsgemeinschaft kommunaler wissenschaftlicher Bibliotheken
Arbeitsgemeinschaft der Parlaments- und Behördenbibliotheken
Arbeitsgemeinschaft pädagogischer Bibliotheken
Arbeitsgemeinschaft der Musikbibliotheken
Arbeitsgemeinschaft der Kunstbibliotheken

For all matters bearing on *local authority public libraries* the central information agency (which will where necessary enlist the help of its study groups or other organisations) is the

Arbeitsstelle für das Büchereiwesen
1000 Berlin 61, Gitschiner Straße 97—103
Head: Klaus-Dietrich Hoffmann.

Information on the special concerns of the *Staatliche Büchereistellen of the Länder*:

Mittelstelle der Fachkonferenz der Staatlichen Büchereistellen.

Denominational libraries

Information on *denominational academic libraries*:
Arbeitsgemeinschaft katholisch-theologischer Bibliotheken
Arbeitsgemeinschaft für das Archiv- und Bibliothekswesen in der evangelischen Kirche, Sektion Bibliothekswesen

Information on *denominational public libraries*:

Deutscher Verband Evangelischer Büchereien e. V.
3400 Göttingen, Bürgerstraße 2
Secretary: Elisabeth Bamberg.

Borromäusverein e. V.
5300 Bonn, Wittelsbacher Ring 9
Director: Dr. Franz Hermann.

St. Michaelsbund zur Pflege des katholischen Schrifttums in Bayern e. V.
8000 München 2, Herzog-Wilhelm-Str. 5.
Director: Hans Schachtner.

For *libraries for children and young people*
Arbeitsstelle für das Büchereiwesen
1000 Berlin 61, Gitschiner Str. 97—103.
The address of the *Internationale Jugendbibliothek* (International Youth Library) is:
8000 München, Kaulbachstr. 40.
Director: Walter Scherf.
Information on *school libraries*:
Arbeitsgemeinschaft pädagogischer Bibliotheken.

For *music libraries*, besides the Arbeitsstelle für das Büchereiwesen:
Internationale Vereinigung der Musikbibliotheken — Deutsche Gruppe BRD (The Federal Republic's section of the Association Internationale des Bibliothèques Musicales).

Enquiries concerning *works libraries*:
Arbeitsgemeinschaft Werkbüchereien für das Bundesgebiet und Berlin e. V.

271

For *armed forces' libraries*:
Bundesminister der Verteidigung
Referat Bibliothekswesen
5300 Bonn, Postfach 161.

For *hospital libraries* and *prison libraries* there are no special information
agencies. Enquiries should be directed to the Arbeitsstelle für das Büchereiwesen and the denominational public library associations.
The central information agency for *libraries for the blind is*:
Arbeitsgemeinschaft Deutscher Blinden-Hörbüchereien
355 Marburg (Lahn), Am Schlag 6 a.

On the libraries of the *Goethe-Institute* and *Deutsche Kulturinstitute*
abroad:
Inter Nationes
5300 Bonn-Bad Godesberg, Kennedyallee 91—103
Section head: Dr. Peter Baudisch.
Goethe-Institut
8000 München 2, Lenbachplatz 3

For the national and international *work of professional organisations*:
Verein Deutscher Bibliothekare e. V.
Verein der Diplom-Bibliothekare an wissenschaftlichen Bibliotheken e. V.
Deutscher Büchereiverband e. V.
Office: 1000 Berlin 61, Gitschiner Str. 97—103.
Verein der Bibliothekare an Öffentlichen Büchereien e. V.
Office: 2800 Bremen 1, Roonstr. 57.

The address of the *Einkaufszentrale für Öffentliche Büchereien (EKZ)* is:
7410 Reutlingen, Bismarckstr. 3.
Executive Director: Herbert Eisentraut.

For the state of *bibliography* in Germany, and bibliographic methods:
Deutsches Bibliographisches Kuratorium.

In the field of *information science*, the competent bodies for matters of
organisation and methods, international co-operation and new developments, are:
Institut für Dokumentationswesen
6000 Frankfurt-Niederrad, Herriotstr.
Director: Dr. Martin Cremer.

Deutsche Gesellschaft für Dokumentation
6000 Frankfurt/Main 1, Westendstr. 19.
Research and development in *mechanised information methods*:
Zentralstelle für maschinelle Dokumentation
6000 Frankfurt-Niederrad, Herriotstr.
Director: Klaus Schneider.
Careers and training of information scientists:
Verein Deutscher Dokumentare
5300 Bonn, Gustav-von-Veit-Str. 15.
The professional associations named above can give information on *librarianship as a career*. General questions concerning the education of public librarians might also be directed to the Konferenz der bibliothekarische Ausbildungsstätten (c/o Bibliothekar-Lehrinstitut in Cologne). Questions about particular details can often only be answered at the level of individual *library schools*, the addresses of which are:
Berlin — Berliner Bibliothekarakademie
1000 Berlin 31, Prinzregentenstr. 33/34.
Head: Ilse Reichel.
Bonn — Staatlich anerkanntes Bibliothekar-Lehrinstitut Bonn
5300 Bonn, Wittelsbacher Ring 9.
Head: Dr. Franz Hermann.
Cologne — Bibliothekar-Lehrinstitut des Landes Nordrhein-Westfalen
5000 Köln 41, Universitätsstraße 33.
Head: Prof. Dr. Werner Krieg.
Frankfurt am Main — Bibliotheksschule
6000 Frankfurt am Main, Bockenheimer Landstr. 134–138.
Head: Prof. Dr. Clemens Köttelwesch.
Göttingen — Evangelisches Bibliothekar-Lehrinstitut
3400 Göttingen, Groner-Tor-Str. 32 a.
Head: Dr. Rudolf Rueppel.
Hamburg — Bibliothekarschule der Freien und Hansestadt Hamburg
Abteilung Wissenschaftliche Bibliotheken
2000 Hamburg 13, Grindelallee 2.
Abteilung Öffentliche Büchereien
2000 Hamburg 13, Grindelhof 30.
Head: Dr. Kurt Richter.
Hanover — Niedersächsische Bibliotheksschule
3000 Hannover, Landesbibliothek, Am Archive 1.
Head: Dr. Wilhelm Totok.

Munich — Bibliotheksschule der Bayerischen Staatsbibliothek
8000 München 34, Ludwigstr. 16.
Head: Dr. Rupert Hacker.
Stuttgart — Süddeutsches Bibliothekar-Lehrinstitut
7000 Stuttgart N, Feuerbacher Heide 40.
Head: Dr. Hermann Wassner.

8.2 Study Tours for Foreign Visitors

Individuals and groups from abroad who wish to study the library scene
in the Federal Republic and West Berlin, and who have no direct contacts with it, can apply to the *Bibliothekarische Auslandsstelle* (present
address: 5000 Köln, Johannisstraße 72/80, tel. 2 21 38 95). The Auslandsstelle advises interested persons and groups on planning the content and
organisation of study visits, and establishes contact with appropriate
libraries and organisations.
It is important to give the Auslandsstelle, even in a preliminary enquiry,
as precise details as possible, particularly about the purpose of any
proposed study visit. Only when it is known what types of library or
other institutions and what particular professional questions are of
special interest, can suggestions be made for a successful study tour.
After this, it is important for the practical preparation of tours to know
the time available, and also to know in good time the exact dates and the
means of transport to be used. In the case of parties, details of the
number and type of participants are needed.
The Auslandsstelle, which functions entirely on the unpaid work of
librarians, is in no position to assume the function of a travel agency,
i. e. to obtain tickets or reserve seats for journeys. Hotel accommodation
can nevertheless be arranged for individual visitors with the help of
local libraries, if exact requirements are given.

8.3 Working Visits for Foreigners

Librarians wishing to work for a time at a library in the Federal Republic or West Berlin can likewise apply to the *Bibliothekarische Auslands-*

stelle (5000 Köln, Johannisstraße 72/80, tel. 2 21 38 95), which will endeavour to find a post. Previous experience has shown that this is possible in certain cases, sometimes by an exchange of posts with German librarians. Students at foreign library schools are also able, on occasions, to gain practical experience in German libraries.

The chief preliminary requirements for a working visit are a command of German and appropriate professional experience. Employment may be under widely varying conditions according to the requirements of the foreign applicant and the aforementioned opportunities. Those interested should therefore give very precise details of their age, education, qualifications, previous professional posts and special experience, knowledge of German, length of time to be spent working, type of library desired, limitation to particular places or regions, purpose of stay and nature of the employment desired, besides the salary expected or required. Where an exchange with a German librarian is proposed, relevant additional information is needed.

It is a good idea to give these particulars in German and to send several copies, which can then be forwarded by the Auslandsstelle to suitable libraries. Further documents, such as copies of certificates, can be submitted later on request.

8.4   Exchange of Publications

Librarians in other countries who wish to obtain by exchange publications appearing in the Federal Republic have numerous, but in a sense restricted, possibilities open to them. They can seek a suitable exchange partner from a great number of academic libraries of every kind, academies of science, learned societies and associations, specialist institutes, archives and museums. They cannot, however, count on obtaining every West German journal and every newly-published monograph by exchange. As a matter of principle each institution conducting exchanges can decide whether and to what extent it wishes to employ this method, but as a rule it can only use certain types of publication for exchange. The guidelines adopted by individual institutions correspond to those internationally accepted and published in Unesco's "Handbook on the international exchange of publications" (3rd ed. 1964).

Exchange of Scholarly Publications

For libraries exchange is a means of acquisition. One of the fundamental rules is that each exchange transaction must be handled individually. This means that the exchange office or exchange department must be staffed with specially well-qualified personnel with a knowledge of languages, and that its working processes cannot be standardised in the way that they can in a purchasing department. Hence, every library examines carefully, before entering into new exchange agreements, whether, on the one hand, the material to be received fits into its own acquisitions policy and is not also obtainable through the book trade; and whether, on the other hand, the German material requested in exchange can be supplied without difficulty. Offers from abroad are accepted or turned down accordingly. A refusal has nothing to do with a low opinion of the partner, but should be understood as a result of the library's adherence to its acquisitions policy and its financial resources.

University libraries, Staats-, Landes- and Stadtbibliotheken generally have material for exchange, composed in varying ways of the types given below. The prospective partner is well advised to request, first of all, the lists of available material which the larger libraries usually compile.

a) The library's own publications, such as annual reports, periodical lists, new accessions lists, exhibition catalogues; sometimes also catalogues of MSS and incunabula and occasionally even editions of MSS.

b) Publications of academies, learned societies or associations in the same town or region.

c) Dissertations.

d) Duplicates.

e) Currently-published monographs or periodicals have to be bought for exchange purposes. Only a few of the larger libraries are in a position to take up requests for this kind of material.

Items c) and d) require some clarification. *Dissertations* are only available for exchange from the libraries of universities and other similar institutions. They are generally exchanged for other dissertations, though in exceptional cases for other publications. Besides the "blanket" exchange of all available dissertations for all those of one's partner university, which was the general practice until recently, the individual exchange of selected dissertations on request is now accepted. Regulations governing the "Druckzwang", that is, the obligation of a candidate for the doctorate to have his dissertation printed, and to fix the number of copies to be supplied, is a prerogative of the faculties. The obligation to print, which was suspended during the war, has now been widely re-introduced, but the supply of copies is subject to varying rules. The libraries are pressing for the supply of 150 copies to the central university library, in consideration of their obligations in Germany and abroad.

Duplicates in the libraries can in principle be used like other disposable material for exchange purposes at home and abroad. Some libraries have joined together in regional or specialised groupings for the exchange of their duplicates. However, the great need for books in Germany itself, as a result of the losses in the war and, later, the founding of new institutions, has so far prevented an organised disposal of duplicates abroad. The libraries department of the Deutsche Forschungsgemeinschaft had assumed this task in the absence of others and in a limited sphere. In 1969 the Staatsbibliothek Preußischer Kulturbesitz began to set up a centre for the exchange of duplicates for academic libraries in the Federal Republic, on the pattern of the Reichstauschstelle in Berlin in the years 1926–1945.

Special libraries may be important potential partners in the same subject field, provided language is no obstacle. Exchanges here can be concluded relatively simply, since frequently only one or a few "house" publications are issued and are willingly disposed of by exchange.

Academies of sciences and learned societies have a special part to play in exchange. Some make use of an academic library in the same town or area to carry out exchanges (cf. b) above). Others maintain exchange arrangements themselves, but dispose of the publications received to another library where they possess no library of their own. Possibilities of exchange with them are limited by the aims of the society and the number of copies in which their publications appear.

A preliminary survey of institutions in the Federal Republic willing to exchange, with their addresses and the titles of currently available publications, is given in the Unesco "Handbook" mentioned above. However, the particulars given no longer show the latest situation; besides which, only a selection of the most important institutions could be included.

Information on other exchange possibilities is obtainable from the *Bibliotheksreferat der Deutschen Forschungsgemeinschaft* (cf. 3.23), which is the centre for the exchange of scholarly publications under the terms of Unesco Convention I (Convention concerning the international exchange of publications) of 1958. From an index arranged by subject interests, the addresses of suitable institutions can be supplied, to whom the interested party should then apply. As the centre for forwarding exchange material from various German institutions to their partners abroad and vice versa, the Bibliotheksreferat maintains contact with national exchange centres in 22 countries. In 1969 about 235,000 items of printed matter and parcels were dispatched in both directions in this way.

For the group of libraries participating in the co-operative acquisition scheme and the central specialist libraries, the Bibliotheksreferat itself maintains direct exchange links. Its partners are currently about 1500 libraries and institutes in 92 countries. Possibilities for offers of exchange are comparatively wide. Copies of monographs and journals published with the support of the Forschungsgemeinschaft are available, besides funds to buy material requested by the exchange partner. As with the libraries, exchanges follow certain lines of policy, so that even the Forschungsgemeinschaft cannot reply positively to every enquiry from abroad. The Bibliotheksreferat only acquires by exchange material of importance for the two groups of libraries named above, and only insofar as this is not obtainable — or obtainable only with particular difficulty — through the book trade. The emphasis is therefore on countries which are difficult of access and where the book trade is not well developed, and on those where trade is restricted through the state's economic policy but the libraries are free to send indigenous publications to recipients abroad. In 1969, 4 325 journals and over 9 400 monographs were received on exchange and passed on to academic libraries. The *Deutscher Büchereiverband* and its *Arbeitsstelle für das Büchereiwesen* dispose of their publications by exchange. Besides this, the Arbeitsstelle is often able to arrange the exchange of publications of individual public libraries and public library organisations, and hence to this extent also exercises certain central functions.

Exchange of Official Publications

The exchange of official and parliamentary publications, regulated by Unesco Convention II of 1958 (Convention concerning the exchange of official publications and government documents between states), is not divided among so many separate points as the exchange of scholarly publications. As with the latter, there are on the one hand the exchange arrangements maintained by the parliamentary and government libraries individually, and on the other an exchange centre. Orientation is more difficult here: the Unesco Handbook does not include these institutions.

Of the parliamentary libraries, the Bundestag Library maintains the most extensive exchange relations with other countries. In government libraries, the need for foreign official publications is limited to the larger libraries (cf. 2.43). The material which they can dispose of in exchange consists of publications of the authority concerned. These can be ascertained from the Verzeichnis Amtlicher Druckschriften, produced by the Deutsche Bibliothek.

The centre is the Internationaler Amtlicher Schriftentausch, which was set up in 1958 at the Staatsbibliothek Preußischer Kulturbesitz in Berlin (cf. 2.12). It has available as exchange material the official publications of the Bund and of Schleswig-Holstein, Berlin and Hesse (statutes of 26. 5. 1964, 25. 7. 1969 and 22. 10. 1969 respectively). By governmental agreements or exchange conventions with the foreign exchange centres concerned, it conducts exchanges with 30 foreign countries. By a resolution of the Kultusministerkonferenz in 1962, this department of the Staatsbibliothek also acts as the central German collecting point for official publications and government documents from Germany and abroad. In this way, individual libraries are largely relieved of the onerous work of acquiring and controlling this voluminous and difficult material.

Appendix I

Länder of the Federal Republic, kreisfreie Städte, Landkreise and kreisangehörige Gemeinden*

Land	Area sq. km.	Pop. in 1000s	Pop. per sq. km.	kreis- freie Städte	Land- kreise	kreis- angeh. Gemeind.
Schleswig-Holstein	15,675.4	2,546.5	162	4	17	1,371
Hamburg	747.2	1,818.6	2,434	1	—	—
Lower Saxony	47,411.7	7,067.2	147	15	60	4,143
Bremen	403.8	755.3	1,874	2	—	—
North Rhine-Westphalia	34,038.8	17,039.4	500	35	56	2,014
Hesse	21,110.0	5,379.1	254	9	39	2,653
Rhineland Palatinate	19,837.0	3,659.5	184	12	28	2,580
Baden-Württemberg	35,749.6	8,822.1	246	9	63	3,366
Bavaria	70,549.7	10,490.3	148	48	143	7,019
Saarland	2,567.8	1,129.0	440	1	7	346
West Berlin	480.1	2,135.1	4,448	1	—	—
Federal territory	248,571.0	60,842.1	244	137	413	23,492

* These terms are explained in the first section of chapter 1. Data taken
  from: Statistisches Bundesamt Wiesbaden. Fachserie A.
      Bevölkerung und Kultur. Reihe 1. III. 30. 6. 1969.
      Stuttgart und Mainz: Kohlhammer (1970).

Appendix II

Gemeinden with their Residential Population in Order of Size*

	Number of Gemeinden	(kreisfreie Städte included in this total)	Population in 1000s	in %
Below 100	812	—	54.9	0.1
100 — 200	2,533	—	386.1	0.6
200 — 500	7,054	—	2,370.6	3.9
500 — 1,000	5,531	—	3,914.2	6.4
1,000 — 2,000	3,713	—	5,169.1	8.5
2,000 — 3,000	1,303	—	3,156.8	5.2
3,000 — 5,000	1,073	—	4,115.1	6.8
5,000 — 10,000	876	—	6,065.4	10
10,000 — 20,000	413	(18)	5,633.7	9.3
20,000 — 50,000	206	(28)	6,455.2	10.6
50,000 — 100,000	56	(33)	3,898.0	6.4
100,000 — 200,000	31	(30)	4,135.2	6.8
200,000 — 500,000	17	(17)	4,934.2	8.1
500,000 — 1,000,000	8	(8)	5,297.5	8.7
1,000,000 and over	3	(3)	5,256.3	8.6
	23,629	(137)	60,842.1	100

* Data taken from: Statistisches Bundesamt Wiesbaden. Fachserie A.
Bevölkerung und Kultur. Reihe 1. IV. 30. 6. 1969.
Stuttgart und Mainz: Kohlhammer (1970).

Appendix III

Halts on a Library Study Tour through the Federal Republic

This selective directory is intended not to replace a general guide-book, but merely to supplement it as far as libraries and librarianship are concerned. It lists towns with noteworthy libraries of all kinds, points of contact and those library organisations that have more than local functions. The result is a small selection of about 70 towns. Apart from these there are however other establishments worth seeing, particularly in medium-sized towns and country districts. It is recommended that intending visitors should get in touch with the offices of the regional union catalogues and the Staatliche Büchereistellen in the case of academic and of public libraries respectively. The locations are listed below, and full addresses can be found in the "Jahrbuch der Deutschen Bibliotheken" or in the "Handbuch der Öffentlichen Büchereien" or obtained from the Arbeitsstelle für das Büchereiwesen in Berlin.

The following marginal abbreviations are intended to facilitate reference:

BL   Bibliothekar-Lehrinstitut (Bibliotheksschule) — library school (cf. 7.3)

BS   Staatliche Büchereistelle — "state public library office" (cf. 2.53)

Ki   Kirchliche Einrichtung — denominational establishment (cf. 2.6)

LB   Staatsbibliothek or Landesbibliothek — "state library" (cf. 2.2)

ÖB   Kommunale Öffentliche Bücherei — "local authority public library" — or Einheitsbücherei — "integrated library" (cf. 1.62, 2.5)

Sp   Spezialbibliothek — special library (cf. 2.4)

St   Wissenschaftliche Allgemeinbibliothek einer Stadt — academic general library in a town (cf. 2.51)

UB   Universitätsbibliothek or Hochschulbibliothek — university library or one of comparable status (cf. 1.22)

ZK   Zentralkatalog — union catalogue (cf. 3.121)

The use of asterisks indicates those libraries and other establishments that appear to be of especial interest for various reasons (e. g. building, organisation, technical projects, or of an unusual structure).

Arrangement

For our purpose the 11 Länder of the Federal Republic are grouped in
5 areas:
North Germany, comprising the coastal Länder of Schleswig-Holstein,
Hamburg, Lower Saxony and Bremen;
West Berlin;
North Rhine-Westphalia;
Central Länder, comprising Hesse, Rhineland Palatinate and the Saar-
land;
South Germany, comprising Bavaria and Baden-Württemberg.
See also the map at the end of the book.

North Germany

Schleswig-Holstein

Schleswig-Holstein (pop. 2.5 million) is largely devoted to agriculture,
and less than a third of the population live in the large towns and cities
of Flensburg, Kiel and Lübeck.
The library service in the Landkreise of the two divisions Schleswig and
Holstein is the concern of the two Büchereizentralen of Flensburg and
Rendsburg, which are well staffed and well supplied with technical services. Through their large-scale experiments with mobile libraries they
have inaugurated a new era in rural library work in the Federal
Republic.

Flensburg (pop. 96,000), Baltic port on the Danish border.
The one town in the Federal Republic to have three library systems: the
ÖB   municipal Stadtbücherei (main building rebuilt 1962), the Nordertor-
ÖB   bücherei (new building 1958), which acts as the central library of the
**BS, *ÖB   Büchereizentrale Flensburg, and the Central Library for the Danish
minority (Dansk Centralbibliothek før Sydslesvig, new building
1958/59).

Kiel (pop. 268,000), Land capital, situated at the mouth of the canal linking the North Sea and the Baltic, ferry port for Scandinavia.

*UB   The Bibliothek der Landesuniversität is housed in a new modern build-
**Sp   ing. In the Institut für Weltwirtschaft there is the Zentralbibliothek der
       Wirtschaftswissenschaften, in its field of economics one of the most im-
       portant collections in the world (new building to be completed in 1971).
LB, ÖB Kiel has also a Landesbibliothek and a municipal library system (includ-
       ing new branch library buildings).

       Lübeck (pop. 243,000), ferry port for Scandinavia.
St, *ÖB The Stadtbibliothek (with stock of historical interest) and the Öffent-
       liche Büchereien are separate institutions. The headquarters of the ÖB are
       in an old civic hall. The unusual branch library buildings are of interest.

       Rendsburg (pop. 38,000).
**BS   Site of the Büchereizentrale for Holstein and also of the mobile libraries
       centre for three Landkreise (there are 3 special mobiles, plate 15). In the
*ÖB   historic "Arsenal" there is an architecturally noteworthy Stadtbücherei,
ÖB   besides one in the neighbouring Gemeinde of Büdelsdorf.

       Hamburg

       The Free Hanseatic City of *Hamburg* (pop. 1.8 million) is the largest Ger-
       man seaport.
*UB   Hamburg possesses important academic libraries. The Staats- und Uni-
       versitätsbibliothek is directly next to the complex of new buildings for
       the University in the centre of the City. After the Library's own new
       building has been finished much of its stock will be on open access. It
ZK   houses also the North German Union Catalogue. The picture is com-
Sp   pleted by comprehensive economics libraries (that of the Hamburg Welt-
Sp   Wirtschafts-Archiv and the Commercial Library) and many special
       libraries, among which should be singled out the architecturally inter-
*Sp   esting law library of the Max-Planck-Institut für ausländisches und inter-
Ki   nationales Privatrecht, and the Landeskirchliche Bibliothek (new build-
       ing).
**ÖB The Hamburger Öffentliche Bücherhallen comprise about 50 open-access
       libraries with full-time staff, besides mobile libraries and about 30 sub-
       urban branches with part-time staff, which are administered from a
BS   central office. The system includes the second largest music library in the
       Republic. A central library is being planned for 1971. Some of the

numerous branch library buildings are full of interest (plate 5). The
BL library schools, formerly separate, have been brought together under one
person and named the "Bibliothekarschule der Freien und Hansestadt
Hamburg". It trains staff for all types of library work.
(Führer durch die Hamburger Bibliotheken. 2. Auflage. Hamburg: Staats- und
Universitätsbibliothek 1957. 103 p.)

Lower Saxony

Lower Saxony (pop.7.1 million), like Schleswig-Holstein largely devoted
to agriculture, was founded after the War out of several formerly independent states and provinces. Here too less than a third of the population live in the 15 major towns and cities.
As far as the public library service is concerned, the 8 Regierungsbezirke
are controlled by 5 "Fachstellen für das öffentliche Büchereiwesen", the
offices of which are at Brunswick, Hanover, Lüneburg, Oldenburg and
Stade.

Brunswick (pop. 227,000).
UB Bibliothek der Technischen Universität (new building under construc-
St tion). Stadtbibliothek (collection of theatre hand-bills), as well as an
*ÖB Öffentliche Bücherei, whose main library building is an interesting com-
BS bination of old and new. A "Fachstelle für das Öffentliche Bücherei-
wesen".

Clausthal-Zellerfeld (pop. 16,000).
*UB Has a Technische Universität (formerly a mining academy) with a new
library building.

Göttingen (pop. 115,000).
**UB Houses the Niedersächsische Staats- und Universitätsbibliothek, one of
the largest German academic libraries with about 2 million volumes.
(Plans are being prepared for an extension next to the new Science
ZK Faculty building). Union Catalogue for Lower Saxony.
*Ki Headquarters of the Deutscher Verband Evangelischer Büchereien (DVEB)
BL and the state-recognised Evangelisches Bibliothekar-Lehrinstitut, which
trains staff for public libraries and for the executive grade in academic
ÖB libraries. There is also a Stadtbücherei.

Hanover. As the Land capital Hanover (pop. 525,000) acts together with Göttingen as a focus for library activity in the Land.

LB   The Niedersächsische Landesbibliothek (collection of Leibniz material);
*UB, **Sp   Bibliothek der Technischen Universität, linked with the Technische Informationsbibliothek (the central specialist Library of technology in the Federal Republic) (both housed together in a remarkable new building,
UB   plate 8); Bibliothek der Tierärztlichen Hochschule ("Library of the
*UB   Veterinary College", housed in a new building of the College); Bibliothek der Medizinischen Hochschule (this Medical College is a new foundation
St   with a new building for the Library), and the Stadtbibliothek with its
**ÖB   valuable historical holdings. The public library system in Hanover, of which the Stadtbibliothek is the headquarters, includes a well-developed network of branches (of architectural interest, plate 9), and mobiles. An extension to the Stadtbibliothek is planned.
BS, BL   Site of a "Fachstelle für das Öffentliche Büchereiwesen" and a Bibliotheksschule connected with the Landesbibliothek (it prepares staff only for the executive grade in academic libraries).
       (Führer durch die Bibliotheken Hannovers. Hrsg. von den Bibliotheken Hannovers. Redaktion: Karl-Heinz Weimann. Hannover 1966. 39 p.)

Lüneburg (pop. 63,000)
In the building of a former Franciscan monastery the remarkable old
St, ÖB, BS   "Ratsbücherei" (stock of historical interest). Site of a "Fachstelle".

Wilhelmshaven (pop. 103,000), North Sea port.
ÖB   Stadtbücherei and evening institute in adjacent new buildings (1960–1962).

Wolfenbüttel (pop. 42,000).
*LB   In the Herzog August Bibliothek (with its memories of Leibniz and Lessing) the town boasts a valuable collection of manuscripts, incunabula and early printed books. Noteworthy conversion: successful modernisation of an older library building (plate 12). In the Landkreis of Wolfen-
ÖB   büttel there is a new mobile library service.

Wolfsburg (pop. 92,000).
This town of the Volkswagen works has achieved with Alvar Aalto's "Kulturzentrum" a splendid cultural focal point. Apart from an evening
*ÖB   institute and a young people's centre it comprises a remarkable Stadtbücherei.

Bremen

The smallest German Land is the Free Hanseatic City of Bremen (pop.
750,000). It is divided into two Stadtgemeinden; Bremen and Bremerhaven.

Bremen (pop. 607,000)

UB, **ÖB   The present Staatsbibliothek is being enlarged to become the Library of
the new University (special structure worth nothing). The former Volksbüchereien — now called Stadtbibliothek — in Bremen are characterised
by an efficient central Library, some large suburban branches (including
some interesting new buildings) and a network of school and youth libraries (plate 10). In this latter field the Bremen public libraries are in the

*   front rank. In Bremen there is the headquarters of the Verein der Bibliothekare an Öffentlichen Büchereien (VBB).

Bremerhaven (pop. 149,000).

*ÖB   Has had since 1965 a new building for its Stadtbibliothek, which houses
also the evening institute.

Berlin

West Berlin (pop. 2.1 million)

**LB   One new building that has already begun to go up is the Staatsbibliothek
Preußischer Kulturbesitz (now about 2.2 million vols., cf. 2.12) (plate 2).
Several departments are already in operation in Berlin, whereas others
are still at Marburg, where there remains a large part of the stock.
Attached to the Staatsbibliothek is the Arbeitsstelle für Bibliothekstech-
nik (see below).

*UB   The Libraries of the Freie Universität and the Technische Universität are
*UB   both in post-War buildings. In the TUB there are interesting experiments
ZK   in library techniques. The FUB houses the Berlin Union Catalogue.

*Ki   Another modern library worth mentioning is that of the (Protestant)
Kirchliche Hochschule.

Sp   Well-known special libraries are the Kunstbibliothek (including the
*Sp   Lipperheide library of costume and a collection of posters) and the Ibero-
Amerikanisches Institut. A special collection of all records of music issued

*   in Germany is housed in the Deutsche Musik-Phonothek, temporarily in
Sp   the building of the Amerika-Gedenkbibliothek. Many other special
libraries.

**ÖB   The Amerika-Gedenkbibliothek (the Berlin Central Library, plate 4), erected in 1954 thanks to a gift of American money, is a milestone in the growth of the modern German public library. Local collection, music library.

*ÖB   The 12 Bezirke have their own library systems with about 100 branches, some of which have new modern buildings.

The following libraries and information centres are of more than local

*   significance: the Arbeitsstelle für Bibliothekstechnik, established in 1969 as a research centre for modern library technology and concentrating on

*   automatic data processing; the Arbeitsstelle für das Büchereiwesen ("Study Centre for Public Libraries", cf. 3.24), linked with the head-quarters of the Deutscher Büchereiverband (DBV) since 1958; and the Deutscher Normen-Ausschuß, together with its numerous specialist committees on standards (cf. 6.224).

BL   Moreover Berlin has a Bibliothekarakademie, which prepares staff for public libraries and also for the executive grade in academic libraries.
       (Verzeichnis der Bibliotheken in Berlin (West). Hrsg. Hildegard Lullies. Berlin: Spitzing 1966. xii, 301 p. [612 libraries with 7,000,000 volumes].)

North Rhine-Westphalia

Almost a third of the inhabitants of the Federal Republic live in North Rhine-Westphalia (pop. 17 million). It is a Land geared to urban and industrial development, in which the agglomeration that is the Ruhr poses particular problems.

Through the concentratet activities of the Verband der Bibliotheken des Landes Nordrhein-Westfalen we have here a model case of library co-operation that transcends local boundaries.

The six Staatliche Büchereistellen are in Aachen, Cologne, Detmold, Essen, Hagen and Münster.
(Die Bibliotheken in Nordrhein-Westfalen. 2. Aufl. bearb. von Klaus Bock. Köln: Westdeutscher Verlag 1964. 149 p.)

Aachen (pop. 178,000).

*UB   Bibliothek der Technischen Hochschule (new building, 1966; a medical department set up near the hospital, electronic data processing for the issue system).

BS, St Staatliche Büchereistelle. Municipal establishments: Stadtbibliothek and
ÖB   Stadtbücherei.

Bielefeld (pop. 171,000).

UB Universitätsbibliothek, at present in its first stage, housed in temporary premises (new University foundation, with decentralised library struc-
ÖB ture). Stadtbibliothek (in new premises since 1969 — a local union catalogue is being set up).

Bochum (pop. 356,000).

**UB Universitätsbibliothek (modern library techniques with electronic data
ÖB processing, plate 16). Stadtbücherei.

Bonn (pop. 296,000), Federal capital.

*UB Universitätsbibliothek in a fine new building. Linked administratively
Sp but not physically is the Zentralbibliothek der Landbauwissenschaft, the central specialist library for agriculture (plans for new building).
Sp The research department of the Deutscher Bundestag has a comprehensive Library (including press cuttings). Also libraries of the Federal Ministries.
St In the municipal sector there is a rather small Stadtbibliothek and a
ÖB Stadtbücherei (note the music library in the Schumann House).
*Ki Bonn is the headquarters of the Borromäusverein, the central office for the Roman Catholic library service. Linked with it is the state-recognised
BL Bibliothekar-Lehrinstitut, which prepares staff for public libraries and the executive grade in academic ones.

Bonn-Bad Godesberg

Headquarters of many Federal authorities with libraries, houses also the
* Deutsche Forschungsgemeinschaft (Bibliotheksreferat). Notable special
Sp libraries are the Bibliothek der deutschen Landeskunde ("Library of German Topography"), with its map collection, and (housed in the same
Sp building) the Bibliothek des Instituts für Raumforschung ("Library of the Institute of Regional Planning"), with its information centres.

Cologne (pop. 866,000).

*UB Universitäts- und Stadtbibliothek (1.5 million vols. New building, 1967).
Sp Medical department now established as central medical library for the
ZK Federal Republic. Union Catalogue of the academic libraries in North Rhine-Westphalia.
Sp Numerous special libraries, including the Kunst- und Museumsbibliothek
Sp ("Fine Arts and Museums Library"), the Germania Judaica (on the

Sp   history of German Judaism), Bibliothek der Sporthochschule ("Library of
Ki   the Physical Education College") and the Roman Catholic Erzbischöf-
    liche Diözesan- und Dombibliothek.
ÖB   Stadtbücherei (Central Library at the planning stage, several modern
BS   branches, 3 mobiles). Staatliche Büchereistelle.
*BL   The Bibliothekar-Lehrinstitut des Landes Nordrhein-Westfalen, the
    largest in the Federal Republic, prepares staff for all categories of library
    service (in new building of the UB).
  *   The administration of the Bibliothekarische Auslandsstelle (cf. 3.22)
    takes place in the Stadtbücherei. A modern works library may be seen
    near Cologne in the Dynamit Nobel AG at Troisdorf.

Dortmund (pop. 649,000).
UB   Universitätsbibliothek (new University, Library being developed in
*St   temporary new premises on the University site); Stadt- und Landesbiblio-
*ÖB, Sp   thek, together with the Stadtbücherei (note new branches) and the Insti-
    tut für Zeitungsforschung ("Institute for Research into Newspapers"),
Sp   are housed in the "Haus der Bibliotheken" (1958). The former Pädagogi-
    sche Zentralbücherei Nordrhein-Westfalen has been renamed the Biblio-
    thek der Pädagogischen Hochschule Ruhr, Abteilung Dortmund ("Library
    of the Ruhr College of Education, Dortmund Division").

Düsseldorf (pop. 674,000), Land capital.
UB   Universitätsbibliothek (Medical and science library of the University;
    new building for the Library dates from 1962 with extension in 1968 for
St   the medical and science faculty). Landes- und Stadtbibliothek (to become
    the main section of the new University Library).
ÖB   Stadtbüchereien (new branches).
Sp   VDI-Bücherei (Library of the Verein Deutscher Ingenieure, "Association
    of German Engineers"), new building. Library of the Verein Deutscher
    Eisenhüttenleute ("Association of German Iron-Workers"). Library of
    the Henkel works.

Duisburg (pop. 460,000).
**ÖB   Stadtbüchereien (fine large Central Library, electronic data processing,
    modern branches).

Essen (pop. 703,000).
St,ÖB,*Sp   Stadtbüchereien (separate academic department), Mining Library (an
BS   extensive special library). Staatliche Büchereistelle.

Hamm (pop. 78,000).
*ÖB Stadtbücherei (in a new building 1966, plate 6).

Hilden (pop. 50,000).
ÖB Stadtbücherei (example of integrated co-operation with school libraries and the evening institute).

Jülich (pop. 20,000).
*Sp Site of the central library of the Kernforschungsanlage, a research library and information centre for nuclear research (new building).

Krefeld (pop. 227,000).
ÖB Stadtbücherei (new building, "Haus der Erwachsenenbildung", 1962).

Leverkusen (pop. 111,000).
*Sp The Kekulé-Bibliothek der Farbenfabriken Bayer AG is one of the largest
ÖB German industrial libraries (about 300,000 vols.). The Stadtbücherei (plans for new building) is supplemented by the large works library of the Bayer firm.

Marl (pop. 78,000).
ÖB Integrated municipal cultural enterprise ("Die Insel"; educational work of the evening institute; and the Stadtbücherei).

Mönchengladbach (pop. 154,000).
*ÖB The Stadtbücherei (new building) houses an extensive special collection on the social sciences (the library of the former Volksverein für das katholische Deutschland) with many unique items.

Mülheim an der Ruhr (pop. 190,000).
ÖB New building of the Stadtbücherei dates from 1968.

Münster (pop. 205,000).
UB A new building for the Universitätsbibliothek has been under construc-
ÖB tion since 1969. The Stadtbücherei in the historic Krameramtshaus is
Sp responsible also for the Blindenhörbücherei Nordrhein-Westfalen (a
BS "listening library for the blind"). Staatliche Büchereistelle.

Oberhausen (pop. 249,000).
ÖB Integrated co-operation between Stadtbücherei and school libraries.

Remscheid (pop. 135,000).
ÖB   Stadtbücherei (new building 1966).

Unna, Landkreis (pop. 240,000).
ÖB   Example of a developing library system in a Landkreis (mobile library
and supplementary library services).

Wanne-Eickel (pop. 103,000).
ÖB   Stadtbücherei (new building 1963).

Central Länder

Hesse

Hesse (pop. 5.4 million), the central Land formed in 1945 out of Hesse-
Darmstadt and the former Prussian provinces of Kurhesse and Nassau.
A quarter of the inhabitants live in the cities of Frankfurt/Main, Wies-
baden, Kassel, Darmstadt and Offenbach. Diversified industry and agri-
culture.
The two Staatliche Büchereistellen are in Darmstadt and Kassel.
(Führer durch die Bibliotheken in Hessen. Wiesbaden: Harrassowitz 1955.
153 p.)

Darmstadt (pop. 141,000).
UB   The Hessische Landes- und Hochschulbibliothek (in the castle) with about
900,000 vols. and 1.2 million patents is the headquarters of the Biblio-
ÖB   graphisches Kuratorium. Stadtbücherei (in the multipurpose "Justus-
BS   Liebig-Haus" with the evening institute). Staatliche Büchereistelle.

Frankfurt am Main (pop. 666,000). Rhine-Main airport. Headquarters of
the Börsenverein des deutschen Buchhandels (cf. 1.3).
**   Deutsche Bibliothek (cf. 2.11): deposit library for works in German
published since 1945, bibliographical information centre, Deutsche Bibliographie, compiled with the aid of electronic data processing. (New building, plate 1).
*UB   Stadt- und Universitätsbibliothek with the main library for the University
hospital services as well as the Senckenbergische Bibliothek (profession-
ZK, BL ally interesting new building 1965). Union Catalogue for Hesse, Biblio-

theksschule (prepares staff for administrative and executive grades in academic libraries).

Of the many special libraries the following are particularly well known:
Sp those of the Deutsches Institut für Internationale Pädagogische Forschung
Sp ("German Institute for International Pedagogical Research"), the Freies Deutsches Hochstift ("Free German Academy") (in the Goethe Museum near the Goethe House, with special collection 1750–1850) as well as
Sp the Gmelin-Institut für anorganische Chemie und Grenzgebiete ("Gmelin Institute for Inorganic Chemistry and Allied Fields").
ÖB Stadtbücherei (new branches and mobile libraries).
* Centre for information services: Institut für Dokumentationswesen; headquarters of the Deutsche Gesellschaft für Dokumentation; Dokumen-
* tar-Lehrinstitut; Zentralstelle für maschinelle Dokumentation (ZMD).

Giessen (pop. 75,000).
UB Universitätsbibliothek (papyrus collection, new building).

Kassel (pop. 214,000).
Sp, St Museum of the Brothers Grimm (fairy tale collection). Murhardsche
ÖB, BS Bibliothek der Stadt Kassel und Landesbibliothek. Stadtbücherei. Staatliche Büchereistelle.

Marburg (pop. 51,000).
LB Staatsbibliothek Preußischer Kulturbesitz (except for the departments already transferred to Berlin); compiles the two union lists of foreign and German periodicals (cf. 3.122).
*UB Universitätsbibliothek (about 1,000,000 vols., notable new building 1967,
Sp plate 3). Library of the J. G. Herder-Institut (Union Catalogue of Academic Works on Eastern and Central Europe [GKO]).
Sp Emil-Krückmann-Bücherei (academic library for the blind).
ÖB Stadtbücherei.

Offenbach am Main (pop. 118,000).
*Sp, ÖB Klingspor Museum (art of writing and the printed book). Stadtbücherei
Sp (in the castle). Bibliothek des Deutschen Wetterdienstes ("Library of the German Weather Service").

Rüsselsheim (pop. 57,000).
ÖB Noteworthy Stadtbücherei (new building 1963).

Rhineland Palatinate

Rhineland Palatinate (pop. 3.7 million), created in 1946 out of the Palatinate and parts of Prussian provinces. Only a sixth of the inhabitants live in the large towns of Ludwigshafen, Mainz, Koblenz, Trier and Kaiserslautern. Agriculture and viticulture.

The two Staatliche Büchereistellen are in Koblenz and Neustadt an der Weinstraße.

Koblenz (pop. 107,000).
*ÖB Stadtbibliothek (Einheitsbücherei in the historic "Alte Burg").
BS   Staatliche Landesfachstelle für Büchereiwesen Rheinland-Pfalz.

Ludwigshafen/Rhein (pop. 176,000).
*ÖB Stadtbücherei (new building 1962, branches). Large works library of the
Sp   BASF (Badische Anilin- und Soda-Fabriken). The BASF has also a research library.

Mainz (pop. 180,000), Land capital.
UB, St Universitätsbibliothek (new building), Stadtbibliothek (stock of historical
ÖB   interest; open-access). Municipal Volksbüchereien.
*Sp   Gutenberg library (in the Gutenberg Museum): international museum of the printed book.

Trier (pop. 106,000).
St   The old Stadtbibliothek, with valuable historical holdings of books and
ÖB   manuscripts, is housed in a new modern building. Next to it is a Stadtbücherei.

Saarland

The Saarland (pop. 1.1 million) was incorporated in 1957 as the youngest member of the Federal Republic. An urban area with coal mining and steel industry.

Saarbrücken (pop. 131,000), Land capital.
*UB The Bibliothek der Landesuniversität has a new building dating from
ÖB   1952; medical section is housed in the medical faculty at Homburg. Stadt-
BS   bücherei, seat of the Staatliches Büchereiamt für das Saarland.

South Germany

Bavaria

Bavaria (pop. 10.5 million, of which only a quarter live in the cities of Munich, Nuremberg, Augsburg, Regensburg, Würzburg, Fürth and Erlangen) is in area the largest Land in the Republic and is mainly agricultural. It offers abundant and valuable collections of books and manuscripts from past centuries, which are preserved by an old tradition of librarianship. The centre of this tradition is the Bayerische Staatsbibliothek, which also co-ordinates the activities of 10 Bavarian staatliche Bibliotheken.

Alongside a rich denominational and private library service there are many local authority libraries, which are partly the responsibility of the 6 Staatliche Beratungsstellen für Volksbüchereien. The latter are situated in Munich (for Upper Bavaria), Regensburg (Lower Bavaria, southern part of the Upper Palatinate), Bayreuth (Upper Franconia, northern part of the Upper Palatinate), Nuremberg (Central Franconia), Würzburg (Lower Franconia) and Augsburg (Swabia).

(Handbuch der bayerischen Bibliotheken. Hrsg. Klaus Dahme. Mit 8 Abb. Wiesbaden: Harrassowitz 166. xx 189 p.) [169 libraries].

Augsburg (pop. 212,000).

St Staats- und Stadtbibliothek (stock of historical interest, Bible collection),
ÖB, BS municipal Volksbücherei, a Staatliche Beratungsstelle.

Bamberg (pop. 75,000).

*LB Staatsbibliothek in the Neue Residenz (stock of historical interest, a
ÖB baroque building recently adapted for the Library (plate 14)). Mobile library service for the Kreis (1966).

Eichstätt (pop. 11,000).

*LB Staats- und Seminarbibliothek, housed since 1965 in a new building
Ki together with the Roman Catholic Bibliothek der kirchlichen Pädagogi-
Ki schen Hochschule, the bischöfliche Seminarbibliothek, and some smaller libraries.

Erlangen (pop. 86,000).

*UB The Universitätsbibliothek Erlangen-Nürnberg (1,200,000 vols., stock of historical interest, collection of the graphic arts, plans for a new ex-

tension) has two external departments, that of the Wirtschaftswissen-
schaftliche Fakultät in Nuremberg and a recently established technical
ÖB   department for the new Technische Fakultät in Erlangen. Stadtbücherei.

Munich (pop. 1,365,000), Land capital.
**LB   The Bayerische Staatsbibliothek (interesting new wing, 1966, to the
       restored building of 1840), is the central Landesbibliothek and research
       library (plate 7), one of the most important general libraries (cf. 2.13)
ZK   (3 million vols.) with the Bavarian Union Catalogue, the Institut für Buch-
BL   restaurierung and the Bibliotheksschule (prepares staff for all grades of
       academic library service).
       In Munich there are many other academic libraries, including that of the
UB, *UB   Universität (new building 1967) and the Technische Hochschule (col-
       lection of atomic energy reports), together with the extensive collections
*Sp   of the libraries of the Deutsches Patentamt (new building 1959) and the
*Sp   Deutsches Museum. Many other special libraries, e.g. those of the
*Sp   Zentralinstitut für Kunstgeschichte ("Central Institute for Art History"),
Sp   the Monumenta Germaniae Historica, the Institut für Zeitgeschichte
Sp   ("Institute for Contemporary History") and the Osteuropa-Institut ("In-
       stitute for East European Studies").
**Sp   International Youth Library.
St, ÖB Stadtbibliothek administered jointly with the Stadtbüchereien. Well-
       developed network of permanent service points and mobile libraries
       (6 vehicles), including libraries in several hospitals and old people's
       homes. Municipal Music Library (largest in the Republic).
BS   Munich is the headquarters of the Ministerialbeauftragter für das Volks-
       büchereiwesen in Bayern and of a Staatliche Beratungsstelle. Central
Ki   office of the Roman Catholic St. Michaelsbund zur Pflege des katholi-
       schen Schrifttums in Bayern.

Nuremberg (pop. 478,000).
*Sp   Bibliothek des Germanischen Nationalmuseums (comprehensive special
       collection on the history of German art, culture and environment; new
       building 1964).
St   Stadtbibliothek (new building 1957) with large collections on Franconia
       and the Eastern Alpine region.
ÖB   Stadtbücherei (3 mobiles).
BS   Staatliche Beratungsstelle.

Regensburg (pop. 129,000).

*UB The Universitätsbibliothek (new University, modern library organisation, electronic data processing) is housed in already completed new premises, which are intended later for one of the future "Bereichsbibliotheken".

LB Staatliche Bibliothek, Fürstlich Thurn- und Taxissche Hofbibliothek,
ÖB, BS Stadtbücherei, Staatliche Beratungsstelle.

Würzburg (pop. 122,000).

UB, *ÖB Universitätsbibliothek, Stadtbücherei (in the Falkenhaus am Markt;
BS rococo style), Staatliche Beratungsstelle.

Baden-Württemberg

Baden-Württemberg (pop. 8.8 million) was formed in 1952 out of Württemberg, Baden and Hohenzollern. Only a fifth of the inhabitants live in the larger towns of Stuttgart, Mannheim, Karlsruhe, Freiburg, Heidelberg, Heilbronn, Ulm and Pforzheim. The Land is characterised by the many small to medium-sized towns. To the south farming and forestry (and viticulture) predominate, to the north industry (consumer goods). Numerous universities and colleges.
The four Staatliche Büchereistellen are in Freiburg, Heidelberg, Reutlingen and Stuttgart.

Freiburg (pop. 163,000).

UB Universitätsbibliothek (1.4 million vols., valuable old collections; plans
ÖB, BS for new building), Stadtbücherei, a Staatliche Büchereistelle.

Heidelberg (pop. 122,000).

*UB Universitätsbibliothek (Library of the oldest University on West German soil, 1.6 million vols., Manessische Handschrift, plans for new extension).
Sp Libraries of the Max Planck Institutes, inter alia Institut für ausländisches
*ÖB öffentliches Recht und Völkerrecht (cf. 6.13). Stadtbücherei with note-
BS worthy new premises (1965), Staatliche Büchereistelle.

Heilbronn (pop. 102,000).

*ÖB Stadtbücherei in the restored Deutschordenshof. To the north of Heil-
ÖB bronn is Bad Friedrichshall with Stadtbücherei (plate 11).

Karlsruhe (pop. 258,400).

*UB, *LB Universitätsbibliothek (new building). Badische Landesbibliothek (new
*Sp building). Libraries of the Deutsches Kernforschungszentrum ("German
Sp Nuclear Research Centre"), the Bundesgerichtshof ("Federal Law Court")
Sp and the Bundesverfassungsgericht ("Federal Constitutional Court") (new
ÖB buildings). Stadtbücherei.

Konstanz am Bodensee (pop. 61,000).

*UB The Universitätsbibliothek (new University, modern administrative
structure for the library system within the University, electronic data
processing) is in temporary premises.
St, ÖB Städtische Wessenberg-Bibliothek, Stadtbücherei.

Ludwigsburg (pop. 79,000).

ÖB The Stadtbücherei moved in 1969 into a splendid multipurpose building
(housing also the evening institute and the young people's centre). In
*Sp nearby Marbach in the Schiller-Nationalmuseum the Bibliothek des
Deutschen Literaturarchivs (literary remains, Cotta papers).

Mannheim (pop. 330,000).

UB The Library of the former Wirtschaftshochschule ("Commercial College",
rehoused in the castle 1968) is being enlarged to form a university library;
St, *ÖB academic Stadtbibliothek; Stadtbücherei (main library in the historic
Dahlberghaus; branches in new premises).

Pforzheim (pop. 91,000).

ÖB Stadtbücherei (main building and new branch).

Reutlingen (pop. 68,000).

ÖB Stadtbücherei (historic building, Bible collection).
BS Staatliche Büchereistelle.
** Einkaufszentrale für Öffentliche Büchereien GmbH (commercial supply
centre for public libraries, wholesale booksellers and wholesale binders,
general library supplies and furniture).
* Publishing house and editorial office of the professional journal, "Buch
und Bibliothek".

Stuttgart (pop. 626,000), Land capital.

*UB, *LB Universitätsbibliothek Stuttgart (new building); Landesbibliothek (new

ZK building) with valuable collection of about 1 million vols. and the Union
Sp Catalogue for Baden-Württemberg, Bibliothek des Instituts für Auslandsbeziehungen ("Library of the Institute for Foreign Relations"),
*Sp Bibliothek für Zeitgeschichte ("Library for Contemporary History"),
UB Bibliothek der Universität (formerly the Landwirtschaftliche Hochschule) in the suburb of Hohenheim (new building).
*ÖB Stadtbücherei (Central Library in the restored Wilhelmspalais 1965, plate 13).
BS, BL Staatliche Büchereistelle and the Süddeutsches Bibliothekar-Lehrinstitut (prepares staff only for public libraries).

Tübingen (pop. 56,000).
*UB Universitätsbibliothek (1.3 million vols., modern wing to a 1912 building).
ÖB Stadtbücherei.

Ulm (pop. 93,000).
UB Universitätsbibliothek under construction (new University devoted to medicine and the sciences; modern administrative structure for the University and the Library).
St, ÖB Stadtbibliothek in the historic Schwörhaus, as is the Städtische Bücherei.

Index

The Index, which is not intended to be exhaustive, supplements the list of Contents. Individual libraries and institutions (except a few major ones), publications and personal names are not covered. For information on individual Länder and towns see Appendix III. The numbers in the entries refer to pages. In filing the Umlaut has been disregarded.